SpringerBriefs in Information Security and Cryptography

The series aims to develop and disseminate an understanding of innovations, paradigms, techniques, and technologies in the contexts of information and cybersecurity systems, as well as developments in cryptography and related studies.

It publishes concise, thorough and cohesive overviews of state-of-the-art topics in these fields, as well as in-depth case studies. The series also provides a single point of coverage of advanced and timely, emerging topics and offers a forum for core concepts that may not have reached a level of maturity to warrant a comprehensive monograph or textbook.

It addresses security, privacy, availability, and dependability issues, also welcoming emerging technologies such as artificial intelligence, cloud computing, cyber physical systems, and big data analytics related to cybersecurity research. Among some core research topics:

Fundamentals and theories

- Cryptography for cybersecurity
- Theories of cybersecurity
- Provable security

Cyber Systems and Secure Networks

- Cyber systems security
- Network security
- Security services
- Social networks security and privacy
- Cyber attacks and defense
- Data-driven cyber security
- Trusted computing and systems

Applications and others

- Hardware and device security
- Cyber application security
- Human and social aspects of cybersecurity

Ernst Piller · Hubert Schölnast

Data Encryption at the Intersection of Mathematics and Physics

Comparing Physical Methods of Cryptography

Ernst Piller
Department of Computer Science
and Security, Institute for IT Security
Research
St. Pölten University of Applied Sciences
St. Pölten, Austria

Hubert Schölnast
Department of Computer Science
and Security, Institute for IT Security
Research
St. Pölten University of Applied Sciences
St. Pölten, Austria

ISSN 2731-9555 ISSN 2731-9563 (electronic)
SpringerBriefs in Information Security and Cryptography
ISBN 978-3-032-24763-6 ISBN 978-3-032-24764-3 (eBook)
https://doi.org/10.1007/978-3-032-24764-3

This work was supported by University of Applied Sciences St. Poelten.

This Springer imprint is published by the registered company Springer Nature Switzerland AG
The registered company address is: Gewerbestrasse 11, 6330 Cham, Switzerland

Competing Interests The authors have no competing interests to declare that are relevant to the content of this manuscript.

Contents

Chapter 1
Introduction

This book is aimed at anyone interested in high data security in telecommunications and data storage, especially procurers, experts, and decision-makers. Anyone involved in procurement in this field makes decisions about algorithms, technologies, and providers, and thus also about infrastructure and security. The generation and distribution of keys for data encryption play a central role in this. Because security assessments for mathematical methods are based on assumptions, physical methods are becoming interesting in the high-security sector. They promise to link security more closely to the laws of nature. This raises the key question: Which technology is suitable for which application scenario, and what assumptions, costs, and operational risks are involved?

This book provides answers and, for the first time, compares QKD (quantum key distribution), RKD (radio signal key distribution), and MKD (memory key distribution) in a common, comprehensible criteria grid: technology-neutral and practical. Secret key rates, ranges/attenuation, robustness, costs/infrastructure, standardization, and risks (implementation, integration, post-processing, side channels) are deliberately evaluated not as a ranking, but as a decision-making aid.

QKD derives its security from the laws of quantum physics, but secret key rates decrease with increasing attenuation. Key management systems connect short QKD distances over longer distances, but only at the cost of additional attack surfaces ("trusted nodes"). Its use for mobile applications fails due to a lack of technical maturity. Very high financial costs and high maintenance requirements for QKD solutions make them not very suitable.

RKD utilizes the reciprocal physical properties of a radio link and scores points for its low technical complexity, excellent suitability for mobile applications (e.g., vehicles or drones), and very low costs. However, RKD falls far short of the key rates achieved by QKD solutions and is still limited to shorter distances. In addition, there is no established infrastructure for distributing key material to more than two partners.

E. Piller and H. Schölnast, *Data Encryption at the Intersection of Mathematics and Physics*, SpringerBriefs in Information Security and Cryptography,
https://doi.org/10.1007/978-3-032-24764-3_1

MKD takes a completely different approach: each party produces key material, stores it on a data carrier, and transports it physically to the other party. Because MKD can securely transfer 16 TB of key material in a single transport, only MKD has the potential to continuously provide a one-time pad (OTP) and thus provably 100% secure data encryption. The price is organizational responsibility: secure generation, storage, transport, and documented chain of custody.

The book examines data security in telecommunications and data storage, discusses three new encryption methods specifically designed for QKD and RKD, and addresses the question of when "OTP-like" security is more practical than theoretical purity. The result of approximately one year of source-critical research and the comparison of literature, manufacturer specifications, and practical observations with systematic cross-checking and our own R&D activities, this book helps to justify architecture and procurement decisions, locate risks (side channels, misconfigurations, logistical vulnerabilities), and separate "security gains" from "new attack surfaces."

1.1 General

Data plays a very important role today, and so does data security. Digitalization, globalization, and global networking require secure telecommunications and data storage, which in turn require secure cryptography. The development of secure data protection procedures for communication and data storage is a key challenge.

The security assessment of current cryptography is based on the assumption that there are mathematical problems that are very difficult for an attacker to solve. In other words, it depends on the computing power of the attackers and their current knowledge of mathematical attack methods. Protection against mathematical attack methods that are still unknown today involves unpublished mathematical methods that can break today's symmetric and asymmetric cryptography and/or post-quantum cryptography. As the past has shown, there have often been unpublished methods with a major impact on cryptography. For example, Mr. Williamson and Mr. Cox developed the Diffie-Hellman and RSA methods in a similar form years earlier and did not publish them, which only became known in 1997 [WP–DH,[1] WP–MJW,[2] Cocks73[3]]. In addition, mathematical methods that were considered sufficiently secure for a long time have repeatedly been found to be insecure at a later date, such as "Supersingular Isogenic Curve Cryptography" (SIKE) in the NIST competition [NIST25].[4]

Anyone who rejects mathematical methods for this reason, especially when it comes to sensitive research data, medical data, confidential data from governments

[1] https://en.wikipedia.org/wiki/Diffie-Hellman_key_exchange.

[2] https://en.wikipedia.org/wiki/Malcolm_J_Williamson.

[3] https://web.archive.org/web/20080227001905/http://www.cesg.gov.uk/site/publications/media/notense.pdf.

[4] https://csrc.nist.gov/pqc-standardization.

and companies, etc., must use physical methods of cryptography. Physical methods introduce a new paradigm of cryptography that differs from today's complexity-based cryptography. The methods are secure against computationally powerful adversaries, such as powerful quantum computers or optical computers (which, according to many predictions, will be many times faster), and against mathematical attack methods that are still unknown to experts today, i.e., secure against as-yet-unpublished mathematical methods that can break today's mathematical methods, including post-quantum cryptography. And this applies not only to data encryption (security goal: confidentiality) and key management, but also to the security goals of integrity and authenticity. In symmetric and asymmetric cryptography today, there are, on the one hand, many mathematical methods that use short keys—usually under 5,000 bits—and their security assessment is based on assumptions. On the other hand, for data encryption, there is one-time pad (OTP) with a very long key, which can reach into the GByte and TByte range, and its security can be proven to be 100% secure. Asymmetric cryptography for key management can be replaced by physical methods such as QKD (Quantum Key Distribution), RKD (Radio-signal Key Distribution), or MKD (Memory Key Distribution) to ensure the highest possible level of security. The physical methods, particularly QKD and RKD, currently provide key sizes that are much too large for mathematical data encryption methods, but are usually too small for the one-time pad. And it is precisely this gap that is covered by two new encryption methods (called OTPH and OTPS) and two new encryption modes of operation (called XTSO and OTPM) described in Chap. 6 of the book and at https://cryptography.study/phys/modes. The key sets achievable with QKD and RKD are perfectly suited to the new encryption methods/modes, and while the security assessment cannot be proven to be 100% secure, it is based on the security of HKDF / hash functions and the XOR operation, which are used in QKD and RKD themselves.

The topic of physical cryptography methods has only become really popular due to the demand for security against quantum computers, but it is a topic that has been just as relevant for decades and still is today because it also affects today's data encryption (storage today, attack in the future). On the other hand, those who are satisfied with today's asymmetric cryptography will also be satisfied with post-quantum cryptography [WP–PQC][5] in the future and will not need physical methods. This also applies to symmetric methods such as AES (Advanced Encryption Standard) [WP–AES].[6]

1.1.1 The Compared Methods/Technologies

This book provides a systematic comparison of physical methods/technologies for generating and distributing cryptographic keys. It examines methods/technologies that are not primarily based on mathematical hardness assumptions, but derive

[5] https://en.wikipedia.org/wiki/Post-quantum_cryptography.

[6] https://en.wikipedia.org/wiki/Advanced_Encryption_Standard.

their security-relevant properties from physical laws. These include three classes of quantum key distribution (QKD) in their practical forms, as well as the generation and distribution of cryptographic keys using radio signals (RKD) and storage media (MKD). The QKD, RKD, and MKD methods/technologies presented each consist of a variety of different individual technologies and methods, which are collectively referred to in this book as methods/technology.

Specifically, the following five methods/technologies of physical cryptography are presented and compared according to practical performance criteria:

1. **DV-QKD (Discrete Variable Quantum Key Distribution)**

   This method exploits the quantum physical properties (specifically: the polarization directions) of indivisible units (specifically, individual photons, i.e., light particles) to generate identical random bit sequences at a transmitter and a receiver. However, the randomness of the key material does not arise "by itself," but must be introduced externally on the sender's side. This random quantum information is transmitted to the receiver via fiber optic cable, free-space channel, or satellite and measured there. Due to the quantum nature of the transmission, any eavesdropping attempt will be detected.
2. **CV-QKD (Continuous Variable Quantum Key Distribution)**

   This works largely like DV-QKD, with the following difference: the carriers of the quantum information are not indivisible units (i.e., not individual photons), but weak light pulses consisting of several photons. As with DV-QKD, randomness is introduced externally at the transmitter and imposed on the individual light pulses as modulation of amplitude (corresponding to the number of photons in the pulse) and phase. This modulation is performed in the same way as in conventional telecommunications. Due to the low intensity of the pulses and a quantum physical relationship between amplitude and phase, eavesdropping attacks can also be reliably detected with this method/technology.
3. **QKD (quantum key distribution) with entanglement**

   In methods of this class, the sender of the quantum information is not one of the two key exchange partners, but a third party that does not need to be trusted. This source generates entangled photon pairs and sends one photon from each pair to the two key exchange partners, who measure these photons. The two partners therefore have equal roles. Another very important difference from the previously mentioned QKD variants is the randomness that arises "by itself" here, i.e., directly from the quantum nature of entanglement. The randomness does not have to be generated by a separate generator. Because an eavesdropping attacker inevitably destroys the entanglement of the two photons, such attacks are reliably detected here as well.
4. **RKD (Radio Signal Key Distribution)**

   RKD uses radio signals above 30 MHz to calculate and distribute cryptographic keys and is known in the literature under various names, e.g., "Physical layer key generation in wireless networks" or "Wireless Physical Layer Key Agreement."

RKD is a physical process based on the reciprocity of radio transmission and measurement of radio channel properties. Both sides of the communication are equal and use the same devices to generate and distribute the cryptographic keys. Randomness arises "by itself" through the process, and protection against eavesdropping is based on the fact that the radio properties of these two locations cannot be reconstructed at locations other than directly at the transmitter or receiver.

5. **MKD (Memory Key Distribution)**

   With MKD, physical distribution is carried out using a storage medium such as high-security smart cards or SSDs (solid-state storage, currently up to 16 TB), which contain at least one integrated AES-256 HW encryption unit and a high-security smart card for key transport for the AES HW encryption integrated in the SSD. Both sides of the communication (Alice and Bob) are equal and use the same devices to generate and distribute the cryptographic keys. Randomness must be introduced from outside. To carry out an eavesdropping attack, an attacker would have to gain physical access to the storage medium and be in possession of the smart card containing the key.

In addition, the QKD variants and RKD also examine the different transmission paths: fiber optic networks (only for QKD), free-space channels, and satellite connections. With MKD, transport is carried out in person or with the help of a personal courier or public parcel service. The terms RKD and MKD were coined by the first author of this book and were chosen in analogy to QKD.

What all the methods considered have in common is that they deal exclusively with the generation and distribution of symmetric keys and are physical methods. The actual data encryption and mechanisms for ensuring integrity and authenticity are considered separately from this conceptually, as they each require additional assumptions, procedures, and system components. The book explicitly does not pursue a product- or manufacturer-specific approach, but analyzes the methods/technologies in terms of their physical principles, systemic properties, and practical feasibility.

1.1.2 Comparison Criteria

The five physical cryptography procedures mentioned above are presented in this book in a generally understandable and technology-neutral manner and compared in a comprehensible way using the following practice-relevant performance criteria:

- IT security
- Market readiness
- Key rate (dependent on distance in the case of QKD)
- Distance (distance between communication partners)
- Cost
- Robustness/susceptibility to interference

- Suitability for mobile devices
- Infrastructural dependencies

The book also contains a technology-neutral analysis of the advantages and disadvantages and, in conjunction with the webpage https://cryptography.study/phys, a current market analysis of the European products/solutions already on offer. Furthermore, the applications *of telecommunications and data storage with physical processes* and the *XOR function* are discussed. In the case of the XOR function, the relationship to physics and the implementation of the security objectives of confidentiality with the one-time pad and integrity and authenticity with the MAC are described.

1.1.3 Fundamentals of Comparability

The comparisons made in this book are based on a systematic compilation of various sources of information and levels of analysis. They are based firstly on the documented state of the art from scientific literature and publicly available research reports, secondly on information provided by manufacturers about their products and systems, and thirdly on experience reports from users who have employed the relevant processes/technologies in real or practical environments.

The significance of the sources used must be evaluated differently.

- Scientific publications generally provide easily verifiable results, but these are often obtained under idealized conditions.
- Manufacturer information is particularly relevant for key technical data, but is naturally subject to marketing-driven distortions and does not always refer to long-term practical operation.
- User reports offer valuable insights into real-world operating conditions, but are often limited to specific configurations and individual cases.

The comparability of the processes/technologies examined is also limited by structural differences. The processes differ fundamentally in terms of physical principles, system architectures, maturity, and context of use. Uniform key figures that would allow direct quantitative comparability exist only to a limited extent. Statements on key rates, ranges, costs, or robustness must therefore always be interpreted in the respective context.

Against this background, the present comparison is not intended as an exact comparison of individual measured values, but rather as a qualitatively sound classification of technological characteristics and framework conditions. The aim is to provide a basis for decision-making and to make the strengths, weaknesses, and dependencies of the processes transparent. In doing so, no attempt is made to feign a level of accuracy that is unattainable given the heterogeneous sources and dynamic technological developments.

1.1.4 Comparison Methods and References

Three methods were used to compare the performance of the various processes/technologies:

1. Process/technology perspective: what is possible with the current state of the art, etc.?
2. Perspective of suppliers of real products on the market
3. Perspective of third parties who act as users of real products on the market

The performance criteria listed above can be compared using these three methods with varying degrees of accuracy and objectivity, i.e., without bias or prejudice. For example, distance and key rate can be compared using all three methods, but the best results come from method 3 (users). Method 3 is also the most suitable for costs, robustness, and market readiness. In contrast, method 1 is best suited for IT security and suitability for mobile end devices.

For method 1, we examined the state of the art in detail and carried out the comparison on that basis. For method 2, we surveyed suppliers of real products and conducted research on the Internet. The results of method 2 had to be treated with caution in some cases, as they often involved marketing statements or tests in laboratory environments. However, the results from methods 2 and 3 were always presented together in the book so that both sides of the argument were visible. For method 3, we surveyed users of real products. However, this was very difficult for some processes/technologies because either there are only a few users or the users have not carried out sufficiently scientifically sound analyses according to these performance criteria and, if they have, they do not release the results.

For QKD, we obtained the results for method 3 from the AIT (Austrian Institute of Technology) as stated in the book. The AIT procured seven different products from the market and tested them extensively and objectively as users in various practical environments. Due to the large number of different products and thus processes/technologies, the AIT was able to compare the various products relatively well according to some performance criteria in this book in a technology-neutral and objective manner in practical environments.

For RKD and MKD, we obtained the results specified in the book for method 3 from the Institute for IT Security Research at the USTP (University of Applied Sciences St. Pölten, Austria).

1.2 Physics and Security

Although physical cryptography methods are based on the laws of physics, as will be explained in detail in the main part of the book, other factors also contribute to security, particularly in QKD (quantum key distribution) and RKD (radio key distribution). The security of a method or technology is always determined by its weakest link, and that is not the physical fundamentals. In QKD and RKD, the concrete implementations, primarily due to hardware design decisions, lead to many real possibilities for side-channel attacks (see Sect. 3.8). The necessary mathematical procedures, which are required for post-processing (error correction and privacy amplification, see Sect. 8), also offer potential points of attack.

In cryptography, what ultimately counts is the security of the procedure and not its complexity or the scientific discipline on which it is based. A good example of this is the simplest method of data encryption, namely the one-time pad [WP–OTP][7,8] (bitwise encryption using the XOR function, see Sect. 6.2), which is the only method that is mathematically provably 100% secure.

Data encryption must always be end-to-end. Since a great deal of sensitive data is generated on an end device (desktop PC, laptop, tablet, smartphone, IoT device, sensor, medical device, etc.), it must also be encrypted sufficiently securely there. For security reasons, the actual encryption often takes place in an HSM (hardware security module) or a cryptobox. Such devices are available on the market at low cost. However, the data may also be encrypted directly on the end device if this is done with a one-time pad and storage media suitable for key transport (see Sect. 5.2) are used. As mobility becomes increasingly important, high-security encryption on laptops, tablets, smartphones, and IoT devices is also becoming more important (e.g., laptops with multisession operation with several parallel virtual workstations with different security levels at the operating system level, from open to closed).

1.3 Economic Aspects of Security

However, the economically reasonable costs necessary to guarantee the required level of encryption security are not based on the price of the end device or the value of an HSM or cryptobox, but primarily on the value of the data. This means that even with a cheap end device, such as a laptop, the total encryption solution per end device may be significantly more expensive than the end device itself if the value of the data, e.g., in the case of very valuable research data or strictly confidential government data, is correspondingly high. However, the total costs must always be taken into account, i.e., the connection costs (fiber optics, satellite, transport of storage media, etc.) and the operating costs, including maintenance costs. These costs can increase quadratically due to the necessary end-to-end connections between all end devices (if no connection can be used twice, the number of connections required for n participants is $\frac{n^2-n}{2}$ connections, i.e., for example, $n = 100$ already requires 4.950 connections).

[7] https://en.wikipedia.org/wiki/One-time_pad.

[8] See Sect. 6.2.

1.4 Objective of the Book

The aim of the comparison is to provide a comprehensible and technology-neutral basis for evaluating these methods. The book is aimed at anyone interested in cryptography, especially procurers, experts, and decision-makers who are faced with the question of whether and to what extent physical cryptography methods should be considered as a supplement or alternative to established mathematical methods. The aim is not to provide an abstract security theory assessment, but rather a classification based on the above criteria.

The comparison does not aim to create a ranking of the methods/technologies examined or to present a single solution as generally superior. Rather, the structural differences, strengths, and weaknesses of the approaches are to be made transparent in order to enable informed decisions in the respective application context. Different application scenarios, such as telecommunications, data storage, highly secure point-to-point connections, and use in mobile devices, place different demands on key rates, range, robustness, infrastructure, and organizational integration, which the methods under consideration meet to varying degrees.

This book does not cover detailed security assessments of individual implementations, the mathematical methods used in the procedures/technologies or products, source code analyses, or certification issues relating to specific products. Similarly, mathematical cryptography, including post-quantum cryptography, is not fundamentally evaluated or placed in competition with physical methods. Rather, it is considered an established frame of reference to which physical methods can be related depending on security assumptions, risk profiles, and use cases. The book is thus intended as a basis for decision-making and orientation, not as a normative guideline for the use of specific methods/technologies.

1.5 Unique Selling Point of this Book

There are many books on cryptography, and some of them also deal with physical methods. In the field of physical cryptography, there are several books on QKD (quantum key distribution). However, RKD (radio signal key distribution) and MKD (memory key distribution) have not yet been covered in books, and there is no performance comparison of these methods/technologies and procedures.

This book is the first internationally to compare these completely different physical cryptography methods in a technology-neutral way and make them generally understandable.

1.6 Reference to the Book's Website

The performance comparisons also included many products from different manufacturers to ensure that the results are comprehensible and manufacturer-neutral. However, because this data is constantly changing—the market is evolving—and because individual results are not very meaningful, the individual results of the products and manufacturers were not included in the book. However, they are available from the St. Pölten University of Applied Sciences via the website https://cryptography.study/phys (the references can be found in the relevant sections of the book) and are considered to be external appendices to the book. This webpage also contains other interesting aspects of the book, including important necessary hardware components (photon sources, detectors, etc.), descriptions of QKD protocols, an overview of random number generators, and a practical RKD implementation, etc. These external appendices therefore represent important additions to the book. Furthermore, four encryption methods/modes developed specifically for QKD and RKD are presented, and a complete eCoC implementation for MKD is discussed.

All supplements and appendices related to this book as well as book proofreading and editing can be found at the following address: https://cryptography.study/phys.

1.7 Origin of the Book, Acknowledgments

The book was written at the St. Pölten University of Applied Sciences, Austria, at the Institute for IT Security Research. It is based on the study "Crypto comparison" and four other projects (KIF, LoRaBridge, RKD, LISA), all of which were funded by the Austrian Research Promotion Agency FFG. The study has been funded by the Austrian security research program KIRAS/K-Pass of the Austrian Ministry of Finance (BMF).

The authors of the book would like to express their gratitude to Simon Tjoa and Henri Ruotsalainen (St. Pölten University of Applied Sciences), Gerald Trost (Federal Chancellery of Austria), Ralf Hammer and Lukas Siebeneicher (Austrian Federal Ministry of Finance), Florian Kutschera (AIT), and the FFG for their support.

References

[WP-DH] Wikipedia contributors, Diffie–Hellman key exchange. Wikipedia, the Free Encyclopedia. https://en.wikipedia.org/wiki/Diffie-Hellman_key_exchange

[WP-MJW] Wikipedia contributors, Malcolm J. Williamson. Wikipedia, the Free Encyclopedia. https://en.wikipedia.org/wiki/Malcolm_J._Williamson

[Cocks73] C.C., Cocks, A Note on 'Non-Secret Encryption. CESG Memo. 20 Nov 1973. https://web.archive.org/web/20080227001905/http://www.cesg.gov.uk/site/publications/media/notense.pdf

[NIST25] National Institute of Standards and Technology (NIST); Computer Security Resource Center (CSRC). PQC Standardization Process (Post-Quantum Cryptography). Created 03 Jan 2017; updated 11 Dec 2025. https://csrc.nist.gov/pqc-standardization

[WP-PQC] Wikipedia contributors, Post-quantum cryptography. Wikipedia, the Free Encyclopedia. https://en.wikipedia.org/wiki/Post-quantum_cryptography

[WP-AES] Wikipedia contributors, Advanced Encryption Standard. Wikipedia, the Free Encyclopedia. https://en.wikipedia.org/wiki/Advanced_Encryption_Standard

[WP-OTP] Wikipedia contributors, One-time pad. Wikipedia, the Free Encyclopedia. https://en.wikipedia.org/wiki/One-time_pad

Chapter 2
General Information about Cryptography

If the security assessments are not trusted, especially in cases of very high data security requirements, physical methods must be used for key generation and distribution, data encryption, and integrity and authenticity procedures. This ensures the confidentiality, integrity, and authenticity of the data against computationally powerful adversaries and mathematical attack methods that are still unknown (unpublished) today. This chapter provides an introduction to these topics, briefly compares mathematical methods, and discusses the generation and distribution of cryptographic keys, as well as QKD (Quantum Key Distribution), RKD (Radio signal Key Distribution), and MKD (Memeory Key Distribution).

2.1 Mathematical Versus Physical Methods in Cryptography

Physical cryptography methods can be used to achieve provably absolute data security in order to ensure the confidentiality, integrity, and authenticity of data, including the necessary key management. However, this statement does not assess the security of the underlying physical laws [Bern18],[1] i.e., the laws of quantum mechanics, the randomness of non-deterministic random number generators, etc. are not questioned.

If, for reasons of security assessment, mathematical cryptographic methods are dispensed with and physical methods are used, mathematics does not have to be dispensed with altogether. This raises the question of which mathematics may still be used. This mainly concerns post-processing in QKD and RKD, which has not yet been sufficiently investigated in terms of security for the individual methods currently in use.

[1] https://doi.org/10.48550/arXiv.1803.04520.

E. Piller and H. Schölnast, *Data Encryption at the Intersection of Mathematics and Physics*, SpringerBriefs in Information Security and Cryptography,
https://doi.org/10.1007/978-3-032-24764-3_2

2.2 Mathematical Methods of Cryptography

Cryptography can be used to achieve three main security objectives: confidentiality, integrity, and authenticity. Confidentiality refers to the encryption of data, while integrity refers to the ability to verify whether the data transmitted during telecommunications or stored during data storage has been altered. Authenticity allows the origin or authorship of the data to be determined.

When using mathematical cryptographic methods, symmetric methods such as AES (Advanced Encryption Standard, ISO/IEC 18033–3) [WP–AES],[2] ChaCha20 (by Bernstein) [WP–CCP][3] etc. are usually used for data encryption because they are much faster than asymmetric methods. In addition, many methods, such as AES-256 (AES with a 256-bit key), are also classified as quantum computer-secure. An assessment of the threat posed by future optical computers is still pending. Integrity and authenticity are usually solved with an electronic/digital signature, which comes from asymmetric cryptography. Today, ECDSA (Elliptic Curve Digital Signature Algorithm, ISO/IEC 14883–3) [WP–ECD][4] is mostly used for this purpose. If quantum computer security is desired, post-quantum cryptography methods must be used. For signatures, these are Crystals Dilithium, Falcon, or Sphincs+, and for asymmetric encryption and key exchange according to Diffie-Hellman (PKCS #3: Diffie-Hellman Key Agreement Standard), Crystals Kyber (ISO/IEC 27001:2022) [WP–Kyb],[5] because these methods have all been selected as quantum computer-secure by the NIST (US National Institute of Standards and Technology) [NIST25].[6] This means that no physical methods are required to achieve quantum computer security, as long as the non-provable security assessments are trusted.

2.3 Physical Cryptographic Methods

If these security assessments are not trusted, especially in cases of very high data security requirements, physical methods must be used for key generation and distribution, data encryption, and integrity and authenticity procedures. This ensures the confidentiality, integrity, and authenticity of the data against computationally powerful adversaries and mathematical attack methods that are still unknown (unpublished) today. These methods are discussed in more detail in the following Sects. 1.4 and 1.5.

All five physical cryptography methods/technologies discussed in the book—QKD in several technological variants, RKD, and MKD—only allow the generation and distribution of symmetric keys. Therefore, only symmetric cryptography

---

[2] https://en.wikipedia.org/wiki/Advanced_Encryption_Standard.

[3] https://en.wikipedia.org/wiki/ChaCha20-Poly1305.

[4] https://en.wikipedia.org/wiki/Elliptic_Curve_DSA.

[5] https://en.wikipedia.org/wiki/Kyber.

[6] https://csrc.nist.gov/pqc-standardization.

methods can be used with QKD, RKD, and MKD. Only symmetric methods can therefore be used to achieve the security objectives of confidentiality, integrity, and authenticity. These cryptographic methods are dependent on the physical methods QKD, RKD, and MKD because they only enable symmetric methods and because the key rates (measured in bits/second) enabled by the various methods and implementations of QKD, RKD, and MKD influence the selection of cryptographic methods.

As already stated above, it is always the case that, in order to ensure a consistently high level of security in terms of confidentiality, integrity, and authenticity, all mathematical cryptographic methods whose security cannot be strictly proven mathematically should be avoided. However, in the case of the physical methods QKD and RKD, mathematical methods must also be used for post-processing in addition to the physical method. These may include, for example, cascade error correction, low-density parity checks (LDPC), or secure sketch for error correction, and universal hash functions with a Toeplitz matrix and the use of a fast Fourier transform (FFT) for privacy amplification.

2.4 Generation of Cryptographic Keys

All mathematical methods for generating cryptographic keys used today are based on complex mathematical problems, such as the discrete logarithm in multiplicative groups or in elliptic curves. The security of post-quantum cryptography (PQC) is based on mathematical problems that are difficult to solve and, from today's perspective, cannot be solved efficiently even with quantum computers. These include, in particular, lattice problems, code-based problems, multivariate equation systems, and hash-based methods. In the case of lattice problems (lattice-based cryptography), these are primarily the shortest vector problem (SVP) and learning with errors (LWE). Code-based problems are based on the difficulty of decrypting linear error-correcting codes. The security of "multivariate quadratic equation systems" is based on the difficulty of solving systems of nonlinear equations over finite fields. Hash-based methods use the one-way properties of cryptographic hash functions.

The security of these methods is based on the assumption that, above certain key lengths, there are no efficient algorithms that can solve these mathematical problems within a reasonable amount of time. Assuming that Moore's Law for the increase in computer processing speed continues to apply, this increase requires that the keys used must be extended by approximately 13 additional bits every 10 years in order to maintain the same level of security. However, with the advent of powerful quantum computers or optical computers, the situation is changing dramatically and requires post-quantum cryptography. However, as this assumption has not yet been proven, these established and mathematically based methods are associated with a degree of uncertainty that is difficult to assess. It is possible that there are as yet unpublished efficient algorithms that can be used to break these mathematical methods.

2.4.1 QKD

Quantum key distribution (QKD; see Chap. 3) takes a fundamentally different approach. Unlike conventional methods, QKD is based on fundamental principles of quantum mechanics. These principles arise from physical laws, such as the fact that measurements on quantum states inevitably change them, or the fundamental impossibility of copying unknown quantum states. Of the QKD technologies discussed in this book, only the "QKD with entangled photons" variant itself provides the entire randomness of the key during key generation, and does so independently on both sides. (Both key exchange partners have identical roles.) In the other two QKD technologies, additional non-deterministic random number generators provide the randomness, and the two key exchange partners have different roles. One of the two is the sole generator of the randomness of the raw key, while the role of the other partner is limited to pure selection, without the possibility of influencing the randomness of the raw key itself. In practical use with independent communication partners, this is unfavorable in terms of security, primarily because a random number generator is used on only one side.

2.4.2 RKD

Another physical method is Radio Signal Key Distribution (RKD, see Chap. 4), where security is also not based on mathematical assumptions, but on fundamental principles of the generation and propagation of electromagnetic waves, in particular ultra-short waves (VHF). In contrast to QKD, which operates with light quanta, RKD uses radio signals above 30 MHz. RKD takes advantage of the unique physical properties of wireless radio channels. RKD is based on two fundamental properties of high-frequency transmission: the inherent unpredictability (randomness) of channel properties and the reciprocity of radio transmission between two communication partners. With RKD, two communication devices transmit radio signals in both directions at approximately the same time and continuously measure the received signal properties. Typically, the signal strength (RSSI–Received Signal Strength Indicator), the phase angle, or the transit time of the signals are recorded. The key principle lies in the reciprocity of the radio channel: since both devices use the same physical transmission path, they measure almost identical channel characteristics. These common measurements form the basis for generating identical cryptographic keys on both sides without having to exchange this information via a separate channel. As with QKD with entangled photons, RKD does not require an additional non-deterministic random number generator for key generation; instead, randomness arises independently on both sides from physics. However, like QKD, RKD also requires mathematical post-processing and mutual data exchange, which makes it much more difficult to assess the security of the overall solution. In contrast to QKD, however, RKD is very cost-effective. QKD and, above all, RKD has a relatively low key rate (bits generated per second).

2.4.3 MKD

In MKD (Memory Key Distribution; see Chap. 5), the communication partners use a non-deterministic random number generator to generate the raw material in the form of very long bit sequences, which are later used as a shared key. This raw material is then stored on suitable, highly secure, transportable storage media—which are inexpensive and available on the global market with high security certification—and physically transported to the future communication partner. When storing data, all users with the same read rights receive the storage media containing the keys. In MKD, randomness comes from additional non-deterministic random number generators that are available on both sides. This means that in MKD, randomness is determined independently by both sides, as in RKD and QKD with entangled photons. Even a faulty or poor-quality random number generator—possibly caused by an attacker or the manufacturer—thus poses no problem, because after an XOR operation, the better of the two generators always determines the minimum quality of the key bits. There are no work steps that would be equivalent to post-processing or other mathematical procedures that would make it difficult to assess the security of the overall solution. Therefore, MKD enables completely math-free key generation and distribution. Because MKD also allows for very long keys (suitable storage media are now available up to 16 TB), data encryption with a one-time pad is also possible, which uses only an XOR operation and is provably absolutely secure.

2.5 Distribution of Cryptographic Keys

2.5.1 Within a Key Exchange Pair

In the case of QKD and RKD, the distribution of the generated key material within the pair that performs the joint key generation is an integral part of key generation and cannot be separated from it. Generating the key and ensuring that both parties receive the same key goes hand in hand with these two types of procedures.

With MKD, generation and distribution are separate steps, because here a key exchange partner generates the key, makes a copy of it, and then physically transports this copy to the other party. To further increase security, the other party can also generate its own key and send a copy to the first party. Each of them then combines the self-generated and received keys into a common key using an XOR operation.

2.5.2 *Distribution to Multiple Communication Partners*

All of the methods discussed in this book involve symmetric encryption, which means that two people who want to communicate with each other must first be provided with identical key material. This can be done through direct key exchange between these two people, but, as will be shown in the following chapters, there are physical distance limits, particularly with QKD and RKD, beyond which direct key exchange is impossible. If the distance between the two communication partners is too great, direct key exchange is not possible.

Trusted Nodes

In such cases, previously generated keys must be distributed via a specially created infrastructure, the essential components of which are trusted nodes. Trusted nodes are nodes in a network through which the key material can be exchanged. New key material is constantly being generated between neighboring trusted nodes, but the endpoints (i.e., the points that actually want to communicate with each other) also generate the key material in pairs with one or more trusted nodes. Some of the key material generated in this network is then used to secure the transport of other key materials through this trusted node network. In this way, the key material can also be transported across physical distance boundaries.

However, this method comes at a price: on the one hand, a significant portion of the key material generated is not used for the intended communication, but rather to secure key distribution. Many consider the need to trust trusted nodes to be a major disadvantage. This is because the trusted nodes' memory stores all the key material used for communication, making these devices desirable targets for attack and requiring them to be specially protected. The necessary maintenance also poses a major challenge here.

MKD

5As shown in the chapter on Multi-Key Distribution (MKD), there are no physical distance limits for MKD, which is why there is no need for trusted node networks with this method/technology.

2.6 Security Objectives

2.6.1 *Security Objective: Confidentiality*

Confidentiality means that protected information can only be read by authorized persons. In other words, the protection goal of confidentiality is considered to have been achieved for encrypted messages if it is impossible to read the plain text without the key.

There is a single encryption method for which the achievement of this protection goal can be proven mathematically. This is the one-time pad (see Chap. 6.2), which is based on the bitwise XOR operation between the plaintext and a key of equal length. An essential additional condition is that each key may only be used for a single message (prohibition of multiple use). A further additional condition is that the key must be truly random, i.e., it must originate from a non-deterministic source (for details, see Chap. 6.2 and https://cryptography.study/phys/XOR).

For all other known encryption methods, it can be proven that there must always be an algorithm that makes it possible to read the plaintext without a key. The simplest algorithm that always works (except for the one-time pad) is to systematically try all possible keys, i.e., a brute force attack.

It is therefore clear that the trust goal of confidentiality cannot be achieved in the strict formulation just used by any other known method other than the one-time pad. In practical application, however, a weakened definition of this protection goal is sufficient in many cases:

Practically achievable confidentiality means that protected information can only be read by unauthorized persons with unrealistically high effort and/or with an extremely low probability of success.

This definition means that the ability of an encryption method to achieve practically achievable confidentiality depends on the algorithmic complexity of the most efficient key-breaking algorithm. In other words, the algorithm that allows an attacker to read the plaintext with the least effort or the greatest probability of success without having to know the key determines the extent of practically achievable confidentiality.

With standardized encryption methods that correspond to the current state of the art, the effort an attacker must expend to obtain the plaintext with a predetermined probability which depends on the length of the key used and, in many cases, also on the type of computer used (classical computer or quantum computer). The most efficient known key-breaking algorithm is used as a basis in each case. The recommended key lengths then correspond to a time expenditure for the attacker that, when using reasonably realistic hardware, is equivalent to a multiple of the age of the universe, or the key lengths correspond to a probability of success that is equivalent to the probability that in an unmanipulated lottery over dozens or hundreds of rounds, exactly the same numbers will always be drawn at random in each draw.

However, there is a problem: practically achievable confidentiality depends on the most efficient algorithm possible. But standardizations necessarily only take known algorithms into account. What if there is a very efficient key-breaking algorithm for an encryption method that is still unknown but will become known tomorrow? Or worse, what if the very party from whom you most urgently want to keep your secrets has discovered a very efficient key-breaking algorithm and can use it without making it public?

It would therefore be very helpful if it could be proven for at least one encryption method that, for fundamental reasons, there cannot be any algorithm for this method whose efficiency exceeds a certain threshold. (In technical terms, this is referred to as algorithmic complexity rather than efficiency.) Experts have been trying to provide such proof for decades, but have not yet been successful. The one-time pad is an exception to this.

There is a widespread belief among experts that such limits do indeed exist for many encryption methods, which is good news for the trust that can be placed in standardized encryption methods. But an opinion is not proof, and based on current knowledge, it cannot be completely ruled out that any standardized encryption method could soon become ineffective because someone has found an efficient way to break it (with the exception of the one-time pad).

The only method that is completely exempted from all these considerations is the one-time pad,[7] for which the achievement of this protection goal can be proven mathematically and is therefore an important data encryption method for MKD.

2.6.2 Security Objective: Integrity

Integrity means guaranteeing that the sender receives exactly the data that the sender sent. Integrity therefore means that it is impossible to manipulate the data during transmission or while it is stored. This goal is achieved by adding checksums and authenticating the sender to the recipient.

The physical cryptography methods currently available only allow symmetric cryptography, but not asymmetric cryptography. Therefore, in addition to data encryption, MACs (message authentication codes for integrity assurance, ISO/IEC 9797–2) [WP–MAC][8] are also possible, which allow integrity and authenticity checks between two communication partners.

Integrity can be easily implemented with a high level of security using a symmetric method. For example, CCM-MAC (Counter with CBC-MAC, specified in RFC 3610), CBC-MAC (Cipher Block Chaining with MAC, ISO/IEC 10116) and GCM-MAC (Galois Counter Mode with MAC, ISO/IEC 13157–3) use the XOR function (see Chap. 6) for MAC calculation. In conjunction with the one-time pad for encryption, these MACs allow for provably absolute integrity security.

2.6.3 Security Goal: Authenticity

Authenticity means the verifiable certainty that a received message actually originates from the claimed sender and has not been generated or falsified by an unauthorized third party.

Asymmetric cryptography can be used to generate digitally signed certificates that allow a person, device, etc. to be assigned to a public key, which in turn can

[7] See Sect. 6.2One-Time Pad.

[8] https://en.wikipedia.org/wiki/Message_authentication_code.

be used to verify any digital signature. Without asymmetric cryptography—as is the case with physical methods—this elegant solution is not possible.

Therefore, physical methods and thus protection against computationally very strong opponents and mathematical attack methods that are still unknown (unpublished) today cannot be used even for blockchains and cryptocurrencies such as Bitcoin, whereby Bitcoin, for example, has not even taken the step towards post-quantum cryptography and thus protection against powerful quantum computers with mathematical methods.

All key exchange procedures discussed in this book generate keys that are intended for symmetric encryption methods. When these keys are used, a symmetric shared secret is usually employed. In conjunction with methods such as the Wegman-Carter method [Weg81],[9] it is possible to ensure not only the integrity of the transmitted data, but also the authenticity of the sending communication partner. However, the shared secret must be exchanged in pairs between all possible communication partners so that each communication partner can reliably identify their counterpart. With n communication partners, this means $n * (n - 1)/2$ shared secrets (e.g., $n = 100$, resulting in 4950 shared secrets). This number can be significantly reduced by forming groups in which several communication partners are assigned to groups. However, this means that it is no longer possible to assign a communication partner directly, but only to assign them to a group. Another option is star-shaped topologies with central communication nodes. Each party communicates directly only with this central server, which forwards all received messages to all participants. This means that with n communication partners, only n shared secrets need to be exchanged. However, each member of this group must then trust that the central node actually verifies the authenticity of all other group participants.

This must be distinguished from key generation. In all the methods presented in the book, key generation takes place in pairs, i.e., between exactly two parties. To ensure authenticity during key generation in the QKD and RKD methods, the Wegman-Carter method (or another equivalent method) is also used. In the case of MKD, the key exchange involves the physical transfer of a data carrier, which enables the use of authentication methods from the physical world, such as high-security smart cards, etc., in conjunction with PIN (personal identification number) or biometric features (two-factor authentication).

2.7 Common Communication Roles (Alice, Bob, Eve, Mallory)

In cryptography, in the field of network protocols, and also in subdisciplines of physics, it is common to talk about communication partners with specific roles or characteristics. Over the past few decades, a few names for recurring roles

[9] https://doi.org/10.1016/0022-0000(81)90033-7.

have become established in international specialist literature and have now become "standard names" [WP–A&B].[10] Four of these names are also used in this book:

2.7.1 *Alice and Bob*

These are the names of the two legitimate communication partners. These two parties do not want other parties to gain possession of information that is the subject of legitimate communication. The names *Alice* and *Bob* are derived from the first two letters of the alphabet, but otherwise have no special meaning.

In many communication protocols, Alice and Bob are not exactly the same. If one of them actively initiates the communication (e.g., by dialing a phone number) and the other responds to this action (e.g., by picking up the phone or accepting the call), then the party that acts first or starts sending is called "Alice" (because A is the first letter of the alphabet). The other legitimate party is then called "Bob."

In the field of quantum key distribution in particular, Alice initiates communication in two of the three methods described. In the third method (QKD with entanglement), in RKD and MKD, the roles of the two communication partners are exactly the same. In this case, it does not matter which of the two has which name. However, the names are still "Alice" and "Bob."

2.7.2 *Eve and Mallory*

The English verb *"to eavesdrop"* means to *listen in on a conversation secretly*. The interception of other people's messages is therefore referred to as *eavesdropping* in technical jargon. Due to the phonetic similarity of the first syllable of these terms to the English first name "Eve," this name has become established as the name for the party attempting to eavesdrop on the communication between Alice and Bob. Eve expressly does not attempt to actively interfere with the communication.

A malicious attacker who intends to alter the content of the transmitted information, inject new information, or block information is given the name *Mallory* (from *malicious attacker*) in this international quasi-standard nomenclature.

In the case of QKD protocols (see Chap. 3), however, a key feature of these protocols is that Eve unintentionally alters information or prevents it from reaching the recipient by eavesdropping. But this is typical of attempts to eavesdrop on quantum information. These changes are not intentional on Eve's part. On the contrary, she would actually prefer it if this did not happen, because her eavesdropping activities are reliably detected precisely by these changes. Due to the lack of intent to manipulate, it is therefore not justified to use the name *Mallory* for someone who unintentionally leaves traces by eavesdropping on the quantum channel. Therefore,

---

[10] https://en.wikipedia.org/wiki/Alice_and_Bob.

in the world of QKD protocols, the name *Eve* is always used for a party whose goal is to passively eavesdrop.

References

[Bern18] Bernstein, D.J., Is the Security of Quantum Cryptography Guaranteed by the Laws of Physics? arXiv preprint, (2018). https://doi.org/10.48550/arXiv.1803.04520

[WP-AES] Wikipedia contributors, Advanced Encryption Standard Wikipedia, the Free Encyclopedia. https://en.wikipedia.org/wiki/Advanced_Encryption_Standard

[WP-CCP] Wikipedia contributors, ChaCha20-Poly1305. Wikipedia, the Free Encyclopedia. https://en.wikipedia.org/wiki/ChaCha20-Poly1305

[WP-ECD] Wikipedia contributors, Elliptic Curve Digital Signature Algorithm. Wikipedia, the Free Encyclopedia. https://en.wikipedia.org/wiki/Elliptic_Curve_DSA

[WP-Kyb] Wikipedia contributors, Kyber. Wikipedia, the Free Encyclopedia. https://en.wikipedia.org/wiki/Kyber

[NIST25] National Institute of Standards and Technology (NIST); Computer Security Resource Center (CSRC), PQC Standardization Process (Post-Quantum Cryptography). Created 03 Jan 2017; updated 11 Dec 2025. https://csrc.nist.gov/pqc-standardization

[WP-MAC] Wikipedia contributors, Message authentication code. Wikipedia, the Free Encyclopedia. https://en.wikipedia.org/wiki/Message_authentication_code

[Weg81] M.N. Wegman, L. Carter, New hash functions and their use in authentication and set equality. J. Comput. Syst. Sci. **22**, 265–279 (1981). https://doi.org/10.1016/0022-0000(81)90033-7

[WP-A&B] Wikipedia contributors, Alice and Bob. Wikipedia, the Free Encyclopedia. https://en.wikipedia.org/wiki/Alice_and_Bob

Chapter 3
QKD

QKD (Quantum Key Distribution) promises information-theoretical security by using quantum states to generate shared cryptographic key material and to reveal eavesdropping attempts through unavoidable physical disturbances. The practical value of this promise depends not only on quantum technologies such as DV-QKD, CV-QKD, entanglement-based QKD, MDI-QKD, and Twin-Field QKD, but also on authentication, post-processing, implementation quality, and operational architecture. Fiber-optic, satellite, and free-space QKD each impose distinct limits on distance, key rate, trusted nodes, costs, and resistance to side-channel attacks.

3.1 What is QKD?

QKD [WP–QKD][1] is a communication method that allows Alice and Bob to generate a shared cryptographic key that can later be used by both parties for symmetric encryption methods. A significant part of the communication takes place via a quantum channel whose physical characteristics can only be described by the theories of quantum physics.

QKD offers perfect information-theoretical security under the following conditions:

- There is a classical accompanying channel (e.g., a normal Internet connection). All QKD methods and protocols assume that Eve can completely eavesdrop on or read everything that happens on this classical accompanying channel. Everything sent via this channel is therefore considered public knowledge.
- Alice and Bob authenticate each other on this classical channel by adding a MAC (Message Authentication Code) [WP–MAC][2] to each message.

[1] https://en.wikipedia.org/wiki/Quantum_key_distribution.

[2] https://en.wikipedia.org/wiki/Message_authentication_code.

E. Piller and H. Schölnast, *Data Encryption at the Intersection of Mathematics and Physics*, SpringerBriefs in Information Security and Cryptography,
https://doi.org/10.1007/978-3-032-24764-3_3

- The devices used by Alice and Bob are optimally configured and perfectly secured against classic eavesdropping attacks such as side-channel attacks.

It is expressly not a requirement that Eve be prevented from eavesdropping on the quantum channel in addition to the classical channel.

Perfect information-theoretical security specifically means that Eve, who is eavesdropping on both the quantum channel and the classical channel, has no way of extracting useful information about the key that Alice and Bob are currently trying to generate on both sides from the intercepted data. This circumstance is often referred to as "eavesdropping security of quantum communication." However, this term does not mean that eavesdropping is impossible, but rather that Eve can eavesdrop on both channels without being able to derive any benefit from what she intercepts. The reason for this is not any special mathematical procedures, but rather the physical nature of the quantum channel used.

In this consideration, the entire mathematical processing (see Chap. 8) required to generate a final cryptographic key is ignored or assumed to be perfectly secure, and possible side-channel attacks are also disregarded (see Chap. 3.8). This means that the security of QKD requires a much more comprehensive consideration than presented above and is usually undertaken in scientific QKD publications or manufacturer presentations.

3.1.1 Eavesdropping on the Classical Side Channel

Alice and Bob consider the classical side channel to be public and do not concern themselves with whether anyone is eavesdropping on the data traffic on this channel. Alice and Bob do not even know if anyone is eavesdropping on this classical side channel. They do not care.

3.1.2 Eavesdropping on the Quantum Channel

The quantum channel is designed in such a way that any attempt to eavesdrop on it will result in the falsification of a large proportion of the transmitted information units (bits [WP–Bit][3] or qubits [WP–Qbit][4]). This falsification is purely random and, due to the laws of physics, cannot be prevented or actively influenced by Eve. Alice and Bob use mathematical and statistical methods to detect these distortions retrospectively and then respond in such a way that Eve cannot obtain any useful information about the key from what she may have picked up on the quantum channel.

[3] https://en.wikipedia.org/wiki/Bit.

[4] https://en.wikipedia.org/wiki/Qubit.

More specifically, if Eve eavesdrops on the quantum channel and thereby obtains information that could potentially be useful to her, she will inevitably be noticed by Alice and Bob. Based on the extent of the perceived interference, the two can estimate the maximum amount of data traffic Eve could have intercepted. Alice and Bob then use appropriate mathematical methods to reduce the length of the shared key, with the result that Eve cannot gain any useful information about the key from what she has learned. The more information Eve intercepts on the quantum channel, the shorter becomes the key generated by Alice and Bob. If Eve exceeds a certain amount of intercepted information, Alice and Bob terminate the key exchange altogether. This means that Eve is effectively carrying out a denial-of-service attack, but in most cases she could do this more easily and cheaply by simply cutting the transmission medium (very often a fiber optic cable, see Chap. 3.4). Apart from that, the damage to Alice and Bob is minor, because the two were not trying to transmit important or urgent information, but only wanted to replenish their shared key stock. So the two have time to find the physical location where Eve carried out her eavesdropping attack. They then secure this location and repeat the key exchange.

3.1.3 Quantum Physics Paradigms

The special type of eavesdropping security offered by the quantum channel is based on physical principles that can only be described by quantum physics theories. In particular, these are the following quantum physics paradigms:

- **Measurement disturbance principle**: Every measurement of a quantum state changes this state with a high degree of probability [WP–MQM].[5]
- **No-cloning theorem**: Unknown quantum states cannot be duplicated. [WP–NCT].[6]
- **Monogamy of entanglement**: Maximum entanglement is only possible between two particles. It is possible to extend entanglement to three or more particles, but then there is no completely shared information between all particles. If you measure the state of one particle in a three-particle entanglement, you do not obtain complete knowledge about the states of the other two particles [WP–QEnt].[7]
- **Superposition**: Quantum states can consist of superpositions of several basis states [WP–QSup].[8]
- **Uncertainty principle**: Complementary observables cannot exist simultaneously with arbitrary precision, but are subject to a fundamental common uncertainty (indeterminacy) that is distributed unevenly between the two observables. This

[5] https://en.wikipedia.org/wiki/Measurement_in_quantum_mechanics.

[6] https://en.wikipedia.org/wiki/No-cloning_theorem.

[7] https://en.wikipedia.org/wiki/Quantum_entanglement.

[8] https://en.wikipedia.org/wiki/Quantum_superposition.

makes it impossible to measure both observables exactly at the same time. Location and momentum, or energy and time, are often cited as such observable pairs, but in the case of QKD, it is the pair of amplitude and phase of an electromagnetic wave that is always subject to such a common uncertainty [WP–Unc].[9]

In addition, there are QKD methods that are currently in the experimental stage or that exist only as ideas on paper, some of which are based on lesser-known paradigms. For the sake of completeness, these methods are briefly mentioned below, but they have not yet reached a level of maturity that would allow them to be used in security-critical applications.

3.2 How Does QKD Work?

3.2.1 Two Communication Channels

As already mentioned, QKD always uses two communication channels:

1. There is a quantum channel through which quantum states are transmitted. Who generates these states, who sends them, and who receives them varies depending on the type of QKD method. What all QKD methods have in common is that eavesdropping on a transmission of quantum states via a quantum channel leads to an increased quantum bit error rate (QBER) due to the measurement disturbance principle, which Alice and Bob can use to detect that the quantum channel is being eavesdropped on. However, a low error rate always occurs even without an actual eavesdropping attempt. Regardless of the true cause, it is always formally attributed to Eve. Correction procedures ensure that Eve cannot use the intercepted information. If the error rate exceeds a certain threshold, the procedure is aborted.

   In all existing QKD procedures, photons are used as carriers of the quantum states. This means that light (or another electromagnetic wave) is sent from a transmitter to a receiver. There are attempts to transfer the quantum states of photons to matter particles (e.g., individual atoms or electrons), for example, to store them there or to transfer them back to another photon in a quantum repeater [QRep],[10] but these technologies are still in the experimental stage and currently have a high error rate.
2. In addition, a classical communication channel is always required for the legitimate communication partners to exchange meta-information. This classical communication is necessary to enable the communication partners to interpret their secretly performed quantum measurements in agreement with the other party. In addition, information is transmitted via this channel that is later used

[9] https://en.wikipedia.org/wiki/Uncertainty_principle.

[10] https://qt.eu/quantum-principles/communication/quantum-repeaters.

for error correction. Nothing transmitted via the classical channel is secret. It is therefore permissible for a potential attacker to read this classical information in its entirety.

3.2.2 Authentication

However, it is of crucial importance that Alice and Bob authenticate each other. Without strict authentication, man-in-the-middle attacks are possible, in which the legitimate communication partners do not actually generate secret keys with the supposed counterpart, but with an unknown third party (with *Mallory,* see Sect. 2.7.2). This mutual authentication is no different from authentication in many other communication protocols, so it will only be discussed very briefly here.

Wegman-Carter authentication [Weg81][11] is commonly used. Alice and Bob must already have a shared secret key before the key exchange process begins (from a previous key exchange, which may have been performed by means other than QKD). From this key, the sender obtains a small subkey for each message packet it sends, which it uses to add a Message Authentication Code (MAC) to the packet before sending it to the recipient via the public channel. The recipient receives the message packet and, in the same way as the sender, has derived the same subkey from the shared key, which it uses to calculate a MAC from the message in the same way. The recipient only accepts the received packet if the MAC it has calculated itself matches the MAC that the sender sent with the message.

Since fresh random bits are used for MAC generation for each transmitted packet (which may not be reused afterwards) and because only Alice and Bob know the secret key, it is guaranteed that Alice and Bob only accept data packets that have actually been authenticated by the other party. Without knowledge of the secret key, a third party cannot manipulate the data traffic on the public channel unnoticed, nor can they impersonate the other party to Alice or Bob.

In practice, this authentication requires an initial key at the beginning, which must have been distributed securely, but once common key material has been generated through ongoing key exchange, a small portion of this fresh key pool is used for authentication. All implementations of key exchange protocols ensure that this happens automatically and that the bit sequences used for ongoing mutual authentication are not added to those bit sequences that are issued as key material.

Although authentication technically only affects the classical side channel, it also indirectly protects the quantum channel from targeted manipulation attempts. No separate authentication is required on the quantum channel itself, as manipulation there would only be useful if it were coordinated with the message traffic on the classical side channel, which is impossible due to the authentication of this channel.

The quantum channel can still be manipulated, but without simultaneous manipulation of the classical accompanying channel, this inevitably leads to an increased

[11] https://doi.org/10.1016/0022-0000(81)90033-7.

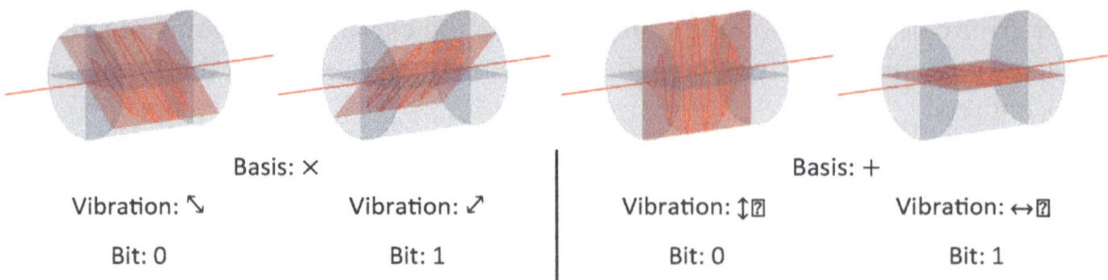

Fig. 3.1 The four oscillation planes in the BB84 protocol

quantum error rate. This reduces the actual key rate generated or even leads to a termination, but in both cases, Eve does not obtain a usable key material.

3.2.3 General Procedure

It starts with someone using a suitable device to generate random quantum information and then sending this information. This quantum information is measured at the receiver after transmission.

This applies to both prepare-and-measure methods and methods using entangled photons. In prepare-and-measure, one of the two key exchange parties generates the quantum information (usually Alice, but in exotic QKD technologies it can also be Bob). When entangled photons are used, there is a third party in addition to the two key exchange parties, namely the source, which neither Alice nor Bob need to trust. This source generates the quantum information and sends it. Both Alice and Bob are the recipients.

However, there are also QKD technologies, such as MDI-QKD (see Chap. 3.3.5), in which both Alice and Bob generate and send quantum information. In this case, the recipient is a third party that neither Alice nor Bob need to trust.

Measurement Bases (Using the BB84 Protocol as an Example)

Measurement bases play a fundamental role in the transmission and reception of quantum information, which will be explained here in brief using the example of the BB84 QKD protocol. (A detailed description of the BB84 protocol can be found together with descriptions of several other protocols on the book's website at.[12])

The BB84 protocol uses linearly polarized photons, and the quantum information is encoded as the direction of oscillation of each individual photon, as shown in Fig. 3.1.

The photon moves along the central red line. At right angles to this is the direction along which the photon oscillates. In the BB84 protocol, this oscillation direction can have the four orientations shown in Fig. 3.1. Two directions that are at right angles to each other form a measurement basis. (⤡ and ⤢ together form the basis ×; ↕

[12] https://cryptography.study/phys/protocol.

and ↔ form the basis +.) The two directions of a basis are interpreted as opposite bit values. This allows both possible bit values to be encoded in both bases.

An example: Alice wants to send Bob the bit value 0 and chooses the measurement basis × for this purpose. (The measurement basis is chosen randomly for each photon beforehand.) Alice therefore imprints the direction ⤡ on the photon. This photon is now the carrier of a quantum bit, or "qubit" for short. The special thing about this quantum bit is that it only corresponds to the value of a classical bit in the measurement basis ×, because it only has the bit value 0 chosen by Alice in this specific measurement basis. In the other measurement basis (the measurement basis +), the bit value of the photon is a quantum physical superposition of the two bit values 0 and 1, each with a weighting of exactly 50%. In other words, the bit value of this photon is completely indeterminate in the measurement basis +.

Bob does not know the measurement basis used by Alice at the time of his measurement and therefore has to guess. (Bob only finds out which basis Alice used after he has measured the photon.) If Bob uses the correct basis × for his measurement, he will (almost) always obtain the correct direction ⤡ and (almost) never the wrong direction as the measurement result, because in the basis × the photon has a clearly defined bit value. (Possible rare measurement errors are discussed in more detail below.) So, if Bob uses the correct measurement basis, he will most likely obtain the correct bit value (in the example: 0).

However, if Bob measures this photon in the wrong measurement basis, i.e., in the basis +, then he will obtain the result ↕ (which he interprets as 0) with a probability of 50% and the result ↔ (which he interprets as 1) with a probability of 50%. This is not because his apparatus would only output these two measurement results, but because the qubit carried by the photon is a superposition of the two possible values 0 and 1 in the wrong measurement basis.

In this case, Bob receives a completely random result. He would also measure the values 0 and 1 with a 50:50 probability if Alice had encoded the value 1 as ⤢.

This means that a matching measurement basis means that both Alice and Bob have the same bit value. (Apart from rare measurement errors, see below.) Different measurement bases, on the other hand, mean that neither Alice nor Bob knows which bit value the other side has generated or measured.

Of course, Bob wants to know which of his measurements were correct and which were random, and Alice also wants to know which of the bits she sent were measured correctly by Bob and which were not. Therefore, Alice and Bob exchange their measurement bases via the public channel, but only after the quantum measurements have already been completed, i.e., when the photons transmitted in the process no longer exist. This curtain is called *sifting* and is described in more detail below.

The security of the protocol is based on the fact that Eve has to guess the measurement basis just as blindly as Bob. However, in order to deceive Bob (and indirectly Alice as well), Eve must send Bob a new photon instead of the measured (and thereby destroyed) one. But Eve not only does not know which basis Alice used, she also does not know which basis Bob will choose when the photon that Eve sends to Bob as a replacement for the measured one arrives. Therefore, Eve is bound to be wrong about the measurement basis in 50% of all cases, which leads to incorrect measurement results for Bob, driving up the quantum error rate. Alice and Bob respond to this increased error rate by making the information Eve has received completely useless to her in the end. This response involves Alice and Bob first performing error correction and then a second processing step called *privacy amplification*. Both processes are described in Chap. 8.

But even if Eve did not destroy the photon during the measurement, but instead forwarded the same photon to Bob after the measurement, it would be of no use to her because the measurement changes the state of the measured photon. This is a fundamentally unavoidable consequence of the measurement disturbance principle.

Preparation, General (All Protocols)

Whether Alice, Bob, or perhaps even an unreliable or untrustworthy source generates and sends the quantum information, and who the recipient is, varies from protocol to protocol. In the BB84 protocol just presented, Alice sends the quantum information and Bob receives it. But in some protocols that work with entangled photons, even an external source that does not have to be trusted is allowed to send the quantum information, and there are even protocols in which unreliable relays measure the quantum information.

In any case, randomness plays an important role in both the creation and measurement of these transmitted states, because ultimately it is precisely this randomness that determines the bit sequence that represents the finished shared key. Therefore, the source of randomness plays a very decisive role in the security of the respective QKD protocol (see https://cryptography.study/phys/TRNG).

In each protocol, Alice and Bob generate bit sequences that they keep secret. However, other bit sequences are also generated, which are sent to the partner via the classical channel from Alice and Bob (sometimes even from an unreliable third party). These public bit sequences are used to decide what to do with the secret bit sequences.

Sifting

This comparison of the secret bit sequence with the help of public bit sequences is called “sifting”. In the first step of the sifting process, Bob sends Alice a list of timestamps or time indices. In all processes, short time slots are defined in advance, which, depending on the process, have a length of a few micro- or nanoseconds. Each second is thus divided into several million time slots. For this reason, it is also important that Alice and Bob synchronize their clocks very precisely with each other. Bob tells Alice in which of these time slots he has measured anything at all. In procedures where Alice is also the recipient, Alice also sends such a list to Bob. Once this has been done, Alice and Bob know which bits from their own secret bit sequence they must discard because there is no matching bit on the other side.

In the second step of sifting, Bob sends the list of the measurement bases he has randomly selected to Alice, and Alice also sends her corresponding list to Bob. In doing so, the two only transmit the data from those time slots that remain after the first step. By comparing the measurement bases, Alice and Bob determine in which time slots they happened to use measurement bases that match each other. They then discard all bits that belong to incompatible measurement bases and retain only those bits from the original sequence of measurements that belong to time slots with compatible measurement bases.

Eve can follow all of this. Eve learns in which time slots there were simultaneous measurements, and she learns in which time slots Alice and Bob are highly likely to have obtained identical measurement results. But after sifting, Eve has no information about the measurement results themselves, because Alice and Bob have not yet revealed anything about the measurement results at this point. Eve only knows how many raw bits Alice and Bob have accumulated.

Error Correction

Quantum states are very fragile and can be easily disturbed, which leads to transmission errors even without the activities of an eavesdropping attacker. Calibrating the devices used before the actual key exchange, which is usually done automatically by the devices, helps against some sources of error, but the effects of some other sources of error cannot be mitigated so easily.

The list of possible sources of error is long, and a complete enumeration would defeat the purpose of this book. Nevertheless, the most important sources of error should be briefly mentioned:

- Normal bending of fiber optics causes polarization and/or phase drift along the fiber. In extreme cases, fiber optics hanging from masts and exposed to wind movement can cause such a high calibration effort due to these drift errors that there is no free time available for the actual key exchange. However, temperature fluctuations, vibrations, and many other influences also cause errors of this type.
- Another common source of error is a time offset in the delimitation of time slots (clock offset and jitter).
- During transmission through the air (direct line of sight, but also connection to a satellite), scattered light (e.g., sunlight) causes errors. In addition, atmospheric influences (rain, fog, dust) can significantly increase signal attenuation in these transmission paths, which is not an error in the true sense, but greatly reduces the key rate because it leads to many non-measurements.
- The measuring devices themselves are also a significant source of errors. Depending on the method/technology, they must be capable of measuring individual photons, or at least very weak light pulses. This can sometimes lead to dark counts (a measurement result is triggered even though no photon has reached the detector) and the overlooking of existing photons.

Because of these and other errors, even without anyone eavesdropping on the quantum channel, after sifting, Alice and Bob usually end up with two bit sequences that match in most places, but not in all. To correct these errors, it is necessary for the two communication partners to perform error correction. The details of this procedure are described in Sect. 8.2

After error correction has been performed, Alice and Bob have identical bit sequences that they could actually already use as keys for symmetric cryptographic procedures.

Privacy Amplification

Due to the data traffic between Alice and Bob required for error correction, which takes place via the public channel, the eavesdropper Eve gains access to information that she could, at least theoretically, use to her advantage. Although Eve cannot reconstruct individual bits of the exchanged key using the intercepted data, she can at least rule out some possible bit sequences as key candidates. To deprive her of this advantage, privacy amplification is performed. This involves mixing and shortening the bit sequences that were created after error correction. The exact procedures are described in Sect. 8.3.

Result (Key Rate)

The more quantum bits Eve intercepts, the more errors she causes in the raw keys. Each error (whether caused by Eve or due to other unavoidable causes) shortens the length of the resulting key in privacy amplification, which is reflected in a reduced secure key rate. This is the number of bits that are generated within a specified period of time (e.g., within one second) and that can actually be used in a symmetric key. It should also be noted that communication via the public channel consumes an approximately constant portion of the generated key material due to the necessary MAC authentication of all data packets.

Even if an attacker intercepts only a sufficiently large fraction of the quantum bits, this can ultimately lead to a situation where, after privacy amplification and after some bits have been reserved for MAC authentication, there are no bits left for a shared key. In practice, however, most protocols terminate earlier, namely when the quantum error rate exceeds a certain threshold or when the key rate falls below a certain lower limit. If this is the case, the attacker has successfully carried out a denial-of-service (DOS) attack, but they could have achieved the same result more cost-effectively by cutting the fiber optic cable, blocking the light beam, turning off the power, or using other simpler methods.

Furthermore, legitimate communication partners do not suffer any major damage as a result of a DOS attack. They can try again at a later point in time to perform a physical key exchange.

3.3 Technology Classes

As already mentioned, there are a variety of different QKD procedures that can be grouped into technology classes based on certain characteristics. The most important of these are briefly presented here.

3.3.1 Prepare & Measure (P&M)

Prepare-and-Measure methods [WP–P&M][13] are the classic basic form of quantum key distribution. Alice generates individual quantum states, typically photons with specific polarizations, intensities, or quadratures, and sends them to the receiver (Bob). Bob measures each of the states immediately upon arrival. Security arises from the fact that each measurement irreversibly changes the quantum state: any attempt at eavesdropping leads to measurable errors. P&M methods also include a classical channel through which Alice and Bob exchange their measurement bases, error rates, and other parameters.

Within P&M, a further distinction is made between DV (Discrete Variable) and CV (Continuous Variable) (see below: Sects. 3.3.2 and 3.3.3). The best-known DV P&M protocol is BB84, and the best-known CV P&M protocol is GG02. P&M is suitable for systems with low complexity, is technologically easy to master, and forms the basis of many commercial QKD products.

3.3.2 DV-QKD

DV stands for "Discrete Variable" [QSNP–DV].[14] Discrete variables refer to physical quantities that can be counted on the basis of specific and indivisible observations, in contrast to the continuous variables (CV) discussed below, which can take any value within a certain range. DV-QKD uses discrete properties of individual photons, such as polarization, time slot, or phase. The receiver measures each photon in a specific basis and obtains discrete values ("0" or "1"). The most commonly used DV-QKD protocol is BB84. Security is based on the impossibility of copying unknown quantum states and on high error rates during eavesdropping. DV-QKD requires single-photon detectors[15] with high sensitivity, low dark rate, and often cryogenic cooling. DV-QKD is well researched, widely used worldwide, and suitable for longer distances (e.g., over longer fiber optic links or satellite). However, it is more cost-intensive and complex than CV-QKD, especially in the detection area. On the other hand, DV is currently the most standardized QKD technology.

Maturity

The technology readiness level (TRL [WP–TRL][16]) of P&M + Discrete Variable can be rated at the highest level, 9. There are several commercial providers of this technology (e.g., IDQ, Toshiba, and others), and this technology is running in projects with metro networks in continuous operation.

---

[13] https://en.wikipedia.org/wiki/Quantum_key_distribution#Quantum_key_exchange.

[14] https://qsnp.eu/glossary/dv-qkd/.

[15] See https://cryptography.study/phys/QKD-HW.

[16] https://en.wikipedia.org/wiki/Technology_readiness_level.

Key Rates Fiber Optics

In laboratory operations under optimal conditions, key rates of around 10 Mbit/s have already been achieved, but such rates cannot be reproduced in field tests. These values are more realistic [Sas11][17]:

up to approx. 50 km: 1–10 kbit/s

up to approx. 200 km: 50 bit/s and below

Key rates for satellite (Micius) [Liao17a][18]

approx. 12 kbit/s at a distance of approx. 645 km

approx. 1 kbit/s at a distance of approx. 1200 km

3.3.3 CV-QKD

CV stands for "continuous variable" [QSNP–CV],[19] [Zha24].[20] CV-QKD uses continuous properties of light, such as the amplitude and phase (quadratures) of an optical carrier. Instead of single-photon detectors, "standard" telecommunications components are used: lasers, modulators, and fast homodyne or heterodyne detectors. The measured values are continuous numbers that are later digitized. CV-QKD is more cost-effective and easier to integrate into existing telecom DWDM networks. The methods are based on Gaussian states (e.g., GG02). The additional challenge lies in the more complex information processing, the higher sensitivity to optical noise, and the more demanding modeling of security proofs. CV-QKD is particularly suitable for urban networks, short to medium distances, and multi-channel coexistence with data traffic.

3.3.4 Entanglement-Based QKD

Entanglement [QSNP–Ent],[21] [WP–QEnt][22] refers to a non-classical correlation phenomenon in which two or more quantum systems are connected in such a way that their properties cannot be described independently of each other. The state of an entangled pair of particles is completely defined, while the values of the individual particles in the pair remain indeterminate until a measurement is made. In

[17] https://doi.org/10.1364/OE.19.010387.

[18] https://doi.org/10.1038/nature23655.

[19] https://qsnp.eu/glossary/cv-qkd/.

[20] https://doi.org/10.1063/5.0179566.

[21] https://qsnp.eu/glossary/entanglement/.

[22] https://en.wikipedia.org/wiki/Quantum_entanglement.

QKD, entangled photons are used to create strong, eavesdropping-proof correlations between the parties. An eavesdropping attacker cannot copy or disrupt entangled states without being noticed. Systems based on entanglement offer particularly high security guarantees. Entanglement is more technically demanding, but offers the most robust theoretical security basis of all QKD approaches.

Entanglement-based QKD methods/technologies use entangled photon pairs instead of prepared states. A central source generates photon pairs that are distributed to Alice and Bob. Both measure their photons independently of each other. The correlations arise solely from quantum entanglement and not from classical preparation. Security is verified using so-called Bell tests [QSNP–Bell],[23] [WP–Bell][24]: Only if the measured non-locality violations are high enough can no eavesdropper possess consistent information. Entanglement-based QKD requires precise sources, extremely stable channels, and highly efficient detectors, but offers a particularly strong theoretical security basis in return. It is also the basis for device-independent QKD and future quantum repeater networks.

3.3.5 MDI Measurement-Device-Independent

MDI-QKD [QSNP–MDI][25] eliminates the biggest point of attack in classical QKD systems: the detectors. In MDI-QKD, both parties send their quantized light signals to an untrusted relay station that only performs Bell measurements. Since detection no longer takes place at the legitimate communication partners, all detector side channels are excluded. The station can even be completely controlled by an attacker without compromising security. MDI-QKD offers very high security, but is technically more complex: it requires interfering signals from both transmitters and high stability of optical paths. MDI-QKD is considered one of the most secure architectures that can be implemented and is a step toward device-independent QKD.

3.3.6 Twin Field

Twin-Field QKD [Ars25][26] is an approach developed in 2018 that dramatically increases the range of QKD. Two remote parties send attenuated coherent light fields to an intermediate station, which causes the fields to interfere. The intermediate station does not need to be trustworthy, as no key materials are present there. The method scales with the square root of attenuation, enabling distances of over 500 km in fiber optics. This is significantly more than classic DV or CV methods/

[23] https://qsnp.eu/glossary/bell-state-measurement/.

[24] https://en.wikipedia.org/wiki/Bell_test.

[25] https://qsnp.eu/glossary/measurement-di-qkd/.

[26] https://doi.org/10.48550/arXiv.2510.26320.

technologies. Twin-Field is a type of MDI-like architecture, but combines the advantages of interference techniques with reduced detector requirements. Technically, the most difficult part is the precise synchronization of photon coherence over long distances.

Twin-Field is an experimental QKD method/technology that can significantly increase the range without trusted nodes. Two remote endpoints send coherent light pulses to a central measuring station. Security is maintained even if this station is untrusted, as the crucial information lies in the interfering fields. With TF-QKD, ranges of over 500 km in fiber optics appear quite realistic without the station in the middle having access to the key.

DI-QKD (Device-Independent QKD)

Device-Independent QKD [QSNP–DI][27] is the most stringent and theoretically secure form of quantum key distribution. Security does not depend on the correct functioning of the devices. Instead, eavesdropping security is guaranteed by the proof of quantum mechanical non-locality (Bell inequalities). As long as the measured violation is sufficiently large, the system remains secure. Even if devices are manipulated, faulty, or built entirely by the attacker. However, DI-QKD requires extremely efficient sources and detectors, low losses, and high-precision entanglement over long distances. Practical DI-QKD systems are still in the early stages of development, but are considered the ideal form of QKD to strive for.

3.4 Fiber Optic QKD

The transmission of quantum information through fiber optics is the most mature and commonly used method of operating QKD.

3.4.1 Rule of Thumb for Attenuation and Distance

In fiber optic QKD, key rates do not actually depend directly on the length of the fiber, but on the attenuation that occurs as the light travels through the fiber. However, since all common single-mode fibers are very similar in terms of attenuation, it is possible to convert between distance and attenuation using a constant factor of 0.2 dB/km or 5 km/dB, as shown in Table 1.1.

It should be noted that ultra-low-loss fibers with lower attenuation per kilometer (less than 0.16 dB/km) are available, but in most cases they are more expensive and often cannot be bent as much. In addition, glass fibers are usually supplied by the manufacturer in lengths between 2 and 4 km and must be joined together by splicing during installation, which leads to additional attenuation at these points. With optimal

[27] https://qsnp.eu/glossary/di-qkd/.

Table 1.1 Rule of thumb for attenuation and distance

Attenuation	Distance
0.2 dB	1 km
1.0 dB	5 km

execution, this amounts to 0.02–0.05 dB per splice, but with poor execution it can be considerably more. Added to this is attenuation that can occur due to minor damage to the fiber, e.g., small kinks that can happen during installation. However, this additional attenuation, which is to be expected, is already taken into account in the distance rule of thumb.

What Does "attenuation" Mean Specifically for QKD?

"Attenuation" is a term that can be easily understood intuitively if one thinks of light flux as something whose intensity can be continuously varied. Light enters a medium on one side with an initial intensity I_0 and exits on the other side with a lower final intensity I. The attenuation factor is then simply $d = \frac{I_0}{I}$.

For QKD, however, in the case of CV-QKD, extremely weak light pulses are used, which contain very few photons per pulse (typically less than 10 photons per pulse), or even only a single photon per pulse, which is the norm for DV-QKD and for methods/technologies with entangled photons.

So, what does "attenuation" mean in this context? Or rather, what is the intensity of light? It is the average number of photons per unit of time. This is because a photon has a constant energy due to its wavelength, which cannot decrease. However, a photon can disappear on its way from the beginning to the end of the fiber optic cable, e.g., through absorption or other effects. Attenuation therefore means that some photons that enter the fiber do not come out at the other end because they disappear in between.

An example: 1000 pulses, each with one photon, are fed into a glass fiber at one end, but after about 50 km, 900 of these pulses are empty and only 100 pulses still contain a photon. The attenuation factor is then $d = \frac{1000}{100} = 0.1$, or 10%, which corresponds exactly to 10 dB. (Decibel is a logarithmic measure. If 10% arrives, that is exactly 10 dB by definition. 1% corresponds to 20 dB and 0.1% is 30 dB. Halving the intensity, i.e., an attenuation factor of 50%, corresponds to approximately 3 dB.)

Security Theory Treatment of Attenuation

It should be mentioned at this point that attenuation is a completely normal and, in practice, unavoidable aspect of the movement of photons through a medium, as are small disturbances in the quantum properties of these photons (e.g., rotation of the polarization direction by a small angle). In the security theory analysis of these processes, however, it is always assumed that all transmission media have completely ideal properties. This includes the assumption that they cause no attenuation and no changes in quantum properties. Instead, the security theory analysis always assumes that an eavesdropping attacker, i.e., Eve, is the cause of all these effects. So, we act as if Eve were able to secretly replace all real components with ideal components in order to divert and evaluate photons unnoticed. Therefore, in error correction and privacy amplification, all disruptive effects (including attenuation) are treated as if Eve were the sole cause.

3.4.2 QKD Fiber Optic Networks

When talking about quantum key distribution (QKD) in the context of fiber optics, in practice we are almost always talking about two things at once: firstly, real physical transmission links (typically telecom fibers, sometimes as dark fiber or as WDM coexistence with classic traffic), and secondly, a network and operating architecture that turns comparatively short QKD links into a widely available service that delivers the key material to applications. This second level, consisting of key management, interfaces, monitoring, operation, robustness against errors, and automatic route selection, has a greater impact on the practical value of QKD than spectacular laboratory values for individual links. This is precisely why QKD networks are particularly revealing as real infrastructure: they show where QKD crosses the threshold from a feasibility demonstration to practical operation.

In field networks, the factors that determine quality are less in pure quantum advantages and more in the classic operating metrics: stability over weeks and months, availability, average secret key rate (SKR), key transfer over multiple hops, and integration into crypto and network components via standardized interfaces (e.g., ETSI APIs).

Another key point is the assumption of trust: all fiber optic QKD networks found during research for this book are implemented as trusted node networks. This means that the key material is processed and recombined in plain text at intermediate nodes, because this is currently the only option that scales well over long distances. This circumstance raises the question of whether a network can be operated "productively" in terms of critical security requirements, and with what organizational protective measures.

Networks that do not require trusted nodes because they can teleport entangled states over long distances with the aid of quantum repeaters are already being tested, proving their basic feasibility [Luo25],[28] but they do not yet enable meaningful key exchange and are still a long way from being ready for use in real security-critical applications. (A single source reports that the system ran for 275 seconds in one day, generating approximately one bit per second as a raw key, which is very little to create a secure key from it [Koz19].[29] All other sources reporting on such experiments contain no references to key rates.)

The following is a list of the most important existing QKD networks and network infrastructures, sorted by region, with a focus on fiber-optic QKD, but also mentioning free-space and satellite links if they are integrated into the network.

[28] https://doi.org/10.48550/arXiv.2504.05660.

[29] https://doi.org/10.1145/3345312.3345497.

China

China appears to be the most influential region for fiber-optic-based QKD networks at present. This became apparent early on with the Beijing–Shanghai Backbone Network, whose construction began in 2013. The backbone route was completed in 2017 with around 2032 km and 32 trusted nodes [Chen25].[30] This backbone infrastructure was explicitly presented in public communications as a national demonstration and application route [CAS17].[31] The technical literature also emphasizes that the backbone and the connected metro networks were used as a platform for application testing (including in the finance and insurance sectors) [Zha18].[32]

The next step was to integrate terrestrial fiber-optic QKD with satellite and free-space QKD. A Nature publication [Chen21][33] describes an integrated network that connects a geographically extensive fiber optic QKD infrastructure with two satellite-based free-space QKD links, demonstrating QKD between more than 150 endpoints over a combined distance of 4600 km. Here, too, the architecture remains essentially trusted-node-based.

In a publication from August 2025 [Chen25],[34] the China Quantum Communication Network (CN-QCN) is described as an operational, trusted-relay-based network that spans 10,000 km, comprises 145 backbone fiber optic nodes and 20 metro networks, and covers 17 provinces and 80 cities. The article explicitly emphasizes operation and maintenance as well as hybrid networking of different QKD types as progress over pure verification networks. It is also interesting to note that, in the same context, the integration of ground stations for the Jinan-1 quantum microsatellite (see Chap. 3.5.2) is already mentioned as a supplement to the terrestrial base.

China is thus most clearly demonstrating the transition from field testing to a permanently operated infrastructure, albeit under the central prerequisite of a trusted node security model. For productive security-critical applications, this is only plausible if the nodes are understood to be highly secure operational locations. However, this architecture does not guarantee end-to-end security and requires additional trust assumptions.

EU testbeds and EuroQCI

At present, the central European goal is not a large EU-wide network, but rather many distributed testbeds with a focus on interoperability and use cases. The EU project OPENQKD (since 2019) [EC24][35] is designed precisely for this purpose: open testbeds are intended to demonstrate network functionality and use cases to stakeholders. In parallel, the EU is pursuing the establishment of a Europe-wide quantum

---

30 https://doi.org/10.1038/s41534-025-01089-8.

31 https://english.cas.cn/newsroom/archive/news_archive/nu2017/201703/t20170324_175288.shtml.

32 https://doi.org/10.1364/OE.26.024260.

33 https://doi.org/10.1038/s41586-020-03093-8.

34 https://doi.org/10.1038/s41534-025-01089-8.

35 https://cordis.europa.eu/project/id/857156.

communication infrastructure with EuroQCI, initially with a strong terrestrial focus [EC25].[36]

Austria

Europe recognized QKD networks as a networking problem (interoperability, routing, key management, multi-vendor integration) at a very early stage. The most visible early example is the SECOQC network in Vienna (2004–2008). This was an EU project with a trusted node-based prototype network that was operational in Vienna in 2008 and was publicly demonstrated, including one-time pad telephony and a video conference secured by QKD keys across multiple nodes [Peev09].[37] This network was a technology and architecture demonstrator: it showed how heterogeneous QKD devices can be orchestrated in a network.

More recently, Austria has been visible primarily in the EuroQCI context through the national deployment project QCI-CAT, which, as Austria's contribution to the European EuroQCI infrastructure, aims to establish a QKD demonstration and testing environment for highly secure communication (especially for public authorities) [AIT26].[38] The project ran from January 2023 to June 2025. In terms of content, the project aimed to set up and test an Austria-wide quantum communication network infrastructure and to evaluate specific security applications such as secret sharing and message authentication. At the same time, QCI-CAT was integrated into the European network (including via PETRUS cross-domain demonstrations).

Switzerland

SwissQuantum was a classic reference network for long-term field operation in Switzerland: it was installed in the Geneva area and ran from the end of March 2009 to the beginning of January 2011 with a key management layer and real-world use via an application layer. The focus was on long-term stability, maintainability, and integration [Stu11].[39]

A special case that is often cited in discussions as evidence of productive use is the use of QKD to protect data transmissions in the context of elections in the canton of Geneva (2007) [OPT07].[40] The manufacturers of the QKD devices used present their use as recurring (in particular as protection for the transmission of election/counting data between locations) [IDQ17].[41]

---

[36] https://digital-strategy.ec.europa.eu/en/policies/european-quantum-communication-infrastructure-euroqci.

[37] https://doi.org/10.1088/1367-2630/11/7/075001.

[38] https://www.ait.ac.at/themen/cyber-security/projects/qci-cat.

[39] https://doi.org/10.1088/1367-2630/13/12/123001.

[40] https://optics.org/article/31646.

[41] https://www.idquantique.com/idq-celebrates-10-year-anniversary-of-the-worlds-first-real-life-quantum-cryptography-installation/.

Spain

One of the most important European case studies for "real-world integration" is the MadQCI project (Madrid Quantum Communications Infrastructure; from 2021 to 2024). The central added value here was not primarily in record key rates, but in the embedding in a real, multi-tenant telecom environment: the network was built with disaggregated components, SDN paradigms, and multi-vendor QKD systems in a real telecom infrastructure, shares infrastructure with commercial traffic, and was tested over a period of approximately three years, with most nodes continuously active [Mar24].[42]

Benelux

A recent European highlight is the cross-border QKD connection between Belgium and Luxembourg as part of BeQCI/LUQCIA, which was communicated as a 132 km link and the first cross-border MDI QKD connection in the region [BEL25].[43] In this project, many weaknesses of real-world QKD implementations were tested by selecting and comparing different methods/technology architectures. This is an important step toward more robust security assumptions, even though overall operation still requires network and site-side trust models.

Germany

Germany is currently positioning QKD networks strongly as a research and testing infrastructure for government agencies and KRITIS scenarios. The QuNET initiative, for example, describes a field experiment that aims to connect multiple users in the Berlin area over 125 km of fiber plus supplementary free-space connections in a quantum-secure manner, with participating locations including Fraunhofer HHI, Deutsche Telekom, and the Bundesdruckerei [QUN24].[44] This project is one of many examples that show that in Europe, QKD networks are increasingly being conceived as hybrid systems in which fiber optic connections dominate but are supplemented by free-space links and satellite links.

Japan

Japan has built one of the best-known metro networks with the Tokyo QKD Network. It was launched in October 2010 and demonstrated as an operational network in the Greater Tokyo Area [NICT11].[45] A publication on the field test describes a mesh network with various QKD systems and cites as a prominent demonstration the world's first secure TV conference over a distance of 45 km [Sas11].[46] Later

[42] https://doi.org/10.1038/s41534-024-00873-2.

[43] https://www.belnet.be/en/news-events/news/new-milestone-quantum-communication-project-beqci-first-cross-border-qkd-network.

[44] https://qunet-initiative.de/en/news-2024/#:~:text=Start%20of%20the%20second%20key.

[45] https://www.nict.go.jp/en/pdf/copy_of_NICT_NEWS_1102_E.pdf.

[46] https://doi.org/10.1364/OE.19.010387.

reviews also highlight that the network was used as a platform for sectoral verifications, including in collaboration with players from the financial sector to assess its practicability [Stan22].[47]

South Korea

South Korea is often cited as the country that, after China, has made the most progress toward a national QKD infrastructure. In 2022, an 800-km QKD infrastructure was reported to connect 48 government organizations via a converged network [KED22].[48] The fact that this infrastructure is explicitly classified as the largest outside China is also found in independent strategy reports [SWNX23].[49]

But here, too, national coverage requires trust in trusted nodes. The fact that this network can be classified as productive is mainly due to the fact that the node locations are part of a government/authority security architecture.

USA

In North America, the best-known real-world QKD network is the DARPA Quantum Network (Boston/Cambridge). The network began operating in 2003 as a laboratory experiment and was shortly thereafter expanded via fiber optics under the streets of Cambridge, Massachusetts, including a multi-node network [Ell18].[50]

Russia

Russia strongly promotes QKD networks as a critical infrastructure application. A concrete, dated milestone is a quantum-encrypted video conference call via a QKD-secured line between Moscow and St. Petersburg on June 8, 2021, in which government officials also participated [ITMO21].[51] In addition, there are official roadmap communications (e.g., expansion targets over several thousand kilometers) [ICT21].[52] Overall, however, the information from Russia is not very transparent.

Overall Impression

The majority of existing QKD networks must currently still be classified as trial, pilot, or demonstration projects, which often follow real operating processes but do not claim to permanently supply the key material for genuine security-critical applications. At the same time, there is some reliable evidence to show that QKD is already being used productively or close to production in niche areas. This is particularly the case where (a) the costs/complexity are justified by high protection requirements and (b) the organizational trust assumptions (trusted nodes, secure locations) are acceptable.

---

[47] https://doi.org/10.1088/1742-6596/2416/1/012001.

[48] https://www.kedglobal.com/tech%2C-media-telecom/newsView/ked202206080023.

[49] https://swissnex.org/app/uploads/2023/05/Report_Epdf_290323_Final-Publish.pdf.

[50] https://doi.org/10.48550/arXiv.quant-ph/0412029.

[51] https://news.itmo.ru/en/science/cyberphysics/news/10393.

[52] https://ict.moscow/en/news/7000-km-of-quantum-networks-to-be-stretched-in-russia-by-the-end-of-2024.

3.4.3 *Performance Data from Publicly Available Sources*

During the research for this book, several specific QKD devices were also examined using publicly available sources. The detailed results of this research, together with all source references, are available on the book's website at.[53] In this book, these results are summarized and grouped according to technology classes.

It should be noted in advance that all manufacturers offer devices of varying quality. Standard configurations and premium variants are often offered, whereby the latter not only have a better success rate in detecting photons due to more sophisticated detector designs, but also have shorter dead times between detection events. Both effects mean that device variants from the same manufacturer can differ by a factor of 10 or more in terms of key rates under otherwise identical conditions. No information on device prices could be found in any of the publicly available sources. Non-binding price information for seven different products was obtained in an interview with a very experienced user with extensive knowledge. This interview is summarized in Chap. 3.4.4.

It should also be mentioned that the key rates specified by the manufacturers themselves often differ significantly from the values published in scientific papers, although some of these publications should be interpreted with caution because the authors are keen to justify the use of funding with good results. This does not mean that incorrect values have been published! However, it can be assumed that particularly low key rates are less likely to be published, while particularly good results are very likely to be published. As a result, there are indeed many publications that demonstrate the general functioning of laboratory and field trials, but when it comes to specifying concrete key rates, many publications provide no information at all, and in many others, the wording is so vague that it often remains unclear whether the raw key rates after sifting but before error correction and privacy amplification, or whether the entire post-processing has been taken into account. This is understandable and comprehensible because many research projects are primarily concerned with demonstrating the feasibility of certain procedures, whereby proof of stable continuous operation over several months can also be considered proof of feasibility.

DV-QKD

By evaluating publicly available manufacturer information, these approximate values were obtained for several different DV-QKD devices:

Distance	Key rate
50 km	Up to 300 kbit/s
60 km	2 kbit/s
65 km	2.2 to 18 kbit/s
90 km	1 kbit/s

(continued)

[53] https://cryptography.study/phys/QKD.

(continued)

Distance	Key rate
120 km	1 kbit/s

These figures illustrate two patterns typical for DV-QKD in fiber optics: First, the systems deliver several kbit/s at average attenuations of 10–15 dB, which corresponds to typical distances of 50–75 km. Second, optimized implementations (process/technology efficiency, clocking, detector technology) can be up to ten times higher at comparable attenuation, and thus in the double-digit to triple-digit kbit/s range. In particular, short distances in special configurations can even reach the Mbit/s range, but it can be assumed that these extremely high rates quoted by manufacturers can only be achieved under particularly controlled conditions that can hardly be expected in productive environments.

However, if we look at the values cited in independent scientific publications, the picture is as follows:

Distance	Key rate	Note
4 to 17 km	0.9 to 2.4 kbit/s	Average value from long-term operation
Approx. 13 km	0.48 to 1.7 kbit/s	24-h average
Just under 50 km	5.4 to 7.4 kbit/s	Stable over several weeks
50 km	36.5 to 63 kbit/s	Optimized device, 24 h
67 km	Approx. 270 kbit/s	Optimized device, 24 h

It is noticeable that the values fluctuate greatly, which is due to the fact that devices from different manufacturers with very different qualities were used for different distances. In some cases, key rates significantly higher than the manufacturer's specifications were even achieved in such test configurations. Unfortunately, it is not always clear whether the specified key rates are raw key rates or secure key rates. Especially at greater distances, a higher quantum error rate is to be expected even without eavesdropping, so that the length of the secure key after privacy amplification may only be a few percent of the raw key length, which means that a raw key rate in the three-digit kbit/s range can quickly become a single-digit secure key rate.

CV-QKD

The manufacturers surveyed who offer devices in this technology class are very reluctant to provide specific information on key rates or the maximum achievable distance.

One manufacturer claims that its current devices can bridge distances of up to 100 km, but without specifying concrete key rates.

Another manufacturer states that its devices can be used for up to 80 km (in fact, an attenuation of 16 dB is specified, which can be converted to 80 km according to the rule of thumb; see Sect. 3.4.1), and it states that speeds of up to 10 kbit/s can be achieved with its devices. However, it is highly likely that the 10 kbit/s applies to very short distances, not to the maximum distance stated.

Unfortunately, independent sources are also not very informative. They only report that CV-QKD devices have been operated successfully over a longer period of time and that the key material generated in the process was distributed to endpoints in larger QKD networks together with the key material from other QKD systems.

QKD with Entangled Photon Pairs

One manufacturer offers a device that is suitable for fiber optic, free-space, and satellite operation, and another that is optimized for medium to long fiber optics. Both devices are specified to achieve 1.5 kbit/s at a distance of 50 km (actually: at an attenuation of 10 dB).

An independent source reported that a key rate of 0.09 kbit/s (i.e., 90 bit/s) was achieved in 10 days of operation at a distance of 70 km, while the manufacturer itself stated that 0.3 kbit/s (i.e., 300 bit/s) could be achieved in the laboratory at an equivalent attenuation. Another source stated that 70 km was the maximum distance that could be bridged.

Another manufacturer offers a device for up to 350 km of fiber optic cable, whereby, according to the manufacturer, approximately 0.007 kbit/s (7 bit/s) can be achieved. The transmitter is located in the middle of the distance, and the two receivers (Alice and Bob) are 350 km apart.

Another device from the same manufacturer is optimized for 10 to 20 km and can achieve up to 120 kbit/s at 10 km (2 dB) and 20 kbit/s at 50 km (10 dB).

It is striking that all public sources found focus heavily on the architecture of QKD networks (star topology, low trusted node density), while concrete secret key rates in kbit/s as a function of attenuation or distance are hardly to be found.

(More detailed reports with references can be found on the book's website at.[54])

MDI-QKD (Measurement Device Independent QKD)

Topologically, MDI systems are structured in exactly the opposite way to entanglement-based systems: there is a receiver in the middle that does not need to be trusted, and Alice and Bob send photons to it.

According to the manufacturer, devices in this category can bridge distances of up to 200 km. At 125 km (25 dB), a key rate of 0.5 kbit/s should be achievable. There are simulations of setups with 16 transmitters and one central receiver, in which each transmitter achieves a key rate of 1.5 kbit/s, but these figures are not based on real-world experiments.

[54] https://cryptography.study/phys/QKD.

3.4.4 User Survey

The Austrian Institute of Technology (AIT)[55] is an internationally established non-university research and technology organization and a key technical and scientific implementation partner of the EU-wide QKD initiative EuroQCI.[56] At the European level, the company is driving forward the integration of fiber optic, free-space, and satellite QKD and is actively involved in the evaluation of trusted node architectures and KMS connections. In Austria, AIT is playing a leading role in the development of national QKD test networks. AIT has been and continues to be significantly involved in many QKD projects, including OPENQKD,[57] eCausis,[58] QCI-CAT,[59] and several others. The company has extensive practical experience with QKD components. It was therefore a great pleasure and very important for the authors of this book to interview Mr. Florian Kutschera, one of the company's QKD network specialists, for this book, for which we are very grateful. In the process, we obtained the following valuable information.

DV-QKD

AIT used devices from three manufacturers that employ methods/technologies from the DV-QKD family. For devices from two of these manufacturers, the following secure key rates were specified depending on distance:

Distance	Key rate
15 km	7 kbit/s
50 km	5.4 kbit/s
65–80 km	2.2 kbit/s

In fact, no distances were mentioned in the interview, only attenuations. They were converted into distances for the book using the formula shown in Chap. 3.4.1. "Secure key rate" refers to the number of bits that are actually provided per second for symmetric encryption after post-processing (i.e., after sifting, error correction, and privacy amplification).

The above table does not include values for a device from a third manufacturer, for which only preliminary values were available at the time of the interview. This device could potentially bridge a distance of up to 150 km (attenuation: 30 dB), but this has not been officially confirmed. This particular device temporarily experienced a problem whereby the keys generated in the device could not be exported.

Approximate prices for the devices used were also quoted. AIT is paid between $140,000 and $220,000 per link for DV-QKD devices, i.e., for all devices at both

[55] https://www.ait.ac.at.

[56] https://petrus-euroqci.eu.

[57] https://www.ait.ac.at/en/research-topics/cyber-security/projects/open-qkd.

[58] http://ecausis.com.

[59] https://qci-cat.at.

ends of a fiber optic cable. According to AIT, equipment from a fourth manufacturer, for which no self-measured key rates were given, is available for around $330,000. Added to this are the costs for maintenance and operation of the equipment and the rental of the fiber optic cable.

It should be noted that these are past costs incurred by a customer with very specific requirements. It is not advisable to base a procurement decision on these individual figures. The costs mentioned here are only given to provide a very rough estimate of the approximate scale of a possible investment. Specific equipment prices must always be requested directly from the manufacturers.

Depending on the manufacturer, the devices are designed for distances of up to 80–150 km, with significantly lower key rates to be expected at greater distances.

For most manufacturers, the bridgeable distance can be increased on the receiver side by using device variants with higher-quality single-photon detectors.[60] However, higher-quality detectors are more expensive and, in most cases, require additional cryogenic cooling, which takes up extra space and consumes a lot of power.

In addition, one device was reported to have software problems and issues with remote maintenance, while another was notable for its highly fluctuating key rates. In one case, the key rates at particularly short distances also fell significantly short of expectations. However, it must be said that these are isolated cases that do not allow conclusions to be drawn about such devices in general. Nevertheless, they show that these are devices with very complex components that can cause problems in real-world operation and also require maintenance, which is a major challenge, especially for trusted nodes.

CV-QKD

In the case of CV-QKD, the AIT provided information on devices from two different manufacturers, with the following key rates being quoted for one device:

Distance	Key rate
15 km	10 kbit/s
25 km	1.4 kbit/s

Technical problems were reported with the other device, the cause of which was not suspected to be the devices themselves, but rather the fiber optic cable, which is why the device delivered only a few bits per second even over very short distances at the time of the interview. However, the same device had previously been able to deliver up to 4 kbit/s of secure key material over an unspecified distance.

In the interview, it was stated that the CV-QKD devices used are suitable for distances of up to 50–80 km, but that key rates in the single-digit bit/s range (i.e., between 0.001 and 0.01 kbit/s) are to be expected.

One of the two CV-QKD devices was described as the most pleasant and stable of the entire device fleet. The other device (the one that produced very low key

[60] See https://cryptography.study/phys/QKD-HW.

rates, presumably due to a faulty fiber optic cable) stood out due to its immature software and the fact that no certificates for the ETSI-014 protocol [ETSI19–14][61] were provided. These certificates are an important basis for the transfer of the key material to an HSM.

A major advantage of CV-QKD is that the quantum channel and the classical communication channel can be routed through the same fiber optic cable, thanks to a multiplexing process.

The acquisition costs were estimated at $180,000 to $200,000, although it should be noted that these are values from a past individual case and do not constitute a reliable basis for any calculations. In addition, several sources have assured us that there will be a significant drop in prices in the future, particularly for CV-QKD devices.

QKD with Entangled Photon Pairs

At AIT, only one device was in use that operated with entangled photons.

Distance	Key rate
A few meters	1 kbit/s
50 km	0.4 kbit/s

The operation of the device was described as very stable, but there were minor problems with the software of a receiver module. The user interface of the software was described as very clear and exemplary. The maximum usable distance mentioned in the interview was 50 km.

The equipment consists of a photon source in the middle of the route (between Alice and Bob) and two receiving stations where the photons are detected. The AIT stated that the cost for this was approximately $275,000. *(Caution: This is a single value from the past as a price range.)*

MDI-QKD (Measurement-Device-Independent QKD)

The AIT also used a device that belongs to the MDI-QKD technology class. Alice and Bob send photons to a central receiving station, which performs Bell measurements and announces the measurement results. Alice and Bob can use this information and the secret parameters they themselves contributed to generate a shared key. However, the publicly announced measurement results alone are worthless, which is why the measuring station does not have to be trusted.

The following preliminary information was provided in the interview, for which there was no official confirmation at the time of the interview, which is why this information is not very reliable: It may be possible to operate the device at an attenuation of up to 40 dB (equivalent to 200 km), and it may be possible to achieve a key rate of 0.5 kbit/s (500 bit/s) at 25 dB (equivalent to 125 km).

It was reported in the interview that a separate 16-amp power line had to be installed for the cryogenic cooling compressor in this device.

---

[61] https://www.etsi.org/deliver/etsi_gs/QKD/001_099/014/01.01.01_60/gs_qkd014v010101p.pdf.

The interview mentioned a price of approximately $410,000 for this. *(Caution: This is a single value from the past as a price range.)*

General Statements from the Interview

There is currently no standardization of QKD methods/technologies. This means that for each link, the devices at both ends of the link must be from the same manufacturer. However, since trusted nodes themselves are not quantum devices, but only connect individual quantum links at a higher level of abstraction, it is still possible to easily implement longer connections with individual links from different manufacturers with the help of trusted nodes. Only the devices at the ends of each individual quantum link must always be from the same manufacturer.

It was also announced that a total of approximately $165,000 had to be paid for the fiber optics for an 18-month trial setup along a 200 km route, which was divided into several links. *But here, too, the costs are from the past and are for a single customer with individual needs.*

3.4.5 Comparison of Specific Devices

This book is based on a study that included detailed descriptions of individual QKD devices. Most of the devices examined were used for fiber-optic QKD, but some devices suitable for free-space QKD or satellite QKD were also described. However, this detailed device comparison would exceed the scope of this book, so the authors decided to move it to the book's website at.[62]

3.5 Satellite QKD

In addition to the transmission of photons through fiber optics, the connection between two ground stations and a satellite also plays an important role. Because the light travels a significant portion of its distance through the Earth's atmosphere, satellite QKD suffers from the same disadvantages as free-space QKD. Since these limitations are more pronounced in free-space QKD than in satellite QKD, this topic is discussed in more detail in Chap. 3.6.

According to publicly available sources, a total of nine QKD-capable satellites have been sent into space to date, two of which have already exceeded their service

62 https://cryptography.study/phys/QKD.

life and have probably already burned up in the atmosphere, namely SpooQy-1 [EOP19],[63] [NanSp][64] (Singapore) and Tiangong-2 [WP–Tia],[65] [N2TG][66] (China).

In December 2025, these seven QKD-capable satellites were in space:

Name	Country	Prepare and measure	Entanglement	Launch	Note
Micius [Lu22],[67] [Liao17b],[68] [Cast17][69]	China	Yes	Yes	2016	Main mission already completed in 2022. Micius is considered as an international QKD reference.
Jinan 1 [Chen21],[70] [Li25][71]	China	Yes	No	2022	"Flying" trusted node
Socrates [WP–Soc],[72] [EOPSoc],[73] [Tak17][74]	Japan	Yes	No	2017	Proof of concept, no operational key exchange, mission completed
QUBE [DLRQub],[75] [FAU25][76]	Germany	Yes	No	Aug. 2024	Technology demonstrator, focus on miniaturization and cost reduction. No results for QKD services

(continued)

[63] https://www.eoportal.org/satellite-missions/spooqy-1.

[64] https://www.nanosats.eu/sat/spooqy-1.

[65] https://en.wikipedia.org/wiki/Tiangong-2.

[66] https://www.n2yo.com/satellite/?s=41765.

[67] https://doi.org/10.1103/RevModPhys.94.035001.

[68] https://doi.org/10.1038/nature23655.

[69] https://doi.org/10.1038/nature.2017.22142.

[70] https://doi.org/10.1038/s41586-020-03093-8.

[71] https://doi.org/10.1038/s41586-025-08739-z.

[72] https://en.wikipedia.org/wiki/SOCRATES_(satellite).

[73] https://www.eoportal.org/satellite-missions/socrates.

[74] https://doi.org/10.1038/nphoton.2017.107.

[75] https://www.dlr.de/en/kn/research-transfer/projects/qkd-quantum-technology-for-secure-communication/qube-satellite-based-quantum-key-distribution.

[76] https://www.fau.eu/2025/08/news/research/global-quantum-encryption-small-satellites-as-quantum-key-generators/.

(continued)

Name	Country	Prepare and measure	Entanglement	Launch	Note
[QUICK3] [Ahn24],[77] [UniJ25][78]	Germany	Yes	No	June 2025	Technology and physics mission, no complete QKD service
SpeQtre [NanSpe],[79] [ISISpe][80]	Singapore + UK	No information	Yes	Nov. 2025	Already in space, but still in the commissioning phase at the time of writing. Operational launch announced for 2026.
Impulse-1 [NanImp][81]	Russia	Yes?	No	2023	Presumably QKD test

3.5.1 *Micius*

This satellite orbits the Earth in a sun-synchronous orbit at an average altitude of 478 km (perigee: 471 km, apogee: 485 km). It takes 94 min to orbit the planet. Figure 3.2 shows the orbit of Micius within one day (24 h).

The yellow spot above Europe in Fig. 3.2 marks the region above which Micius must be located in order to be seen from a ground station in Vienna (Austria). From Vienna, Micius can therefore only be seen in those sections of the orbit that are shown here in thicker and darker lines than the rest of the orbit. A simple geometric estimate shows that, under ideal conditions, Micius is visible from Vienna for a maximum of approximately 50 min within 24 h, divided into typically 6 overflights per day with a visibility duration per overflight of between 0 s and a maximum of 11 minutes and 16 s. Similar figures also apply to other regions of the world, with the total visibility time per day being shortest at the equator and longest at the poles.

Figure 3.3 shows the orbit of Micius in a true-to-scale comparison with the size of the Earth. It also shows how large a portion of the Earth's surface Micius sees at any given time. (Note: Micius' orbit does not pass exactly over the Earth's poles,

---

[77] https://doi.org/10.48550/arXiv.2301.11177.

[78] https://www.physik.uni-jena.de/en/iap/26345/quick3-mission-quantensatellit-mit-jenaer-know-how-startet-ins-all.

[79] https://www.nanosats.eu/sat/speqtre.

[80] https://www.isispace.nl/project/speqtre/.

[81] https://www.nanosats.eu/sat/impuls-1.

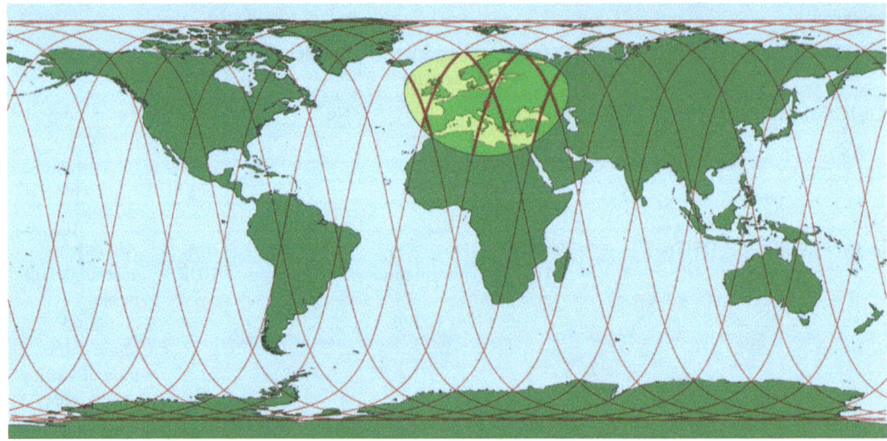

Fig. 3.2 Trace of the Micius satellite above the ground within one day

as Fig. 3.3 might suggest. The figure is only intended to show the relative sizes correctly. The exact course of the satellite's orbit above the Earth's surface is shown in Fig. 3.2.)

A total of six ground stations participated in the experiments with Micius. Four of them were in China (Xinglong, Lijiang, Nanshan, and Delhi), and the other two

Fig. 3.3 True-to-scale representation of the orbit (red circle) compared to the size of the Earth

were in Austria (in Graz and Vienna). There was also a smaller observation station in Ngari, Tibet [Liao18].[82]

Micius masters prepare-and-measure, but can also send entangled photons to two different ground stations.

Prepare and Measure

In Prepare-and-Measure, the satellite takes on the role of Alice in relation to both ground stations. Both ground stations then take on the role of Bob. However, this also means that the two ground stations do not exchange keys directly with each other; instead, each ground station exchanges keys separately with the satellite. The key material is therefore generated in the satellite, which thus also assumes the role of a trusted node. This creates a QKD network between the ground stations and the satellite, and the participants in this network obtain a negotiated key via the protocols of this network. This approach also means that it is not necessary for the two ground stations to exchange keys at the same time. For example, a ground station in China first performs a key exchange, and hours later, when the satellite becomes visible over Europe, a station in Austria performs a key exchange and then obtains the key that China received from the satellite, and a few hours later, a ground station in China obtains the key that was generated between Austria and the satellite.

The first publication on experiments with Micius from 2017 [Liao17a, Liao17b][83] reported that a total of 300,939 usable key bits were generated during a 273-second time slot (4 min, 33 s). This corresponds to 1.1 kbit/s during this time slot. Considering that the satellite typically flies over a ground station 6 times per day, this would result in a maximum of approximately 1.8 Mbit per day. From this, a long-term average of 21 bits/s can be calculated. However, only 4 flyovers within 23 days could actually be used in this experiment, which can be extrapolated to 1.2 Mbit in 23 days or 0.6 bits/s.

Four years later, in 2021, 47.8 kbit/s were published during a "typical" flyover, but these were raw key bits, before error correction and privacy amplification [Chen21].[84] However, in 2024, it was reported that during a 220-second flyover, a secure key material with a length of 310,400 bits was obtained, which corresponds to 1.4 kbit/s and is more in line with the 2017 value [Khm24].[85] But even the peak raw key value from 2021, when extrapolated to a full day under ideal conditions, averages only about 900 bits/s over the entire day.

QKD with Entanglement

In this variant, the satellite generates entangled photon pairs, which it sends to two ground stations. (One photon from each pair to Alice, the other to Bob.) For this to work, the satellite must be visible above the horizon from Alice's point of view and at the same time from Bob's point of view. The two ground stations must therefore

[82] https://doi.org/10.1103/PhysRevLett.120.030501.

[83] https://doi.org/10.1038/nature23655.

[84] https://doi.org/10.1038/s41586-020-03093-8.

[85] https://doi.org/10.1364/OE.511772.

not be too far apart. Two stations that are more than approximately 4800 km apart never see the satellite at the same time and therefore cannot exchange keys via the satellite using entanglement. (Compare this with Fig. 3.2.)

In an experiment conducted with Micius, both ground stations were in China, one in Lijiang and the other in Delhi. For key exchange to be possible, the satellite must have both ground stations in its field of view at the same time. Since these two locations are 1203 km apart, according to the publication [Yin17],[86] this was only possible once a day (at approximately 1:30 a.m. local time, i.e., at night) for a duration of 275 seconds (approx. 4½ minutes) each time. (It can be assumed that there were also flyovers during daylight hours when the satellite had both ground stations in its field of view at the same time, but this was not reported. Presumably, the scattered light from the sun was so strong during the day that key exchange was only possible at night, but again, nothing was reported about this.) In fact, in one case, measurements were taken for approximately 250 seconds, and 134 photon pairs were found to have matching polarization. Thus, after sifting, a raw key length of 134 bits was achieved. Unfortunately, despite intensive research, nothing could be found about how many bits remained after error correction and privacy amplification, or whether these steps were even performed. The sources found suggest that three such experiments were conducted on three different nights, but exact figures could only be found for one experiment [Lu22].[87]

This means that the raw key rate (before error correction and privacy amplification) for satellite-based entanglement QKD is 134 bits per day, which corresponds to approximately 0.0015 bits per second.

Criticism of Micius

In the entangled photon mode, Micius does not achieve a usable key rate and can only be considered a feasibility study.

When implemented in prepare-and-measure mode, analyses by research teams revealed a clearly measurable design flaw that is relevant to security: Micius uses the BB84 protocol with decoy states. The purpose of the decoy states is to detect an eavesdropper performing a photon number splitting (PNS) attack. However, this only works if the eavesdropper cannot distinguish signal pulses from decoy pulses. Micius uses different laser diodes for the two types of pulses, for which a clearly different timing behavior could be demonstrated. This enables the attacker to distinguish signal pulses from decoy pulses, to which they could then react. However, this means that an attacker remains undetected when carrying out a PNS attack, despite the decoy pulses. Under the usual security models, the implementation used can therefore no longer be considered information-theoretically secure [Mil25].[88]

[86] https://doi.org/10.1126/science.aan3211.

[87] https://doi.org/10.1103/RevModPhys.94.035001.

[88] https://doi.org/10.48550/arXiv.2505.06532.

3.5.2 *Jinan-1*

Jinan-1 is newer than Micius, but does not have a source of entangled photons on board. Jinan-1 can only be operated in prepare-and-measure mode. Its trajectory data is very similar to that of Micius. This satellite weighs only about 4% of Micius (Micius: 640 kg, Jinan-1: 23 kg) and costs only about 2.2% of the price of Micius. Unlike the Micius research satellite, Jinan-1 was developed with a greater focus on practical application. This satellite is also supposed to be able to work with portable ground stations. Such portable stations weigh around 100 kg.

The design of Jinan-1 avoids the flaw made with Micus, as Jinan-1 only has one photon source that is used for both types of pulses. This means that signal and decoy pulses cannot be distinguished by an attacker.

With Jinan-1, a peak value of up to 1.07 Mbit of secure key material was generated per flyover of a ground station. This results in up to approximately 5 Mbit per day, which averages out to just under 60 bits/s over an entire day. Other studies mention approximately 400,000 bits per flyover, which amounts to 2 Mbit per day and a daily average of 23 bits/s [Li25].[89]

3.5.3 *Other Current QKD Satellites*

The three satellites Socrates, QUBE, and [QUICK3] are (or were) primarily technology and feasibility demonstrators, i.e., not "productive" QKD satellites like Micius or Jinan-1, which deliver measurably large amounts of keys for real-world applications.

Socrates did not implement error correction or privacy amplification and, as a pure technology demonstrator, was only intended to show that certain QKD variants can be implemented in satellites [Car18].[90]

QUBE was also intended solely to demonstrate a specific technology, namely miniaturization. Although full-fledged key exchange is possible in principle with QUBE, this is not one of the objectives of the research project, and no publications on this topic could be found [LMU24].[91]

[QUICK3] is used for basic physics research, as this satellite is testing how a novel photon source (a dye center in a boron nitride crystal) functions in zero gravity. In principle, the satellite could be used for key exchange, but this is not mentioned as a mission objective in publicly available sources [QUICK3].[92]

SpeQtre is only the second satellite after Micius that will be able to emit entangled photon pairs. (The SpooQy-1 satellite, which has since burned up, also had an

[89] https://doi.org/10.1038/s41586-025-08739-z.

[90] https://doi.org/10.1117/12.2309624.

[91] https://www.lmu.de/en/newsroom/news-overview/news/global-quantum-key-encryption-nano-satellite-qube-launches-into-space-66e31186.html.

[92] https://www.quick3.de.

entangled source on board, but only used it to perform on-board measurements.) It was launched into space shortly before this book was completed, on November 28, 2025, and is undergoing a test phase during the completion of the book to test the functionality of all subsystems. Initial QKD experiments with ground stations in Singapore and the United Kingdom have been announced for spring 2026. All available sources refer to entangled photons. There is no information on whether SpeQtre can also be operated in prepare-and-measure mode [QZ25].[93]

However, SpeQtre is also designed as a demonstrator, not as a satellite for permanent production operation.

Impuls-1 is not actually a QKD satellite, as the main task of this Russian satellite is to observe the sun in the soft X-ray range. However, it also carries the "Vektor" laser communication payload, whose exact purpose is unclear. In any case, the Nanosats database tags Impuls-1 with "QKD – Quantum Key Distribution" and the mission text in this database reads: "solar activity monitoring in soft X-ray range, laser and quantum communications development." Unfortunately, no further information about Impuls-1 could be found [NanImp].[94]

All of the satellites mentioned are in a similar orbit to Micius (LEO = Low-Earth Orbit, between 450 and 600 km above the ground).

3.5.4 Planned QKD Satellite Missions

EAGLE-1 is a planned QKD demonstrator from the ESA (European Space Agency) and is to be used for EuroQCI. The aim of this pilot project is to offer genuine end-to-end QKD services for users in the EU. The launch of this mission was originally scheduled for fall 2024, but has already been postponed several times. Currently (January 2026), all that is known is that the launch is scheduled for "late 2025 or early 2026." Like all previous QKD satellites, EAGLE-1 will also have a low orbit (LEO) [ESA1].[95]

Eagle neXt is a planned follow-up mission to EAGLE-1. There are still no clear statements as to whether Eagle neXt will launch a single QKD satellite into space or several. However, ESA has stated its goal of having several QKD satellites orbiting the Earth at the same time in order to establish a QKD network in space, specifically mentioning the Eagle-1, Eagle neXt, SAGA, and QKDSat missions in this context [SES24].[96]

SAGA is another project by ESA and EuroQCI that is explicitly aimed at European government users. The system design is currently being developed, so there is only a

---

[93] https://quantumzeitgeist.com/speqtre-quantum-quantum-comms/.

[94] https://www.nanosats.eu/sat/impuls-1.

[95] https://www.esa.int/Applications/Connectivity_and_Secure_Communications/Eagle-1.

[96] https://www.ses.com/newsroom/eagle-1-advancing-europes-leadership-quantum-communications#tab-eagle-next.

preliminary draft at this stage. According to publicly available sources, nothing has been built yet, and a launch date has not yet been announced [ESA19].[97]

QKDSat is another QKD project by ESA that aims to launch an operational trusted node into space to provide governments and commercial users with secure keys. The satellite is scheduled to launch in 2027. ("QKDSat" is also the name of an older QKD project on which ESA and the British company ArQit worked. It ran from 2017 to 2021 but did not result in a satellite.) [ESA2].[98]

QKD-GEO/Caramuel will be a Spanish-led QKD satellite in geostationary orbit, with Thales Alenia Space and Hispasat as the two main players. "Geostationary" means that it will orbit the Earth directly above the equator at an altitude of 35,786 km and that it will take exactly 24 h to complete one orbit around the Earth. It will therefore be permanently visible from Europe. This means that QKD-GEO will not be subject to any restrictions due to short overflight times. However, the satellite is about 75 times farther from Earth than Micius or any other LEO satellite, which is likely to cause new problems. This is because the solid angle at which a satellite dish with a diameter of 1 m, for example, appears from the position of QKD-GEO is 5625 times smaller than the solid angle from the position of a LEO satellite. The loss of photons flying just past the receiver dish will be correspondingly higher. QKD-GEO will be the first geostationary QKD satellite and is to be integrated into the EuroQCI architecture. There is no official date for the launch into space yet, but the project was started in 2025 and the development time was predicted to be 2 years [Alv22].[99]

QEYSSat is a Canadian QKD project that aims to provide a fully developed key exchange, including with entangled photons. The launch is announced for the end of 2026 [Jen24].[100]

SpeQtral-1 is a planned QKD project from Singapore that aims to offer QKD services to commercial partners in the form of a pilot project. SpeQtral-1 will operate without entangled photons, but a follow-up project that will also use entangled photons is already planned [SPEQ].[101]

NICT–JAXA is a Japanese QKD project that began in 2025. Information about it is still sparse, in particular there is no launch date yet [VIA25].[102]

SAQTI is a possible name for an Indian QKD project, about which all that is known so far is that the program is scheduled to run until around 2030 or 2031 [Redd].[103]

---

[97] https://www.esa.int/ESA_Multimedia/Images/2019/04/SAGA_for_quantum_key_distribution.

[98] https://www.esa.int/Applications/Connectivity_and_Secure_Communications/QKDSat_Secure_communication_via_quantum_cryptography.

[99] https://doi.org/10.1109/ICSOS53063.2022.9749720.

[100] https://doi.org/10.48550/arXiv.2306.02481.

[101] https://speqtralquantum.com.

[102] https://www.satellitetoday.com/technology/2025/08/28/sky-perfect-jsat-joins-quantum-cryptography-satellite-rd-project.

[103] https://www.reddit.com/r/ISRO/comments/1gczzq5/planned_satellite_for_quantum_key_distribution_is/

China is currently working on several QKD satellite projects. Among other things, a quantum communication mega-constellation is planned, which will consist of several QKD satellites in low orbit and will be operated in cooperation with the BRICS countries. Two to three satellites are to be launched as early as 2026. China also plans to launch a geostationary QKD satellite into space in 2027 or 2028 [[CAS25],[104] [CRF25],[105] [TQI25],[106] [YIC24],[107] [SCM25][108]].

Russia tends to focus on terrestrial projects in the field of QKD, but is collaborating with other BRICS countries on Chinese projects. There are also plans to test QKD services from the ISS space station. Russia has had its own satellite (Impuls-1, see above) in space since 2023 with the potentially QKD-capable payload Vektor, which also points to its own initiatives in this area, but little information about this is publicly available. [[MER24],[109] [JRC19],[110] [TAS18][111]].

USA: In an official paper [NSA],[112] the [NSA] warns of practical limitations of QKD and recommends that US national security systems focus on post-quantum cryptography until the known QKD problems (scaling, infrastructure, trust assumptions) are solved. Therefore, at least from the government's perspective, QKD is not a central pillar of a crypto strategy in the US. Nevertheless, DARPA has developed a roadmap for quantum communication between ground stations and LEO and MEO satellites (MEO = Medium Earth Orbit, i.e., orbits at altitudes between 2000 and 36,000 km; often with a period of 12 h and a highly elliptical orbit), but has not yet named any specific QKD missions [[NAS24],[113] [NSc05].[114]

However, there are commercial companies in the US that see satellite QKD as a lucrative market and are therefore investing in such projects. For example, following its acquisition of Capella Space, IonQ plans to build a "global space-to-space and space-to-ground satellite QKD network," and Boeing is distributing PR material about the Q4S satellite, which is scheduled to launch in 2026 to demonstrate

[104] https://english.casad.cas.cn/newsroom/ma/202503/t20250325_908666.html.

[105] https://www.crfindia.org/-/media/Project/ChintanResearchFoundation/Publications-PDF/19-Sep/Chinas-Ascent-as-a-Quantum-Space-Power.ashx.

[106] https://thequantuminsider.com/2025/03/14/china-established-quantum-secure-communication-links-with-south-africa.

[107] https://www.yicaiglobal.com/news/china-is-likely-to-build-global-quantum-communication-network-in-near-future-scholar-says.

[108] https://www.scmp.com/news/china/science/article/3315963/new-dawn-pan-jianwei-reveals-high-orbit-quantum-satellite-global-network.

[109] https://merics.org/sites/default/files/2024-12/MERICS%20China%20Tech%20Observatory%20Quantum%20Report%202024.pdf.

[110] https://doi.org/10.2760/38407.

[111] https://tass.com/science/1008731.

[112] https://www.nsa.gov/Cybersecurity/Quantum-Key-Distribution-QKD-and-Quantum-Cryptography-QC/.

[113] https://ntrs.nasa.gov/api/citations/20240003113/downloads/AQCF_March2024_SCaNPresentation.pdf.

[114] https://www.newscientist.com/article/dn7484-quantum-cryptography-network-gets-wireless-link/.

"quantum networking in space." However, apart from such marketing statements, no concrete information has yet been forthcoming. [Ion25],[115] [Boe].[116]

Brazil: The situation here is very similar to that in all other BRICS countries: the focus is on terrestrial QKD projects (e.g., "Rio Quântica" [Fon24][117]), and satellite QKD projects are being left to China. Apart from concept studies, no concrete evidence of Brazil's own efforts in this direction could be found. Instead, the intention is to communicate with Chinese QKD satellites from Brazilian ground stations [MER24].[118]

3.6 Free-Space QKD (Line-of-Sight Connection through the Air)

In addition to fiber optics and satellite connections, this is the third way to transport photons from a transmitter to a receiver. It should be noted that in satellite QKD, the photons also travel part of their distance through layers of air, so all the problems mentioned here for free-space QKD also apply to satellite QKD.

The following rule of thumb applies: The entire column of air above a point on the ground (up to outer space) contains approximately the same amount of air as between two points on the ground that are 10 km apart. Since satellites are only in exceptional cases located exactly vertically above a ground station, the photons in satellite QKD usually move diagonally upward through the air, so that the path between the ground station and the satellite can be roughly estimated at an air distance of approximately 15 km [OU23].[119]

Almost all known QKD applications use wavelengths in the near-infrared range. Although this light is not visible to the human eye, it shares many properties with visible light. Some research groups even use wavelengths in the visible range. In the case of free-space QKD in particular, the situation is roughly comparable to someone trying to observe the glow of a very faint candle at a great distance with binoculars. This does not work in fog, rain, or snowfall. Smog can also impair visibility, especially in cities. When looking up (at a satellite), clouds block the view, and during the day, the air between the candle and the binoculars deflects so much sunlight into the binoculars as scattered light that the light from the candle is lost in this scattered

[115] https://www.ionq.com/news/ionq-completes-acquisition-of-capella-space-advancing-vision-for-space-based.

[116] https://www.boeing.com/space/quantum.

[117] https://revistapesquisa.fapesp.br/en/brazils-first-quantum-cryptography-network-is-expected-to-connect-five-research-institutions/.

[118] https://merics.org/sites/default/files/2024-12/MERICS%20China%20Tech%20Observatory%20Quantum%20Report%202024.pdf.

[119] https://www.open.edu/openlearn/science-maths-technology/engineering-environmental-fluids/content-section-3.1.

light. And on hot days, heated air causes turbulence that also makes it impossible to observe the candle [Vas17].[120]

Therefore, both free-space and satellite QKD work best on starry, cold nights.

3.6.1 Current and Completed Free-Space Projects

- A paper published in 2023 entitled "Towards metropolitan free-space quantum networks" [Krz23][121] by authors from the German Fraunhofer Institute and the Austrian AIT reports on a free-space project in **Jena** (Germany). The research group bridged a distance of 1.7 km with mobile QKD devices using entangled photons. A key rate of "up to 5.7 kbit/s" was achieved at night. During daylight hours, 2.5 kbit/s was measured. The same group had already demonstrated the feasibility of entangled free-space QKD on a 300-meter distance in Bonn (Germany) in 2021. The project is clearly designed as a network testbed. The keys generated are processed using a simple KMS with a network stack. As far as can be seen, however, no permanently productive critical application is planned. The project is a demonstrator for future EuroQCI-type infrastructures.
- Back in 2007, Austrian researchers (University of Vienna; IQOQI) demonstrated that a distance of 144 km between the two Canary Islands **of La Palma and Tenerife** could be bridged using free-space QKD. A key rate of 12.8 bits/s was achieved. This unique experiment was a historically important milestone in QKD research [Schm07].[122]
- Since 2023, a research group led by Nobel Prize winner Anton Zeilinger (Austria) has been operating a 10.4 km free-space link between a transmitter on Bisamberg (a hill north of Vienna) and a receiver on the roof of the University **of Vienna**. The research group is using this to test new entanglement-based methods/technologies and has also demonstrated the fundamental feasibility of QKD over 10.4 km of free space. The publications focus on the entanglement quality and stability of the connection. Explicit long-term key rates are not highlighted [Bul23].[123]
- **AirQKD** is an open-air QKD project that has been running in the United Kingdom since 2020 over a 135-meter open-air distance in Suffolk. Key rates of "up to" 84.3 kbit/s have already been achieved. The goal of the project is to secure the last mile in 5G networks. Unfortunately, long-term averages could not be found. The project can be seen as a pilot or field trial in which very specific 5G use cases are to be demonstrated [Zha25].[124]
- In Italy, at the University of Padua, the "**Full daylight QKD at 1550 nm**" project has been running since 2021. The test track runs between two roofs in Padua

---

[120] https://doi.org/10.1103/PhysRevA.96.043856.

[121] https://doi.org/10.1038/s41534-023-00754-0.

[122] https://doi.org/10.1103/PhysRevLett.98.010504.

[123] https://doi.org/10.1103/PhysRevX.13.021001.

[124] https://doi.org/10.1364/JOCN.553171.

and is 145 meters long. Key rates of 30 kbit/s on average are achieved in bright daylight. In principle, the keys generated could be fed directly into an HSM, but the project is not about practical usability, but rather about demonstrating daylight robustness [Ave21].[125]

- An Italian-Austrian research group also attempted to demonstrate **daylight robustness** in 2021 (publication in 2022/23), but with entangled photons. The group conducted several experiments at different distances (mostly between 300 and 500 meters) and obtained raw key rates of around 100 bit/s and a secure key rate of 12 bit/s after sifting [Bas23].[126]
- Several European research groups have collaborated with partners in **China** and achieved key rates between 100 and 400 bits/s over distances between 500 meters and approximately 1 km [Gon18],[127] [Shen18].[128]
- Also in **China**, a 53 km free-space link was operated as a technology demonstrator in 2017 with the aim of simulating QKD connections between satellites. In 1756 seconds (approximately half an hour), 157,179 bits were generated, from which a key rate of 90 bits/s can be calculated [Liao17a, Liao17b].[129] This was followed in 2024 by a follow-up project that achieved a key rate of 495 bits/s over a distance of 20 km on a daily average (day and night operation) [Cai24].[130]
- As early as 2002, a 10 km long free-space link was tested in **Los Alamos (USA)**. Key rates in the single-digit kbit/s range were achieved, and a strong dependence of the key rate on the weather and the time of day was reported. The keys generated in this test were actually used to initialize real crypto devices, but this project was also designed as a test only [Hug02].[131]

There are a number **of other free-space projects worldwide** that have published similar results to the examples cited here. All of these projects are research projects focused on feasibility and on operating such applications in daylight conditions. The distances bridged are usually in the range of 1 km or even significantly less, and the key rates rarely exceed the 1 kbit/s limit. As far as could be ascertained, at the time of completion of this book, there are no free-space QKD applications in productive continuous operation for security-related applications.

[125] https://doi.org/10.1038/s41534-021-00421-2.

[126] https://doi.org/10.1088/2058-9565/acae3d.

[127] https://doi.org/10.1364/OE.26.018897.

[128] https://doi.org/10.1103/PhysRevA.100.012325.

[129] https://doi.org/10.1038/nphoton.2017.116.

[130] https://doi.org/10.1364/OPTICA.511000.

[131] https://doi.org/10.1088/1367-2630/4/1/343.

3.6.2 QKD Projects with Planned Free-Space Components

- **MOZART** (a K-PASS project of the FFG) is an AIT project whose project description was published in October 2025 and which is just getting underway at the time of this book's completion. The aim of the project is to develop requirements and feasibility for future QKD-based connections between the Vienna government network and the federal fallback system in St. Johann (Austria). A large part of the project will be implemented using fiber optics, but the project description also explicitly mentions the use of free-space QKD. Whether this will be done on a section between Vienna and St. Johann or whether it will be used to connect buildings within Vienna could not be determined from publicly available sources. MOZART is the only publicly known QKD project in Austria that refers to free-space QKD [KPa25].[132]
- **LAiQa** is a Horizon Europe project led by Greece with the participation of the Austrian company QTLabs. The project has been running since January 2024 and has, among other things, a 2.5 km free-space link and a ground-to-satellite connection on its to-do list, but no results have been published yet [COR25].[133]
- **QuFree** is a QKD project launched in 2023 in northern Italy, which also plans to test free-space QKD connections. Many fiber optic connections have already been put into operation, and in February 2025 it was reported that work on the free-space connection would begin soon, including the installation of receivers on ships. More recent information could not be found [Uni25].[134]
- There are **many other ongoing QKD projects** in which free-space links are also being tested "on the side," but the associated publications usually only mention the results on fiber optic links, so it is unclear for many ongoing projects whether testing on free-space links has even begun. Pure, permanently operated free-space QKD infrastructures without integration into other technologies are currently hard to find; they are usually test beds or field trials. It should also be mentioned that all projects mentioned so far use DV-QKD, i.e., QKD with single photons. However, there are also free-space research projects that work with CD-QKD.

3.6.3 Free-Space QKD with Mobile Devices

For some time now, attempts have been made to carry out quantum key distribution using balloons, drones, aircraft, and ships. However, it must be strongly emphasized that all experiments in this direction are still purely research-based and that, as far

132 https://www.k-pass.at/en/financed-proposals/detail/mozart-requirements-for-quantum-communication-solutions-for-connecting-the-vienna-public-authority-network-and-the-zas-st-johann/.

133 https://cordis.europa.eu/project/id/101135245.

134 https://portale.units.it/en/news/quantum-link-over-fibre-optics-inaugurated-between-units-and-uniud.

as can be gleaned from the researched material, no devices for continuous use can be purchased now or in the coming years.

In 2021, a Chinese research group published a survey paper on this topic [Xue21].[135]

In it, they define "airborne QKD" on the one hand as an intermediate stage between satellite QKD and terrestrial QKD variants (fiber optics, free beam), but on the other hand also as a variant of free beam QKD with mobile transmitters or receivers, some of which have relatively high relative speeds. A distinction is made between:

- **UAVs/drones**: "last mile" relays, temporary nodes in inner-city or field networks.
- **Slow-flying aircraft**: greater ranges, longer visibility windows, tactical applications.
- **HAPs/stratospheric platforms**: relays between satellite and ground, large-area coverage.

The survey paper describes several experiments conducted between 2013 and 2021 using drones and balloons. In an experiment conducted in 2015, a key exchange was even carried out using a moving pickup truck. (The car on which Bob was mounted drove past Alice at a speed of 33 km/h at a distance of 650 m, during which a 4-second key exchange session was successful, yielding 160 bits [Bou15].[136])

The authors report that distances of 200 m to 20 km were covered in such experiments and that key rates in the order of up to approx. 300 bit/s were achieved, in some cases at relative speeds of up to approx. 260 km/h. In addition to the physical characteristics of such approaches, the authors also briefly touch on the security aspect of such mobile QKD applications and mention device imperfections in particular as a possible source of side-channel attacks, but security is only a marginal topic in this paper.

In 2024, another research group published a similar paper [Dub24].[137] It addresses many technical and physical challenges, such as atmospheric effects (turbulence, humidity) and weather dependence, coupling problems, target tracking, stabilization, synchronization, and timing. The authors also outline visions for the future, such as QKD networks implemented with drone swarms.

In their conclusion, the authors emphasize that they see great potential for military applications, but also for other field operations (e.g., natural disasters), but that there is still a long way to go before such systems reach a level of maturity that allows them to be used in real-world scenarios. The specific key rates and distances cited by the authors in this comprehensive survey paper are similar to those described in the paper mentioned above for moving transmitters and receivers. In an experiment, the authors of the survey paper claimed that a key rate of 868 kbit/s was achieved with an aircraft, which would be a very high value even for a fiber optic connection. However, the abstract of the original paper [Pug17][138] correctly states that the key

[135] https://doi.org/10.3788/COL202119.122702.

[136] https://doi.org/10.1364/OE.23.033437.

[137] https://doi.org/10.1016/j.physo.2024.100210.

[138] https://doi.org/10.1088/2058-9565/aa701f.

material with a total length of 868 kbit was collected "in a few minutes." There appear to be several such errors in the survey paper, but it nevertheless provides a good overview of current efforts in this field of research.

3.7 Trusted Nodes and KMS Networks

Trusted nodes [QNu][139] play a central role in today's large-scale QKD infrastructures. In China in particular, there are networks with more than 40 nodes, some of which bridge distances of several thousand kilometers [Che21],[140] [CAS17],[141] and almost every country in Europe also operates such a network. Initial plans are already in place to connect these national networks into a large pan-European QKD network, which will then consist of hundreds of such trusted nodes [EC25].[142]

Trusted nodes serve as intermediate stations where the key material is received, temporarily decrypted, re-encrypted, and forwarded to the next station. Their existence is due to the physical limitations of today's QKD systems: the losses of optical fibers increase exponentially with distance, and the range of pure end-to-end QKD is therefore typically limited to a few hundred kilometers. Free-space and satellite QKD can also only enable point-to-point key exchange. To bridge very large distances, such as continental or national backbone routes, chains of QKD links are therefore established, which are connected to each other via trusted nodes.

The key advantage of this architecture lies in its technical feasibility and scalability: trusted node networks can already be set up today using commercially available QKD systems and enable the cascading of the key material over hundreds or even thousands of kilometers. They form the backbone of many current demonstrators and pilot networks, including European, Asian, and North American QKD initiatives. At the same time, a new type of critical infrastructure is emerging: since trusted nodes have access to plaintext key material, they must be operated under strict security conditions. Physical security, access control, protection against manipulation, trusted modules for key processing, and organizational measures are essential, because even a single compromised trusted node can jeopardize the entire network path.

Trusted nodes are therefore both a technical necessity and a security vulnerability in current QKD networks. In the long term, they should be replaced or at least relieved by new concepts, such as interferometric methods like twin-field QKD, or by real quantum repeaters, which would enable entanglement-based quantum networking without trust assumptions. Since such technologies are being researched

---

139 https://www.qnulabs.com/glossary/trusted-nodes-quantum-network-architecture.

140 https://doi.org/10.1038/s41534-021-00474-3.

141 https://english.cas.cn/newsroom/archive/news_archive/nu2017/201703/t20170324_175288.shtml.

142 https://digital-strategy.ec.europa.eu/en/policies/european-quantum-communication-infrastructure-euroqci.

in experiments but are still far from being commercially viable, trusted nodes will continue to be the dominant architectural principle of large QKD networks in the coming years.

3.7.1 Important Terms and Definitions

Trusted Node

A trusted node is an intermediate station in a QKD network that processes key material in plain text. The node receives the key generated by QKD from a quantum link, stores it, combines it with other keys, and forwards the combined keys to other trusted nodes or end nodes via a classical channel. The security of the entire path depends on each individual node being completely trustworthy and physically and organizationally protected. An attacker who compromises a trusted node can access the key material of all passing connections [ETSI19–14].[143]

Quantum Repeaters [QSNP–QR].[144]

A quantum repeater is a device that enables entangled quantum states to be distributed over very long distances without intermediate stations gaining access to Technically, a quantum repeater does the following:

- It generates entanglements,
- it distributes the entanglements across multiple segments,
- it connects segments using entanglement swapping,
- it uses quantum memories to temporarily store quantum states without measuring them.

A functioning quantum repeater would make trusted nodes superfluous, as no intermediate station would need to know the keys. However, only laboratory prototypes exist so far. Intensive work is being done on quantum repeaters worldwide, including in China, Europe, the US, and South Korea. However, no fully practical implementation is available yet.

KMS

This is the abbreviation for *Key Management System*. This refers to the way in which multiple trusted nodes, connected to each other via quantum links, interact with each other to distribute shared key pairs to the endpoints of such a network without requiring a direct quantum link between these endpoints. In addition to distribution across multiple trusted nodes, a KMS typically also includes the secure

[143] https://www.etsi.org/deliver/etsi_gs/QKD/001_099/014/01.01.01_60/gs_qkd014v010101p.pdf.

[144] https://qsnp.eu/glossary/quantum-repeater/.

storage, management, deletion, and assignment of keys to specific applications [ETSI20–04],[145] [ETSI22–18].[146]

3.7.2 How a Trusted Node Works

A trusted node is the endpoint of two or more quantum links belonging to different terminals. For example, the trusted node named "Tom" may be connected to Alice via a fiber optic link running the BB84 protocol and to Bob via a satellite station, with the satellite emitting entangled photons and Tom and Bob using the E91 protocol to generate shared key material. (In this example, therefore, no key material is generated in the satellite.)

Over time, Alice and Tom have generated a large number of key bits, which they combine into key packets. Packets of 256 bits each are very common and can be used for AES encryption, for example. Alice and Tom have generated the key packets S_{a1}, S_{a2}, S_{a3}, etc. in this way. The keys S_{b1}, S_{b2}, S_{b3}, etc. are generated between Bob and Tom via the satellite link. This means that Tom knows all the keys mentioned and that Alice and Bob do not (yet) have a shared key.

If Alice wants to send a message to Bob, she needs a key that Bob knows. Therefore, Alice requests such a key from Tom. Tom now takes a key that Alice and Tom know (e.g., S_{a1}) and a key that Bob and Tom know (e.g., S_{b1}) and combines them with an XOR operation[147] to obtain S_{a1b1} with this formula: $S_{a1b1} = S_{a1} \oplus S_{b1}$. This is known as one-time pad encryption (OTP), and in OTP-terminology, S_{b1} is the plain text, S_{a1} is the secret key, and S_{a1b1} is the cypher text.

Tom sends the bit sequence S_{a1b1} to Alice, and Alice also performs an XOR operation with S_{a1} to obtain S_{b1} as follows: $S_{b1} = S_{a1} \oplus S_{a1b1}$. The key S_{a1} is now used up, which means that Alice and Tom delete this key from their memory. More importantly, Alice and Bob now both know the key S_{b1}, which they can use for their intended purpose. Typically, Alice and Bob do not use the key S_{b1} for one-time pad encryption, but for AES or, a comparable encryption method. Nevertheless, the key S_{b1} is removed from the KMS network because there are now two endpoints that share it.

And in the same way as in this simple example, where there was only one trusted node between Alice and Bob, there can also be a chain of several trusted nodes between Alice and Bob, for example: Alice—T_1—T_2—T_3—Bob. If Alice needs one of Bob's keys, she sends the request to T_1, which forwards the request along the chain to T_3, and from there the key is forwarded in the opposite direction to Alice,

[145] https://www.etsi.org/deliver/etsi_gs/QKD/001_099/004/02.01.01_60/gs_qkd004v020101p.pdf.

[146] https://www.etsi.org/deliver/etsi_gs/QKD/001_099/018/01.01.01_60/gs_qkd018v010101p.pdf.

[147] See Chap. 6.

with one key being used on each section of the route. In this way, extensive QKD networks can be implemented.

However, there are other methods for supplying the endpoints of a QKD network with shared keys. In this case, the keys generated by quantum physics are not used for OTP encryption (where they are consumed), but new keys are generated in the trusted nodes with the aid of random number generators, which are distributed to the end points, and the "real" quantum keys are used as AES keys to secure transport between neighboring trusted nodes. No "real" quantum keys are consumed in this process, and only keys that originate directly from the random number generators of the trusted nodes reach the end points. This prevents key scarcity in a QKD network, but it does create new attack vectors that jeopardize the security of the entire network. To mitigate this problem somewhat, the real quantum keys are also considered "used up" after a certain period of time (or after a certain number of uses) and are deleted.

3.8 Implementation and Side-Channel Attacks on QKD Systems

The basis for the description of implementation and side-channel attacks on QKD systems is a study by the German Federal Office for Information Security (*Bundesamts für Sicherheit in der Informationstechnik*—BSI) entitled "Implementation Attacks against QKD Systems," which was published in fall 2023. Details on implementation and side-channel attacks can therefore be found there [BSI23].[148]

3.8.1 Theoretical QKD Security Versus Real Systems

The implementation and side-channel attacks investigated by the BSI highlight the need to distinguish between the theoretical security of QKD methods/technologies and the security that can actually be achieved by real QKD systems. Security assurances derived from formal models and physical assumptions apply under idealized conditions. They assume that all components involved correspond exactly to the assumed security model and also operate within defined parameters.

Real QKD systems inevitably deviate from this. Hardware components have imperfections, additional functions are required to ensure stability and availability, and ongoing operation requires calibration, monitoring, and control mechanisms. The security that can actually be achieved therefore does not result solely from the method/technology used, but from the specific design of the overall system, including hardware, software, control logic, and operating processes.

[148] https://www.bsi.bund.de/SharedDocs/Downloads/EN/BSI/Publications/Studies/QKD-Systems/QKD-Systems.pdf.

Side-channel attacks exploit precisely this difference between model and implementation. They do not attack the QKD method/technology itself, but exploit deviations, side effects, or additional functions of real implementations. The BSI study shows that such attacks are not exceptional cases of individual faulty systems, but are structurally related to the complexity of modern QKD implementations. As the range of functions and automation increase, so does the potential attack surface.

A key conclusion of the analysis is that security in QKD cannot be understood as an inherent property of a process/technology. Rather, it is the result of a specific implementation and continuously monitored operation. Theoretical security guarantees remain ineffective without appropriate technical and organizational measures if real systems are operated outside of idealized assumptions.

3.8.2 Typical Points of Attack and Affected System Components

Real QKD systems consist of a variety of specialized hardware and software components whose interaction enables functioning key generation. The BSI study shows that side-channel attacks typically do not target abstract protocol steps, but rather specific system elements whose physical properties, control logic, or integration requirements deviate from the idealized assumptions of the security models. The attack surface results less from individual components than from the interaction of complex integrated components and operating mechanisms.

Interface Between the Quantum World and Classical Processing

One particularly relevant area concerns the interfaces between quantum physical signal processing and subsequent classical processing. *Time and clock synchronization, trigger and gating mechanisms, signal and power monitoring,* and *digital evaluation of measurement* results form a transition area in which measured values are interpreted, filtered, and prepared for further processing.

The BSI study shows that attacks that influence *calibration and estimation processes* in these paths can lead to noise, loss, or error parameters being systematically misjudged. Such manipulations often remain within plausible operating limits and are therefore not necessarily recognized as a malfunction.

Downstream *classic processing* also represents a relevant point of attack. Implementations of parameter estimation, error correction, key compression, and authentication can unintentionally reveal information about runtime, memory, or access patterns. (See Chap. 8 Postprocessing).

In addition, the BSI study considers scenarios with *maliciously modified hardware or software components* that can leak security-relevant information via covert communication channels. Although such attacks do not affect the quantum physical processes themselves, they can completely undermine the practical security gains.

Attack Paths Close to the Sender and Receiver

A central block of the attack paths analyzed in the BSI study concerns components of real QKD systems close to the sender and receiver. On the receiver side, detector-related attack classes such as

- targeted blinding by feeding in bright light
- efficiency mismatch attacks
- time-dependent effects
- correlations due to dead times
- after-gate pulses, and
- nonlinear detector behavior

are described.

In addition, *backflash* and *breakdown flash effects* are discussed, in which optical emissions generated during the detection process can reveal information about internal states. Characteristically, these attacks exploit permissible operating states that are not covered by the idealized security model.

At the transmitter and modulator level, the study deals with *Trojan horse attacks,* in which light is deliberately fed into optical modules and reflected signals are evaluated in order to reconstruct internal settings such as modulation states or phase positions.

Closely related to this are *laser damage attacks,* in which detectors or photodiodes are deliberately damaged, or their characteristics altered in order to facilitate subsequent attacks or circumvent monitoring mechanisms.

In addition, *transmitter- and source-proximal side channels* are analyzed, in which secondary information in frequency, phase, wavelength, temporal structure, or intensity can undermine statistical assumptions of the process/technology without directly violating it.

The majority of attack vectors documented in the BSI study relate to *discrete QKD implementations (DV-QKD),* while significantly fewer specific attacks have been described for continuously variable systems to date. Entanglement-based QKD approaches, on the other hand, are hardly addressed, as they are currently only available in a few, predominantly experimental implementations and, at least at the time of completion of the BSI study in fall 2023, there was correspondingly little reliable attack literature available.

CV-QKD-Specific Attacks

For continuously variable QKD systems, the BSI study describes its own attack paths that target *calibration and reference assumptions* in particular. These include saturation attacks and manipulations of reference signals and noise estimates, which can lead to security parameters being systematically overestimated.

Random Number Generators

Another security-relevant component is random number generators, which are used for base selection, modulation, and process/technology parameters. Even with quantum-based random sources, real implementations can be influenced by hardware-related limitations, manufacturing influences, or targeted manipulations during integration and maintenance without producing immediately noticeable deviations. The BSI has examined random number generators in separate documents and proposed a classification of these devices [BSI24].[149] (See also https://cryptography.study/phys/TRNG.)

Trusted nodes, KMS, and Operating Environment

Trusted node architectures and higher-level key management infrastructures extend the attack surface beyond individual QKD links. In such systems, key material is temporarily stored, redistributed, or re-encrypted, creating additional security-critical components and interfaces.

Practical security here depends on the entire end-to-end chain of physical protection, access control, key handling, process/technology integration, and organizational measures. Vulnerabilities in management and orchestration layers can neutralize the security gains of the underlying QKD connections without attacking the process/technology itself.

Other Vulnerabilities

Finally, the BSI's analysis makes it clear that side channels do not only arise during operation. Attack vectors during development, manufacturing, integration, and maintenance are equally relevant. The combination of high technical complexity, specialized hardware, and limited transparency favors scenarios in which vulnerabilities remain permanent and inconspicuous (see Sect. 7.2).

3.8.3 Practical Implications and Limitations of Countermeasures

Successful side-channel attacks on QKD systems do not typically manifest themselves in practice as immediate system failure or clearly recognizable security incidents. Rather, there is a gradual loss of assumed security, in which information about the generated key can leak out unnoticed. The systems often remain within specified operating parameters and continue to generate keys. The error monitoring provided in QKD systems is designed to detect disturbances in the quantum channel and does not offer any inherent mechanism for reliably detecting side-channel attacks or subsequently identifying compromised keys.

The BSI study describes a variety of countermeasures that operate at different levels. Technical hardening measures aim to make known attack paths more difficult, for example through improved optical isolation, shielding against electromagnetic radiation, robust design of sensitive components, or limiting the external signals that can be applied. In addition, surveillance and monitoring approaches are discussed that

[149] https://www.bsi.bund.de/SharedDocs/Downloads/EN/BSI/Certification/Interpretations/AIS_31_Functionality_classes_for_random_number_generators_e_2024.pdf.

are designed to continuously record operating parameters such as optical power, electrical signals, or temporal characteristics in order to reveal deviations from expected behavior. Furthermore, conceptual approaches are considered in which certain attack surfaces are reduced by alternative variants or system architectures, for example, by changing the distribution of security assumptions across system components.

At the same time, the study makes it clear that these measures have narrow limits. For the majority of the documented attack paths, there are several proposed countermeasures, but their effectiveness is based on different assumptions and cannot yet be evaluated comparatively or quantitatively. The BSI study explicitly points out that attack assessments were carried out independently of implemented countermeasures, as there are no reliable statements about their effectiveness. In addition, many protection mechanisms themselves require complex additional functions that introduce new sources of error, additional attack surfaces, or increased calibration and maintenance costs.

Overall, it is clear that countermeasures do not fundamentally eliminate side-channel attacks, but rather make them more difficult to exploit or address individual known attack paths. The practical security of QKD systems therefore does not result from a closed catalog of measures, but from the ongoing interaction of system design, monitoring, updating, and the consideration of new attack findings, as documented in the BSI study.

3.8.4 Consequences for the Procurement, Evaluation, and Operation of QKD Systems

The attack vectors and countermeasures documented in the BSI study show that side channels are not a one-off problem, but rather a permanent operational risk for real QKD systems. The attack surface continues to evolve with the system configuration, operating mode, and the state of attack research. Security-relevant deviations can arise without immediately manifesting themselves in malfunctions or noticeable operating parameters.

The study by the German BSI also highlights the limitations of traditional assessment tools. Certificates, laboratory tests, and manufacturer specifications inevitably refer to a defined system state and a known set of assumptions. They can document that a system meets specified requirements under certain conditions, but they do not reflect the dynamics of operation or the full spectrum of possible implementation attacks. Such evidence provides only a snapshot, especially for side channels, the exploitation of which often lies outside the modeled threat scenarios.

Against this background, characteristics that go beyond the individual product are becoming increasingly important. These include the traceability of the system architecture, the ability to analyze security-relevant components and interfaces, and clearly defined concepts for updating, maintenance, and responding to newly identified vulnerabilities. Equally relevant are continuous monitoring mechanisms and procedures that can be used to evaluate and address conspicuous deviations.

Overall, QKD is thus classified as a security-critical special component whose benefits can only be realized in conjunction with suitable system integration and continuous operation. The results presented in the BSI study underscore that the practical security gain does not arise from the isolated consideration of individual components, but from the ongoing control of a complex, changing system.

3.8.5 Meta-Information on the BSI Study

The BSI study comprises around 250 pages and evaluates more than 300 scientific papers. A total of 49 specific attack paths with known attack sequences are described, 35 of which are specific to the currently most widely used QKD family of discrete QKD systems (DV-QKD). In addition, 9 further vulnerabilities are listed for which no complete attack path has been documented to date. Furthermore, the study identifies 18 general countermeasures and assigns them to the various attack classes.

The attack options are also evaluated in terms of the effort required, including the expertise, time, and technical resources needed. These evaluations show that many attacks require considerable skills and resources on the part of the attacker, but this does not mean that the all-clear can be given. The study makes it clear that the assessment of attacks is deliberately carried out independently of implemented countermeasures and that even complex attacks remain relevant in the context of highly secure systems as soon as the necessary skills or motivation are available. The assumption of highly capable attackers follows the established security methodology of not tying threat models to current practical limitations. Especially in the context of information that needs to be protected in the long term, the multitude of documented attack paths should therefore be understood less as a theoretical limit and more as a realistic description of the existing and growing attack surface on QKD systems.

3.9 Summary QKD

3.9.1 Fiber Optics

In the following comparison, a strict distinction must be made between peak results measured and published by research groups in one-off experimental setups under optimal conditions and values that can be achieved with commercially available equipment. In addition, information was obtained exclusively for this study from users, which paints a different picture.

Comparison of Peak Values from Research Groups

- Prepare-and-measure with continuous variables (**CV-QKD**)

  In 2022, a research group published 190.5 Mbit/s for 5 km, 137.8 Mbit/s for 10 km, and 52.5 Mbit/s for 25 km [Wang22].[150] In 2024, another group increased this record to 0.7 Gbit/s at 5 km and 0.3 Gbit/s at 10 km [Haj24].[151] However, research groups consistently report that although CV-QKD achieves significantly higher secure key rates than DV-QKD over short distances, this rate also drops much faster than with DV-QKD as the distance increases because CV-QKD is much more sensitive to a deteriorating signal-to-noise ratio. There are statements that CV-QKD can hardly be used effectively at distances of more than 30 km. Nevertheless, there are also attempts to use CV-QKD over long distances. In 2020, a research group succeeded in doing so over a distance of 202.81 km. They achieved a key rate of 6.2 bit/s [Zha20].[152]
- Prepare-and-measure with single photons (**DV-QKD**)

  In 2023, a research team reported a secure key rate of 115.8 Mbit/s at a distance of 10 km, 22.2 Mbit at 50 km, and 2.6 Mbit/s at 101 km [LiW23].[153] Another group reported 233 bit/s at 328 km, and a third group even succeeded in exchanging keys over a distance of 405 km at 6.5 bit/s.
- **With Entangled Photons**:

  Raw key rates of 151 kbit/s have already been achieved over distances of 20 km, and even at a distance of 40 km, a raw key rate of 40 kbit/s has already been achieved. In a more practical application, these raw keys would then have to be post-processed with error correction and privacy amplification, which could significantly reduce the secure key length.

  For entangled photons, experiments have already been conducted in which, at great expense, a secure key rate of 440.8 bit/s was achieved at 201 km, 1.87 bit/s at 301 km, and 0.0015 bit/s at 404 km [Zhu25][154] (corresponding to 5 bits per hour).

No information could be found on the amount of money that had to be spent to achieve these peak results. It was also not possible to find out any operating costs in this regard. However, several articles report that special detectors were used that require complex cryogenic cooling.

Especially in experiments involving long distances, glass fibers that have actually been laid between two measuring stations at this distance are not usually used. Instead, glass fiber coils supplied directly by the manufacturer of the glass fibers

[150] https://10.1038/s42005-022-00941-z.

[151] https://doi.org/10.1364/OPTICA.530080.

[152] https://doi.org/10.1103/PhysRevLett.125.010502.

[153] https://doi.org/10.1038/s41566-023-01166-4.

[154] https://doi.org/10.1103/PhysRevLett.134.230801.

are used. Although it would be possible to lay such fibers, they are left wound on the drums for the experiments. This prevents the risk of kinks or other disturbances in the fiber optic cable, which can lead to additional attenuation in fibers that are actually laid.

Comparison of Manufacturer Specifications

- **Continuous Variables (CV-QKD)**

  For CV-QKD systems in fiber optic environments, manufacturers specify key rates in the range of approximately 10 to 100 kbit/s for short to medium distances (typically 10–20 km). However, the 100 kbit/s is probably a raw key rate (after sifting; before error correction and privacy amplification).

  For longer distances of up to about 50 to 80 km, key rates in the lower kbit/s range are still specified, i.e., about 1 to 10 kbit/s.

  In this borderline range of 80 to 100 km of fiber optic cable, the explicitly stated key rates are around 1 kbit/s or less.

  According to current research, there appear to be no manufacturers offering devices with CV technology for fiber optic distances of more than 100 km.
- **Discrete Variables (DV-QKD)**

  Only a few manufacturers provide explicit specifications for short distances (10 to 20 km; or attenuations corresponding to these distances). When they do, they mention a few kbit/s, but they also like to refer to products designed purely for research purposes, specifying key rates in the range of 100 to 400 kbit/s.

  For medium distances of around 50 to 80 km, most manufacturers quote typical key rates in a range of 1 to 5 kbit/s. However, there are also high-performance variants that promise key rates of 10 to 300 kbit/s for such distances (or for the corresponding attenuations).

  For distances in the range of around 100 to 150 km, the manufacturer's specifications typically range from 150 to 1700 bit/s.

  In long-range configurations for 200 km and more, key rates of several hundred bit/s are still specified. Variants with measuring device-intensive architectures (e.g., MDI-QKD) specify key rates of more than 500 bit/s at these distances.
- **Entanglement-Based QKD**

  Over short distances of around 10 km, key rates of up to 120 kbit/s are sometimes reported. For medium distances of around 50 km, manufacturers typically report rates in the range of approximately 1.5 to 20 kbit/s.

  There is one system that can also bridge distances of up to 300 km, for which the manufacturer specifies a key rate of approximately 7 bit/s.

	Manufacturer specifications key rate fiber optic		
Distance	CV-QKD	DV-QKD	Entanglement**
10–20 km	Over 10 kbit/s	Typical: 1–20 kbit/s high-end*: 300–400 kbit/s	Approx. 120 kbit/s
50–80 km	1–10 kbit/s	Typical: Approx. 1–5 kbit/s high-end*: Approx. 18–300 kbit/s	Approx. 1.5–20 kbit/s
Approx. 100 km	Maximum range Rate below 1 kbit/s	Typical: Approx. 1.7 kbit/s	No information
Approx. 150 km	No products available	Typical: Approx. 0.5 kbit/s	No information
Approx. 200 km	No products available	High-end: Approx. 0.04–0.4 kbit/s	0.007 kbit/s

*These values are manufacturer specifications for peak configurations that are otherwise very uncommon on the market
**Due to the still low level of technological maturity and the mainly experimental use under very different conditions, the values for entanglement solutions vary greatly

Detailed manufacturer-specific reports are provided together with all source references on the book's website at.[155]

References

[WP-QKD] Wikipedia contributors, Quantum key distribution. Wikipedia, the Free Encyclopedia. https://en.wikipedia.org/wiki/Quantum_key_distribution

[WP-MAC] Wikipedia contributors, Message authentication code, Wikipedia, the Free Encyclopedia. https://en.wikipedia.org/wiki/Message_authentication_code

[WP-Bit] Wikipedia contributors, Bit, Wikipedia, the Free Encyclopedia. https://en.wikipedia.org/wiki/Bit

[WP-Qbit] Wikipedia contributors, Qubit, Wikipedia, the Free Encyclopedia. https://en.wikipedia.org/wiki/Qubit

[WP-MQM] Wikipedia contributors, Measurement in quantum mechanics. Wikipedia, the Free Encyclopedia. https://en.wikipedia.org/wiki/Measurement_in_quantum_mechanics

[WP-NCT] Wikipedia contributors, No-cloning theorem. Wikipedia, the Free Encyclopedia. https://en.wikipedia.org/wiki/No-cloning_theorem

[WP-QEnt] Wikipedia contributors, Quantum entanglement. Wikipedia, the Free Encyclopedia. https://en.wikipedia.org/wiki/Quantum_entanglement

[WP-QSup] Wikipedia contributors, Quantum superposition. Wikipedia, the Free Encyclopedia. https://en.wikipedia.org/wiki/Quantum_superposition

[WP-Unc] Wikipedia contributors, Uncertainty principle. Wikipedia, the Free Encyclopedia. https://en.wikipedia.org/wiki/Uncertainty_principle

[QRep] Quantum Flagship, Quantum Repeaters, Quantum Technology (Quantum Principles; Communication), no date. https://qt.eu/quantum-principles/communication/quantum-repeaters

[Weg81] M.N. Wegman, L. Carter, New hash functions and their use in authentication and set equality. J. Comput. Syst. Sci. **22**, 265–279 (1981). https://doi.org/10.1016/0022-0000(81)90033-7

[155] https://cryptography.study/phys/QKD.

[WP-P&M] Wikipedia contributors, Quantum key distribution; Quantum key exchange; Prepare-and-measure protocols. Wikipedia, the Free Encyclopedia. https://en.wikipedia.org/wiki/Quantum_key_distribution#Quantum_key_exchange

[QSNP-DV] Quantum Secure Networks Partnership (QSNP), DV QKD, QSNP Glossary, no date. https://qsnp.eu/glossary/dv-qkd/

[WP-TRL] Wikipedia contributors, Technology readiness level; Quantum key exchange; Prepare-and-measure protocols. Wikipedia, the Free Encyclopedia. https://en.wikipedia.org/wiki/Technology_readiness_level

[Sas11] M. Sasaki et al., Field test of quantum key distribution in the Tokyo QKD network. Opt. Express **19**(11), 10387–10409 (2011). https://doi.org/10.1364/OE.19.010387

[Liao17a] S.-K. Liao et al., Satellite-to-ground quantum key distribution. Nature **549**(7670), 43–47 (2017). https://doi.org/10.1038/nature23655

[QSNP-CV] Quantum Secure Networks Partnership (QSNP), CV QKD, QSNP Glossary, no date. https://qsnp.eu/glossary/cv-qkd/

[Zha24] Y. Zhang et al., Continuous-variable quantum key distribution system: Past, present, and future. Appl. Phys. Rev. **11**(1) (2024). https://doi.org/10.1063/5.0179566

[QSNP-Ent] Quantum Secure Networks Partnership (QSNP), Entanglement. QSNP Glossary, no date. https://qsnp.eu/glossary/entanglement/

[QSNP-Bell] Quantum Secure Networks Partnership (QSNP), Bell state measurement, QSNP Glossary, no date. https://qsnp.eu/glossary/bell-state-measurement/

[WP-Bell] Wikipedia contributors, Bell test. Wikipedia, the Free Encyclopedia. https://en.wikipedia.org/wiki/Bell_test

[QSNP-MDI] Quantum Secure Networks Partnership (QSNP), Measurement-DI QKD. QSNP Glossary, no date. https://qsnp.eu/glossary/measurement-di-qkd/

[Ars25] Arslan, Syed M., et al., Twin-Field Quantum Key Distribution: Protocols, Security, and Open Problems. arXiv preprint https://arxiv.org/abs/2510.26320 (2025). https://doi.org/10.48550/arXiv.2510.26320

[QSNP-DI] Quantum Secure Networks Partnership (QSNP), DI QKD, QSNP Glossary, no date. https://qsnp.eu/glossary/di-qkd/

[Luo25] Luo, Xi-Yu, et al., Entangling quantum memories over 420 km in fiber. arXiv preprint https://arxiv.org/abs/2504.05660 (2025). https://doi.org/10.48550/arXiv.2504.05660

[Koz19] W. Kozlowski, S. Wehner, Towards large-scale quantum networks, in *Proceedings of the sixth annual ACM international conference on nanoscale computing and communication*, (2019). https://doi.org/10.1145/3345312.3345497

[Chen25] H.-Z. Chen et al., Implementation of carrier-grade quantum communication networks over 10000 km. NPJ Quantum Inf. **11**(1), 137 (2025). https://doi.org/10.1038/s41534-025-01089-8

[CAS17] Chinese Academy of Sciences, Beijing-Shanghai Quantum Communication Network Put into Use. (News Updates). 01 Sep 2017. https://english.cas.cn/newsroom/archive/news_archive/nu2017/201703/t20170324_175288.shtml

[Zha18] Q. Zhang et al., Large scale quantum key distribution: Challenges and solutions. Opt. Express **26**(18), 24260–24273 (2018). https://doi.org/10.1364/OE.26.024260

[Chen21] Y.-A. Chen et al., An integrated space-to-ground quantum communication network over 4,600 kilometres. Nature **589**(7841), 214–219 (2021). https://doi.org/10.1038/s41586-020-03093-8

[EC24] European Commission (CORDIS), Open European Quantum Key Distribution Testbed (OPENQKD)—Project fact sheet (Horizon 2020), 25 Jun 2024. https://cordis.europa.eu/project/id/857156

[EC25] European Commission, European Quantum Communication Infrastructure—EuroQCI. 8 Jul 2025. https://digital-strategy.ec.europa.eu/en/policies/european-quantum-communication-infrastructure-euroqci

[Peev09] M. Peev et al., The SECOQC quantum key distribution network in Vienna. New J. Phys. **11**(7), 075001 (2009). https://doi.org/10.1088/1367-2630/11/7/075001

[AIT26] AIT Austrian Institute of Technology GmbH. QCI-CAT: Quantenkommunikations-Infrastruktur für hochsichere behördliche Anwendungen in Österreich (project page), no date. https://www.ait.ac.at/themen/cyber-security/projects/qci-cat

[Stu11] D. Stucki et al., Long-term performance of the SwissQuantum quantum key distribution network in a field environment. New J. Phys. **13**(12), 123001 (2011). https://doi.org/10.1088/1367-2630/13/12/123001

[OPT07] optics.org. Cryptography secures Swiss elections. Historical Archive, 29 Oct. 2007.; https://optics.org/article/31646

[IDQ17] ID Quantique SA. IDQ Celebrates 10-Year Anniversary of the World's First Real-Life Quantum Cryptography Installation (news post). 23 Nov. 2017. https://www.idquantique.com/idq-celebrates-10-year-anniversary-of-the-worlds-first-real-life-quantum-cryptography-installation/

[Mar24] V. Martin et al., MadQCI: A heterogeneous and scalable SDN-QKD network deployed in production facilities. NPJ Quantum Inf. **10**(1), 80 (2024). https://doi.org/10.1038/s41534-024-00873-2

[BEL25] Belnet. New milestone in quantum communication project BeQCI: first cross-border QKD network established (news post). 5 Jun. 2025. https://www.belnet.be/en/news-events/news/new-milestone-quantum-communication-project-beqci-first-cross-border-qkd-network

[QUN24] QuNET. Start of the Second Key Experiment of the QuNET Initiative for Secure Quantum Communication (news post). Berlin, 19 Sep. 2024. https://qunet-initiative.de/en/news-2024/#:~:text=Start%20of%20the%20second%20key

[NICT11] National Institute of Information and Communications Technology (NICT). NICT NEWS, No. 401 (Feb. 2011): Features on: Quantum cryptography. NICT, 2011. https://www.nict.go.jp/en/pdf/copy_of_NICT_NEWS_1102_E.pdf

[Stan22] Stanley, Manoj, et al. Recent progress in quantum key distribution network deployments and standards. Journal of Physics: Conference Series. Vol. 2416. No. 1. IOP Publishing, 2022. https://doi.org/10.1088/1742-6596/2416/1/012001

[KED22] KED Global (The Korea Economic Daily Global Edition). SK Broadband applies quantum cryptography to Korea network. 9 Jun. 2022. https://www.kedglobal.com/tech%2C-media-telecom/newsView/ked202206080023

[SWNX23] Swissnex Network in Asia and Australia. nexttrends Asia Regional Report 2022: The state of quantum technologies in the APAC region: Views from Asia and Australia. Swissnex Network in Asia, 2023. https://swissnex.org/app/uploads/2023/05/Report_Epdf_290323_Final-Publish.pdf

[Ell18] C. Elliott, The DARPA quantum network, in *Quantum Communications and Cryptography*, (CRC Press, 2018), pp. 91–110. https://doi.org/10.48550/arXiv.quant-ph/0412029

[ITMO21] ITMO University News. First-Ever "Quantum Call" Between Moscow and St. Petersburg Conducted. 8 Jun. 2021. https://news.itmo.ru/en/science/cyberphysics/news/10393

[ICT21] ICT.Moscow. 7 Thousand km of Quantum Networks to be Stretched in Russia by the End of 2024 (news post). 18 Oct. 2021. https://ict.moscow/en/news/7000-km-of-quantum-networks-to-be-stretched-in-russia-by-the-end-of-2024

[ETSI19-14] European Telecommunications Standards Institute (ETSI). ETSI GS QKD 014 V1.1.1 (2019-02): Quantum Key Distribution (QKD); Protocol and data format of REST-based key delivery API. ETSI Group Specification, Feb. 2019. https://www.etsi.org/deliver/etsi_gs/QKD/001_099/014/01.01.01_60/gs_qkd014v010101p.pdf

[EOP19] eoPortal. SpooQy-1 CubeSat Mission (Satellite Missions database entry). 17 Dec. 2019. https://www.eoportal.org/satellite-missions/spooqy-1

[NanSp] nanosats.eu. SpooQy-1 (satellite page). no date. https://www.nanosats.eu/sat/spooqy-1

[WP-Tia] Wikipedia contributors, Tiangong-2, Wikipedia, the Free Encyclopedia. https://en.wikipedia.org/wiki/Tiangong-2

[N2TG] N2YO.com. Tiangong-2, Satellite details (NORAD ID 41765/2016-057A). no date. https://www.n2yo.com/satellite/?s=41765

[Lu22] C.-Y. Lu et al., Micius quantum experiments in space. Rev. Mod. Phys. **94**(3), 035001 (2022). https://doi.org/10.1103/RevModPhys.94.035001

[Cast17] D. Castelvecchi, China's quantum satellite clears major hurdle on way to ultrasecure communications. Nature **15** (2017). https://doi.org/10.1038/nature.2017.22142

[Li25] Y. Li et al., Microsatellite-based real-time quantum key distribution. Nature, 1–8 (2025). https://doi.org/10.1038/s41586-025-08739-z

[WP-Soc] Wikipedia contributors, SOCRATES (satellite), Wikipedia, the Free Encyclopedia. https://en.wikipedia.org/wiki/SOCRATES_(satellite)

[EOPSoc] eoPortal. SOCRATES (Space Optical Communications Research Advanced Technology Satellite) (Satellite Missions database entry). no date. https://www.eoportal.org/satellite-missions/socrates

[Tak17] H. Takenaka et al., Satellite-to-ground quantum-limited communication using a 50-kg-class microsatellite. Nat. Photonics **11**(8), 502–508 (2017). https://doi.org/10.1038/nphoton.2017.107

[DLRQub] Deutsches Zentrum für Luft- und Raumfahrt (DLR), Institute of Communications and Navigation. QUBE – Satellite-based Quantum Key Distribution (project page). no date. https://www.dlr.de/en/kn/research-transfer/projects/qkd-quantum-technology-for-secure-communication/qube-satellite-based-quantum-key-distribution

[FAU25] Friedrich-Alexander-Universität Erlangen-Nürnberg (FAU). Global quantum encryption: small satellites as quantum key generators (FAU news, Research). 11 Aug. 2025. https://www.fau.eu/2025/08/news/research/global-quantum-encryption-small-satellites-as-quantum-key-generators/

[Ahn24] N. Ahmadi et al., QUICK 3 ^3-Design of a Satellite-Based Quantum Light Source for quantum communication and extended physical theory tests in space. Adv. Quantum Technol. **7**(4), 2300343 (2024). https://doi.org/10.1002/qute.202300343

[UniJ25] Friedrich-Schiller-Universität Jena; Institut für Angewandte Physik (IAP), QUICK3-Mission: Quantum Satellite with Jena Expertise Launches into Space (news post). 24 Jun. 2025. https://www.physik.uni-jena.de/en/iap/26345/quick3-mission-quantensatellit-mit-jenaer-know-how-startet-ins-all

[NanSpe] nanosats.eu. SPECTRE (QKD Cubesat) (satellite page). no date. https://www.nanosats.eu/sat/speqtre

[ISISpe] ISISPACE, SPEQTRE (project page) no date. https://www.isispace.nl/project/speqtre/

[NanImp] nanosats.eu. Impuls-1 (satellite page). no date. https://www.nanosats.eu/sat/impuls-1

[Liao18] S.-K. Liao et al., Satellite-relayed intercontinental quantum network. Phys. Rev. Lett. **120**(3), 030501 (2018). https://doi.org/10.1103/PhysRevLett.120.030501

[Khm24] A. Khmelev et al., Eurasian-scale experimental satellite-based quantum key distribution with detector efficiency mismatch analysis. Opt. Express **32**(7), 11964–11978 (2024). https://doi.org/10.1364/OE.511772

[Yin17] J. Yin et al., Satellite-based entanglement distribution over 1200 kilometers. Science **356**(6343), 1140–1144 (2017). https://doi.org/10.1126/science.aan3211

[Mil25] A. Miller, Micius, the world's first quantum communication satellite, was hackable, in *2025 International Conference on Quantum Communications, Networking, and Computing (QCNC)*, (IEEE, 2025) https://doi.org/10.48550/arXiv.2505.06532

[Car18] A. Carrasco-Casado et al., QKD from a microsatellite: The SOTA experience, in *Quantum Information Science, Sensing, and Computation X*, vol. 10660, (SPIE, 2018) https://doi.org/10.1117/12.2309624

[LMU24] Ludwig-Maximilians-Universität München (LMU Munich), Global quantum key encryption: Nano-Satellite QUBE launches into Space (news post). 10 Jul. 2024. https://www.lmu.de/en/newsroom/news-overview/news/global-quantum-key-encryption-nano-satellite-qube-launches-into-space-66e31186.html

[QUICK3] Technische Universität München (TUM), QUICK3—QUantum phonIsChe Komponenten für sichere Kommunikation mit Kleinsatelliten (project website), no date. https://www.quick3.de/

[QZ25] Quantum Zeitgeist (Quantum News), SpeQtre Quantum Comms Satellite Launched Successfully. 1 Dec.2025. https://quantumzeitgeist.com/speqtre-quantum-quantum-comms/

[ESA1] European Space Agency (ESA). Eagle-1 (web page), no date. https://www.esa.int/Applications/Connectivity_and_Secure_Communications/Eagle-1

[SES24] SES S.A. EAGLE-1: EAGLE-neXt; Advancing Europe's Leadership in Quantum Communications (newsroom page). 22 Apr. 2024. https://www.ses.com/newsroom/eagle-1-advancing-europes-leadership-quantum-communications#tab-eagle-next

[ESA19] European Space Agency (ESA), SAGA for quantum key distribution (news post), 08 Apr. 2019. https://www.esa.int/ESA_Multimedia/Images/2019/04/SAGA_for_quantum_key_distribution

[ESA2] European Space Agency (ESA), QKDSat: Secure communication via quantum cryptography (web page). no date. https://www.esa.int/Applications/Connectivity_and_Secure_Communications/QKDSat_Secure_communication_via_quantum_cryptography

[Alv22] A. Alvaro et al., Caramuel: The future of space quantum key distribution in geo, in *2022 IEEE International Conference on Space Optical Systems and Applications (ICSOS)*, (IEEE, 2022) https://doi.org/10.1109/ICSOS53063.2022.9749720

[Jen24] T. Jennewein et al., QEYSSat 2.0—White paper on satellite-based quantum communication missions in Canada. Can. J. Phys. **103**(4), 328–376 (2024) https://doi.org/10.48550/arXiv.2306.02481

[SPEQ] SpeQtral Pte. Ltd., Securing Global Networks in the Quantum Era. Website. no date. https://speqtralquantum.com/

[VIA25] R. Jewett, SKY Perfect JSAT Joins Quantum Cryptography Satellite R&D Project. Via Satellite (SatelliteToday.com) (2025) https://www.satellitetoday.com/technology/2025/08/28/sky-perfect-jsat-joins-quantum-cryptography-satellite-rd-project/

[Redd] Ohsin, Planned satellite for Quantum Key Distribution is called SAQTI. Reddit, r/ISRO (post). no date. https://www.reddit.com/r/ISRO/comments/1gczzq5/planned_satellite_for_quantum_key_distribution_is/

[CAS25] Chinese Academy of Sciences (CAS), Academic Divisions (CASAD). USTC Demonstrates Successful Satellite-Enabled Quantum Key Distribution (Member Activities). 24 Mar 2025. https://english.casad.cas.cn/newsroom/ma/202503/t20250325_908666.html

[CRF25] Anand, V., China's Ascent as a Quantum Space Power. Issue Brief, Chintan Research Foundation (CRF) (2025). https://www.crfindia.org/-/media/Project/ChintanResearchFoundation/Publications-PDF/19-Sep/Chinas-Ascent-as-a-Quantum-Space-Power.ashx

[TQI25] M. Swayne, China establishes quantum-secure communication links with South Africa. Quantum Insid. (2025) https://thequantuminsider.com/2025/03/14/china-established-quantum-secure-communication-links-with-south-africa/

[YIC24] Tongxin, Q., China Is Likely to Build Global Quantum Communication Network in near Future, Scholar Says. Yicai Global (Yicai). 8 Oct 2024. https://www.yicaiglobal.com/news/china-is-likely-to-build-global-quantum-communication-network-in-near-future-scholar-says

[SCM25] Xin, L, China's New Dawn: Pan Jianwei Reveals High-Orbit Quantum Satellite for Global Network. South China Morning Post (SCMP). 26 Jun 2025. https://www.scmp.com/news/china/science/article/3315963/new-dawn-pan-jianwei-reveals-high-orbit-quantum-satellite-global-network

[MER24] Jeroen Groenewegen-Lau; Antonia Hmaidi, China's long view on quantum tech has the US and EU playing catch-up. MERICS Report, Dec 2024. https://merics.org/sites/default/files/2024-12/MERICS%20China%20Tech%20Observatory%20Quantum%20Report%202024.pdf

[JRC19] M. Travagnin, A. Lewis, Quantum key distribution in-field implementations, in *Publications Office of the European Union*, (Luxembourg, 2019). https://doi.org/10.2760/38407

[TAS18] TASS Russian News Agency. Russia to test quantum data transmission from space station in 3 years. 8 Jun. 2018. https://tass.com/science/1008731

[NSA] National Security Agency/Central Security Service (NSA/CSS), Quantum Key Distribution (QKD) and Quantum Cryptography (QC) (cybersecurity guidance web page). no date. https://www.nsa.gov/Cybersecurity/Quantum-Key-Distribution-QKD-and-Quantum-Cryptography-QC/

[NAS24] Nasser Barghouty, NASA SCaN and Space-Based Quantum Communications and Navigation: Towards A Vision (presentation). NASA Technical Reports Server (NTRS), Document ID 20240003113, acquired 13 Mar 2024. https://ntrs.nasa.gov/api/citations/20240003113/downloads/AQCF_March2024_SCaNPresentation.pdf

[NSc05] Will Knight, Quantum cryptography network gets wireless link. New Scientist (Info-Tech). 07 Jun 2005. https://www.newscientist.com/article/dn7484-quantum-cryptography-network-gets-wireless-link/

[Ion25] IonQ, Inc. IonQ Completes Acquisition of Capella Space, Advancing Vision for Space-Based Quantum Communications (press release). 15 Jul 2025. https://www.ionq.com/news/ionq-completes-acquisition-of-capella-space-advancing-vision-for-space-based

[Boe] The Boeing Company, Q4S–A quantum entanglement swapping experiment in space (web page). no date. https://www.boeing.com/space/quantum

[Fon24] Renata Fontanetto. Brazil's first quantum cryptography network is expected to connect five research institutions. Revista Pesquisa FAPESP, 342 (2024). https://revistapesquisa.fapesp.br/en/brazils-first-quantum-cryptography-network-is-expected-to-connect-five-research-institutions/

[OU23] The Open University (OpenLearn), Engineering: environmental fluids Section 1.1 The properties of the atmosphere. 12 Dec 2023. https://www.open.edu/openlearn/science-maths-technology/engineering-environmental-fluids/content-section-3.1

[Vas17] D. Vasylyev et al., Free-space quantum links under diverse weather conditions. Phys. Rev. A **96**(4), 043856 (2017). https://doi.org/10.1103/PhysRevA.96.043856

[Krz23] A. Kržič et al., Towards metropolitan free-space quantum networks. npj Quantum Inf. **9**(1), 95 (2023). https://doi.org/10.1038/s41534-023-00754-0

[Schm07] T. Schmitt-Manderbach et al., Experimental demonstration of free-space decoy-state quantum key distribution over 144 km. Phys. Rev. Lett. **98**(1), 010504 (2007). https://doi.org/10.1103/PhysRevLett.98.010504

[Bul23] L. Bulla et al., Nonlocal temporal interferometry for highly resilient free-space quantum communication. Phys. Rev. X **13**(2), 021001 (2023). https://doi.org/10.1103/PhysRevX.13.021001

[Zha25] P. Zhang et al., Daylight quantum key distribution over free-space optics for future security networks. J. Opt. Commun. Netw. **17**(6), B61–B70 (2025). https://doi.org/10.1364/JOCN.553171

[Ave21] M. Avesani et al., Full daylight quantum-key-distribution at 1550 nm enabled by integrated silicon photonics. npj Quantum Inf. **7**(1), 93 (2021). https://doi.org/10.1038/s41534-021-00421-2

[Bas23] F.B. Basset et al., Daylight entanglement-based quantum key distribution with a quantum dot source. Quantum. Sci. Technol. **8**(2), 025002 (2023). https://doi.org/10.1088/2058-9565/acae3d

[Gon18] Y.-H. Gong et al., Free-space quantum key distribution in urban daylight with the SPGD algorithm control of a deformable mirror. Opt. Express **26**(15), 18897–18905 (2018). https://doi.org/10.1364/OE.26.018897

[Shen18] Shen, Shi-Yang, et al., Free-space continuous-variable quantum key distribution of unidimensional Gaussian modulation using polarized coherent-states in urban environment. arXiv preprint https://arxiv.org/abs/1810.00408.(2018). https://doi.org/10.1103/PhysRevA.100.012325

[Liao17b] S.-K. Liao et al., Long-distance free-space quantum key distribution in daylight towards inter-satellite communication. Nat. Photonics **11**(8), 509–513 (2017). https://doi.org/10.1038/nphoton.2017.116

[Cai24] W.-Q. Cai et al., Free-space quantum key distribution during daylight and at night. Optica **11**(5), 647–652 (2024). https://doi.org/10.1364/OPTICA.511000

[Hug02] R.J. Hughes et al., Practical free-space quantum key distribution over 10 km in daylight and at night. New J. Phys. **4**, 43 (2002). https://doi.org/10.1088/1367-2630/4/1/343

[KPa25] K-PASS, Cybersecurity research funding program, MOZART: Requirements for quantum-communication solutions for connecting the Vienna public authority network and the ZAS St. Johann. 2025. https://www.k-pass.at/en/financed-proposals/detail/mozart-requirements-for-quantum-communication-solutions-for-connecting-the-vienna-public-authority-network-and-the-zas-st-johann/

[COR25] European Commission (CORDIS), *Leap in Advancing of crItical Quantum Key Distribution-spAce Components (LaiQa). Project Fact Sheet* (Horizon Europe, 2025) https://cordis.europa.eu/project/id/101135245

[Uni25] University of Trieste, Quantum link over fibre optics inaugurated between UniTS and UniUD (news post). 14 Feb 2025. https://portale.units.it/en/news/quantum-link-over-fibre-optics-inaugurated-between-units-and-uniud

[Xue21] Y. Xue et al., Airborne quantum key distribution: A review. Chin. Opt. Lett. **19**(12), 122702 (2021). https://doi.org/10.3788/COL202119.122702

[Bou15] J.-P. Bourgoin et al., Free-space quantum key distribution to a moving receiver. Opt. Express **23**(26), 33437–33447 (2015). https://doi.org/10.1364/OE.23.033437

[Dub24] U. Dubey et al., A review on practical challenges of aerial quantum communication. Physics Open **19**, 100210 (2024). https://doi.org/10.1016/j.physo.2024.100210

[Pug17] C.J. Pugh et al., Airborne demonstration of a quantum key distribution receiver payload. Quantum Sci. Technol. **2**(2), 024009 (2017). https://doi.org/10.1088/2058-9565/aa701f

[QNu] QNu Labs., Trusted Nodes (Quantum Network Architecture) (glossary entry). no date. https://www.qnulabs.com/glossary/trusted-nodes-quantum-network-architecture

[Che21] T.-Y. Chen et al., Implementation of a 46-node quantum metropolitan area network. NPJ Quantum Inf. 7:134, 07 Sep 2021. https://doi.org/10.1038/s41534-021-00474-3

[QSNP-QR] Quantum Secure Networks Partnership (QSNP), Quantum repeater. QSNP Glossary, no date. https://qsnp.eu/glossary/quantum-repeater/

[ETSI20-04] European Telecommunications Standards Institute (ETSI), ETSI GS QKD 004 V2.1.1 (2020-08): Quantum Key Distribution (QKD); Application Interface. ETSI Group Specification (2020). https://www.etsi.org/deliver/etsi_gs/QKD/001_099/004/02.01.01_60/gs_qkd004v020101p.pdf

[ETSI22-18] European Telecommunications Standards Institute (ETSI), ETSI GS QKD 018 V1.1.1 (2022-04): Quantum Key Distribution (QKD); Orchestration Interface for Software Defined Networks. ETSI Group Specification (2022). https://www.etsi.org/deliver/etsi_gs/QKD/001_099/018/01.01.01_60/gs_qkd018v010101p.pdf

[BSI23] BSI, *Implementation Attacks against QKD Systems. Study (BSI Publications—Studies)* (Bonn, Germany, 2023). https://www.bsi.bund.de/SharedDocs/Downloads/EN/BSI/Publications/Studies/QKD-Systems/QKD-Systems.pdf

[BSI24] BSI, A Proposal for Functionality Classes for Random Number Generators (scheme interpretation/certification guidance). 10 Sep 2024. https://www.bsi.bund.de/SharedDocs/Downloads/EN/BSI/Certification/Interpretations/AIS_31_Functionality_classes_for_random_number_generators_e_2024.pdf

[Wang22] Heng Wang, et al., Sub-Gbps key rate four-state continuous-variable quantum key distribution within metropolitan area. Commun. Phys. 5, 162, 25 (2022). https://doi.org/10.1038/s42005-022-00941-z

[Haj24] A.E. Adnan, Hajomer, et al., Continuous-variable quantum key distribution at 10 GBaud using an integrated photonic-electronic receiver. Optica **11**(9), 1197–1204 (2024). https://doi.org/10.1364/OPTICA.530080

[Zha20] Yichen Zhang, et al., Long-distance continuous-variable quantum key distribution over 202.81 km of fiber. Phys. Rev. Lett., 125, 010502. 30 Jun. 2020. https://doi.org/https://doi.org/10.1103/PhysRevLett.125.010502

[LiW23] Wei Li, et al., High-rate quantum key distribution exceeding 110 Mb s−1. Nat. Photonics 17, 416–421. 13 Mar. 2023. https://doi.org/10.1038/s41566-023-01166-4

[Zhu25] Shi-Chang Zhuang, et al., Ultrabright entanglement based quantum key distribution over a 404 km optical fiber. Phys. Rev. Lett., 134, 230801. 09 Jun. 2025. https://doi.org/10.1103/PhysRevLett.134.230801

Chapter 4
RKD (Radio-Signal Key Distribution)

RKD (radio-signal key distribution) is a physical method for the secure generation and distribution of cryptographic keys. RKD uses radio signals above 30 MHz to calculate and distribute the keys and is known in the literature under various names, e.g., "physical layer key generation in wireless networks" or "wireless physical layer key agreement."

RKD exploits the unique physical properties of wireless radio channels. The method is based on two fundamental properties of high-frequency transmission: the inherent unpredictability (randomness) of channel properties and the reciprocity of radio transmission between two communication partners.

4.1 How Cryptographic Keys Are Generated and Distributed

The basic prerequisite for RKD is a direct bidirectional communication link between two wireless devices, as shown in Fig. 4.1. In everyday use, this type of communication mode is often referred to as ad hoc communication, as in WLAN networks, or simply as peer-to-peer communication. For simplicity, these two wireless devices will henceforth be referred to as Alice and Bob. While these two devices exchange wireless packets, the RF receivers [WP-RF][1] on both sides measure the characteristics of the RF channel, with the most common measure in the terrestrial domain being the received signal strength, or RSSI [WP–RSSI][2] for short. After a certain communication time, Alice and Bob have collected RF channel measurements that are *random* and show a high degree of *similarity*.

[1] https://en.wikipedia.org/wiki/High_frequency.

[2] https://en.wikipedia.org/wiki/Received_signal_strength_indicator.

E. Piller and H. Schölnast, *Data Encryption at the Intersection of Mathematics and Physics*, SpringerBriefs in Information Security and Cryptography,
https://doi.org/10.1007/978-3-032-24764-3_4

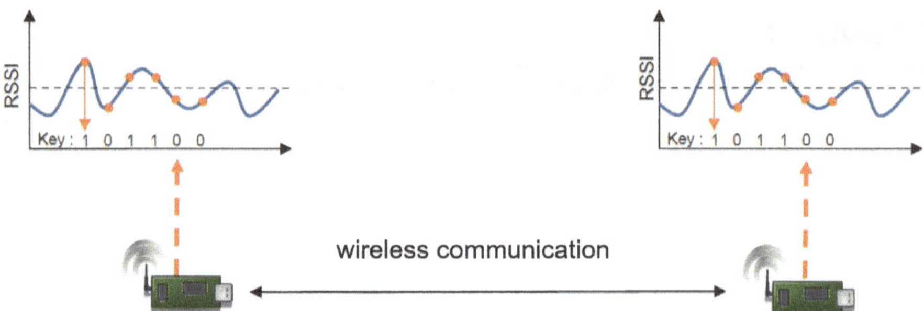

Fig. 4.1 Wireless communication

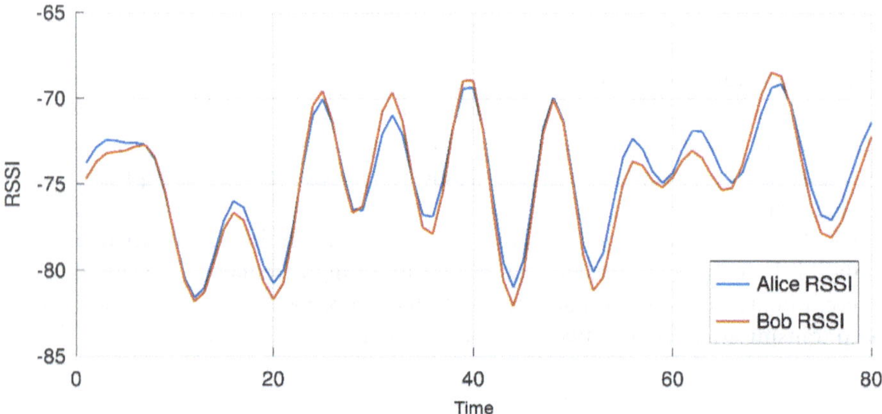

Fig. 4.2 Randomly fluctuating RSSI values for two wireless devices communicating directly with each other

Due to the similarity (see Fig. 4.2), such measurements can be converted into random bit sequences for both Alice and Bob, which differ by only a few bits. After performing error correction, Alice and Bob have the same random bit sequence, which can later be used as a secret cryptographic key on both sides. Cryptographic keys were generated and distributed based on physical properties.

The original idea of RKD dates back to 1993 [Mau93],[3] and some of the first demonstrations of its application to wireless channels took place in the early 2000s. Since the publication of this groundbreaking work, the rapid proliferation of wireless networks has led to extensive experimental research.

[3] https://doi.org/10.1109/18.256484.

4.1.1 Properties and Measurements of Wireless Channels

In order for two users to obtain similar channel measurements from which the secret key bits are derived, certain requirements must be met by a wireless channel and its measurements.

1. **The measurements must be unpredictable**. This guarantees strong, randomly generated keys that cannot be determined by an attacker. In a wireless channel, this randomness can occur in various ways. When an RF wave is transmitted from Alice's transmitting antenna, it is reflected and attenuated by various obstacles/materials, resulting in large fluctuations in the RF wave received by Bob's receiver. Thus, when Alice or Bob moves, the measured channel characteristics are subject to constant change, ultimately resulting in randomness of the secret keys. If there is no movement, changes in the environment, such as a moving object or person near a receiving/transmitting antenna, have a similar effect. In an urban environment with buildings, cars, etc., such effects are more common than in rural environments.
2. **The measured channel parameters for Alice and Bob must be nearly identical**. In point-to-point communication, i.e., when Alice talks directly to Bob and vice versa, the random channel properties are symmetric (reciprocal). In other words, reflections and attenuation are independent of the direction of propagation of the RF waves between Alice and Bob. Since Alice and Bob do not measure the channel at exactly the same time due to communication latency, their measurements show some discrepancies.
3. **An eavesdropper Eve must not be able to obtain measurements similar to those obtained by Alice or Bob**. This condition has been investigated experimentally, and it has been shown to hold true if Eve's location is at least more than a quarter of the wavelength away from both legitimate antennas (Alice's and Bob's) [Ruo18].[4] In practice, this means that for frequencies commonly used for RKD, starting at around 800 MHz, a wavelength of less than 375 cm and, consequently, a minimum distance of at least approximately 100 cm between Eve and Alice or Bob. Outside this range, i.e., at a distance of more than 100 cm from Alice and Bob—and while Alice or Bob (or both at the same time) are moving for several minutes—Eve's chances of extracting the legitimate key are practically the same as for a key generated by random guessing. At higher radio frequencies, Eve can even get closer to Alice or Bob.

As for the measurements themselves, Alice and Bob must set up a rapid exchange of wireless messages, e.g., a query from Alice to Bob and an immediate confirmation from Bob to Alice. Depending on the movement of their transceivers, the time that elapses between the two messages must not exceed a certain limit. For example, at a walking speed of 2–5 km/h, a few milliseconds are tolerable, while at speeds of moving cars (approx. 50–100 km/h), the time window for measurement is reduced

[4] https://doi.org/10.1145/3230833.3232803.

to 50–500 μs. The more time spent exchanging messages, the greater the deviation between measurements, which later leads to bit errors in the key extraction phase. It is therefore common practice to use very short user-defined wireless payloads for measurements. In addition, the center frequency for communication should be set to a fixed value, such as a specific Wi-Fi channel, in both directions.

In modern RF transceivers (WLAN/LoRa/Bluetooth), the most commonly available channel measurement is the received signal strength indicator (RSSI). It is typically calculated from the digitized RF waveform amplitude at the RF receiver and made available for each individual radio packet. The main advantage of RSSI is that it is easily accessible, as almost every radio equipment manufacturer provides RSSI querying as part of the device drivers. On the other hand, many RSSI measurements are typically required to extract a single secret key, as a single RSSI measurement corresponds to approximately one key bit. To increase the key generation rate, wireless technologies that use broadband signals such as Wi-Fi offer an alternative measurement called channel state information (CSI) [WP–CSI].[5] The original intended use of CSI is to enable an RF receiver to correct for random noise in the received signal. Since CSI contains finer amplitude information over a large bandwidth, e.g., 20 MHz, more key bits can be generated per measurement.

To provide insight into what measurements look like in real-world situations, three different RSSI curves from Alice (blue line) and Bob (red line) are shown here. In the first diagram (Fig. 4.3), Alice and Bob are stationary and their RF channel characteristics do not change. Therefore, the measurements revolve around a single RSSI value that has virtually no randomness. Keys derived from such measurements can be easily guessed by an attacker because they consist of long strings of zeros and ones. The second diagram (Fig. 4.4) shows measurements with good randomness, but the individual RSSI values between Alice and Bob differ from each other. Such deviation can be caused by rapidly changing RF channel conditions (e.g., due to rapid movement) or by noise at Alice and Bob's RF receivers. Although such deviations in the measurements can be corrected digitally to a certain extent, their presence can lead to errors in the extracted key bits, ultimately causing the key agreement to fail because the keys at Alice and Bob are not the same. Finally, Fig. 4.5 shows RSSI values that exhibit a high degree of randomness and similarity. Such measurements are best suited for key agreement because the resulting keys are random and contain few bit errors.

4.1.2 Physical Principles of Randomness

The randomness required for key generation arises, for example, when using signal strength due to continuous fluctuations in signal strength caused by a variety of physical factors:

[5] https://en.wikipedia.org/wiki/Channel_state_information.

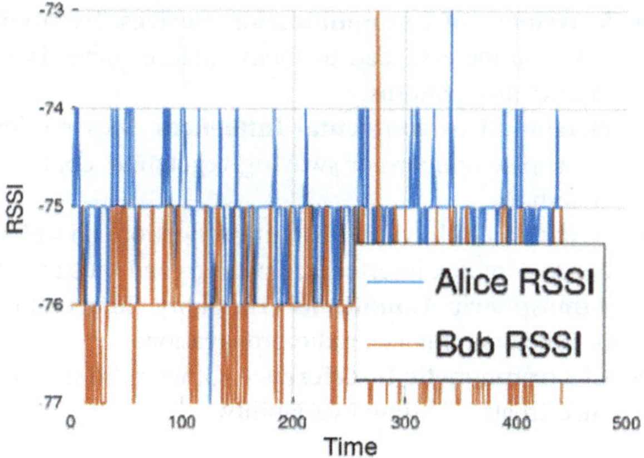

Fig. 4.3 RSSI when Alice and Bob are stationary

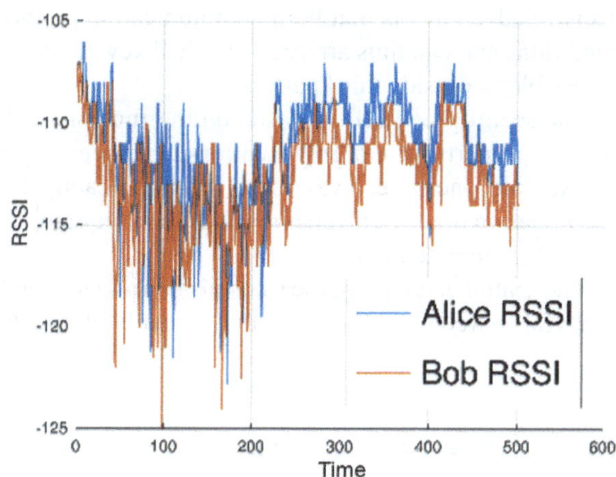

Fig. 4.4 RSSI when moving too fast

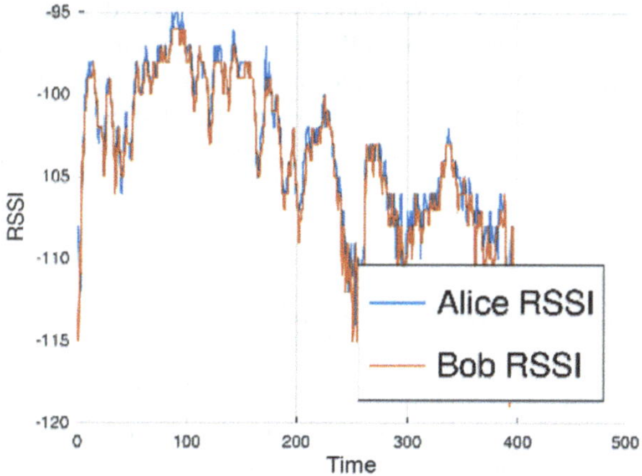

Fig. 4.5 RSSI under optimal conditions

- **Movement of Communication Devices**: Even minimal changes in position (a few centimeters) lead to measurable changes in signal strength due to altered interference patterns.
- **Dynamic Environmental Influences**: Moving devices in the radio field, such as people, vehicles, or swaying vegetation, continuously change the propagation conditions.
- **Reflection Behavior**: Changing reflections on walls, buildings, and other surfaces create complex interference patterns and thus affect signal quality.
- **Atmospheric Conditions**: Humidity, temperature, and other meteorological parameters influence radio propagation.
- **Electromagnetic Interference**: Other radio signals and electromagnetic interference create additional variability.

A cryptographic key can be calculated from these purely physical changes. The decisive advantage is that both communication partners measure the same physical conditions and can thus arrive at identical key material, while this information is not accessible to outside third parties.

The security of RKD is based on the fundamental physical principle that radio channel properties are highly location-dependent. A potential attacker (Eve) located, for example, one meter away, measures significantly different values due to the spatial decorrelation of the radio channel and therefore cannot obtain any usable information about the generated key.

The spatial diversity of the transmission and the random movement patterns create a natural source of randomness that virtually eliminates man-in-the-middle attacks.

4.1.3 Dynamic Requirements

Successful key generation requires a certain degree of dynamics in the transmission path. This occurs naturally due to changes in the distance between communication partners, movements in the environment, or changing reflection conditions. In static scenarios, this dynamic must be generated artificially in some cases, e.g., through controlled movement of one of the devices or through the use of reconfigurable antennas.

4.1.4 Summary of Findings

In RKD, two communication devices (Alice and Bob) transmit radio signals with frequencies of at least 30 MHz (usually above 800 MHz) in both directions and continuously measure the received signal characteristics. Typically, the signal strength (RSSI), phase angle, or signal propagation time are recorded. Since signal strength is usually measured in direct radio (free-space) channels, this text refers to signal strength. An exception to this is the application with satellite connections, where signal strength can only be used for key exchange between Earth and satellite because the satellites amplify the signals with their transparent transponders.

The central principle lies in the reciprocity of the radio channel: since both devices use the same physical transmission path, they measure almost identical channel characteristics. These common measurements form the basis for generating identical cryptographic keys on both sides without having to exchange this information via a separate channel. With RKD, identical non-deterministic random numbers are generated on both sides (at Alice and Bob), which derive their entropy directly from the physical properties of the radio transmission.

RKD thus generates and distributes keys between two sides based on physical processes. These measured radio channel parameters are only available to the two devices involved in the transmission and cannot be measured by a third party (the eavesdropper, Eve). Changes in the measurements are mainly caused by the dynamics of the transmission path (changes in distance, reflections, etc.), which must be generated artificially in some cases when the devices are stationary. In the case of satellite connections, the dynamics result from the movement of the satellites in the LEO range (at an altitude of approx. 1000 km), which, however, can cause quality problems later on due to randomness. RKD is not well-suited for direct communication via a satellite because signal strength cannot be used as a signal property and the satellite always acts as a man-in-the-middle. Using runtime measurements as a signal property is hardly sufficient to defend an attacker. However, RKD could represent a cost-effective alternative to QKD for direct satellite communication between satellites and Earth, because MKD (see Chap. 5) is not applicable here and signal strength can be used as a signal property.

The advantage of RKD lies primarily in its cost and robustness, especially for moving devices. The necessary transmitting/receiving stations are available on the market at low cost as SDR (Software Defined Radio [WP–SDR][6]). These devices can be used not only for radio transmission, but also for sufficiently accurate measurements.

In contrast to free-space and satellite QKD, atmospheric influences such as aerosols, fog, clouds, etc. do not hinder or prevent key generation in RKD, but are part of the key generation process because the key is determined, among other things, from the changing attenuation.

The disadvantage of RKD is the extremely slow key generation resulting from the dynamic requirements. A maximum of a few bits per second are possible. However, this is sufficient for using AES-256 for data encryption and/or for a MAC calculation for integrity assurance. The same applies to the four new encryption methods/modes described in Sect 6.4.

[6] https://en.wikipedia.org/wiki/Software-defined_radio.

4.2 Practical Criteria

4.2.1 *Economic and Technical Advantages*

RKD offers exceptionally low equipment costs and very high system robustness for mobile applications. The hardware required for RKD is based on commercially available LoRa modules [WP–LoRa][7] or software-defined radios (SDRs), which are available from around $250, including power supply, housing, and software. These cost-effective components enable both radio transmission and precise recording of the channel measurements required for key generation, right through to the cryptographic key. In terms of hardware, RKD only contains robust mass-produced components from the global market, which has a very positive effect on the price, availability, deliverability, maintenance, service, and manufacturer or supplier changes.

RKD is particularly well-suited for use in mobile devices such as transport infrastructure (road, rail, water, air), mobile IoT devices, drones, military units, laptops, etc. No additional non-deterministic random number generator is required because the randomness is derived from the random measured values.

For applications with extended range requirements via satellite connections, the system costs rise to several thousand dollars per terminal, as additional signal amplifiers and high-quality antennas are required. However, the satellite-based infrastructure is already in place, as only transparent transponders are needed in LEO and GEO satellites, which already exist, meaning that no new infrastructure is required in space. However, there is still insufficient scientific, technical, and practical knowledge about RKD in conjunction with satellites.

RKD thus enables the cost-effective and mass-market-ready random generation and highly secure distribution of symmetric keys based on physical processes, followed by end-to-end data encryption.

4.2.2 *System Limitations*

The main limitation of RKD is the low key generation rate, which is limited to a maximum of 2–8 bits per second due to the nature of the system. This limitation results from the dynamic requirements of the system and the necessary correlation time between channel measurements. This rate is sufficient for symmetric encryption methods such as AES-256 or Message Authentication Code (MAC) calculations. However, it is not sufficient for a one-time pad, for which RKD is not suitable.

[7] https://en.wikipedia.org/wiki/LoRa.

4.2.3 Application Domains and Areas of Use

RKD is particularly suitable for applications with existing mobility, as the system requires channel dynamics for key generation. Primary areas of application include the following:

- **Transport Infrastructure**: road, rail, water, and air transport.
- **Mobile IoT Systems**: Mobile sensor networks and autonomous devices.
- **Unmanned Systems**: drones and autonomous vehicles.
- **Military and Security Applications**: Mobile communication units.

4.2.4 Security Considerations

The security analysis of RKD systems requires a differentiated consideration of various attack scenarios. Due to inherent measurement inaccuracies and the probabilistic nature of radio channel characteristics, passive man-in-the-middle attacks are theoretically possible if an attacker (Eve) can position themselves in a spatially optimal position relative to one of the legitimate communication partners.

For a successful attack from a distance (several meters away), an attacker would have to place at least three to four calibrated receivers in different spatial positions around Alice or Bob. This measurement at multiple points would be necessary to capture the three-dimensional components of the radio field distribution and to reconstruct the signal characteristics at the target location (Alice or Bob) using spatial interpolation. This scenario works without taking reflections into account, i.e., for example, in an open field without buildings, trees, etc.

The technical effort required for this attack is considerable: all receiving devices would have to be precisely synchronized in time, have identical calibration, and continuously determine their exact spatial positions relative to the target object. In moving scenarios—which are common with RKD—this complexity increases exponentially, as the entire measurement system would have to follow the movement in real time while maintaining spatial correlations. These practical limitations make coordinated spatial attacks in real environments, especially when reflections occur, unfeasible, particularly in the typical mobility scenarios for which RKD is primarily designed.

Experimental validations under controlled conditions have shown that even at distances of 50 cm to 1 m between Eve and the legitimate communication partners, significant spatial decorrelation of the channel measurements occurs. In these worst-case scenarios, Eve exhibits a two to three times higher bit error rate compared to Alice and Bob, confirming the locality of the channel characteristics.

Privacy amplification methods based on the leftover hash lemma offer information-theoretical security even in the event of partial compromise of the raw key material. An initially counterintuitive aspect of the system is its tolerance for a large number of publicly disclosed bits. In fact, it does not pose a security problem if up to 80% of the original key material is publicly communicated during cascade correction. This robustness results from the information-theoretical foundations of privacy amplification. The following example calculation illustrates this:

- Raw key: $n_{raw} = 2000$ *Bits*.
- Publicly transmitted bits: $n_{pub} = n_{raw} \times 80\ \% = 1600$ *Bits*.
- Bits not transmitted: $v = n_{raw} - n_{pub} = 400$ *Bits*.
- Security margin: $s = 50$ *Bits*.
- Secure key: $n_{secure} = n_{raw} - v - s = 2000 - 1600 - 50 = 350$ *Bits*.

Even an attacker with knowledge of over 1600 bits (80%) of the original key material cannot draw any conclusions about the final 256-bit key. This property is based on the information-theoretical guarantees of the Leftover Hash Lemma and ensures that the remaining entropy is completely extracted into the secure key.

In satellite-based RKD implementations, the satellite acts as a transparent repeater that amplifies and retransmits received signals. By definition, this represents a man-in-the-middle scenario, making the trustworthiness of the satellite infrastructure a system requirement.

Alternative security architectures can address this problem by restricting secure communication to direct satellite-ground station connections, with end-to-end security between terrestrial endpoints ensured by downstream cryptographic protocols.

4.2.5 Market Readiness

Systematic analysis of the state of research revealed a significant implementation gap between theoretical findings and practical market applications. Although RKD has been an established field of research for two decades and there is extensive scientific literature available, only a single commercial product could be identified that enables RKD to generate and distribute cryptographic keys for end users. (Manufacturer: insitu[8]) This means that RKD lacks practical, marketable solutions. As part of this book, extensive practical tests were carried out with this single RKD product on the market in order to obtain practical data in real environments. This product is a LoRa-based RKD system and includes a complete implementation, whereby the LoRa modules autonomously collect measurement data and, after connection via the USB interface, e.g., to a laptop, RKD software, which is also part of the solution, performs key generation. The RKD hardware is housed in a small enclosure (see Fig. 4.6), is mobile, very robust, and contains a battery in addition to a USB interface for key delivery. When connected to a laptop, for example, the RKD device continuously generates key bits as soon as it is in motion (e.g., when the laptop user is on the move). When the laptop is in use, which usually happens when it is stationary, the RKD device again supplies new key material. The inner workings of the RKD device can also be integrated into other devices (e.g., IoT devices, drones, etc.)—it consists

[8] https://www.insitu.software.

Fig. 4.6 RKD device

exclusively of globally available mass-market products—or connected to mobile devices in its current form.

The software is available in two versions, which pursue different approaches. Since the current state of research covers many different approaches (see Sect. 1.8; literature analysis), all of which have their advantages and disadvantages depending on the application environment, but which are often only recognizable to a limited extent in the publications, two approaches were selected for the RKD product.

In relation to this book, this means that the extensive practical tests could be designed to be somewhat broader, resulting in even better practical data in real environments. Based on the literature analysis, this was only possible to a limited extent and with great uncertainty.

The introductory text on RKD only provided a general description of this technology. Readers who would like to learn more about how RKD works and do not want to work through the extensive scientific literature can find a more detailed description on the book's website at.[9]

4.2.6 Distance

The distance is limited to around 15 kilometers for direct radio-based RKD systems, although much greater distances are possible under excellent conditions. The LoRa-based system available as a product can reach up to several kilometers with good line of sight, although the distance is limited by the transmission power and technology standards permitted in the respective region. The range limitations result from several regulatory and technical factors: LoRa modules operate in the license-free ISM band (e.g., 863–870 MHz in Europe) [WP–ISM][10] with a maximum effective transmission power of 25 mW ERP [WP–ERP][11] according to EU regulations. This

[9] https://cryptography.study/phys/RKD.

[10] https://en.wikipedia.org/wiki/ISM_radio_band.

[11] https://en.wikipedia.org/wiki/Effective_radiated_power.

power limitation, combined with the precision of RSSI measurements required for RKD, significantly limits the practical range. Theoretically, ranges of up to 5 km are possible with high-quality antennas and optimal propagation conditions, but this reduces the measurement accuracy of the signal strength, which is essential for key generation. The spatial correlation of channel characteristics between Alice and Bob decreases with distance, causing the error rate in key generation to increase exponentially. The documented LoRa distance record is 1336 km (achieved on the open sea under perfect propagation conditions). It is not verifiable whether there would be sufficient RSSI fluctuations at such extreme distances to derive secure keys.

The ranges can be significantly improved by using more expensive SDRs (software-defined radios) instead of LoRa modules, but this also increases the cost of the RKD device.

LEO satellite connections enable global ranges of several thousand kilometers between any two points on Earth. However, for key generation, both communication partners must be able to connect via a satellite in both directions at roughly the same time, which limits the duration of the satellite connection and thus the key generation, as well as the maximum distance between the two communication partners. Furthermore, security risks arise because the satellite acts as an unavoidable man-in-the-middle and requires the trustworthiness of the satellite infrastructure. In practice, this means a connection time of around 5–15 min per satellite overflight for LEO satellites (approx. 1000 km flight altitude).

4.2.7 Cost

The costs of RKD in the terrestrial sector with LoRa modules, as used in this RKD device, are low due to the inexpensive, commercially available components on the mass market:

- Hardware: Approx. $60 to $150, for longer ranges up to $1500 (for details, see the book's website at[12]).
- RKD Software: Due to the currently low number of units, higher amounts are still required here.

4.2.8 Compatibility

Since RKD has currently only been implemented by individual research groups and a single provider, there is no established compatibility between different systems. Each implementation uses proprietary methods/technologies for synchronization, key generation, error correction, and verification.

[12] https://cryptography.study/phys/RKD.

Only the hardware components that make up the RKD hardware are mass-produced goods from the global market. They therefore do not pose a compatibility problem. The compatibility problem only applies to the RKD software. The RKD software does not run on the RKD hardware and can therefore be easily replaced.

4.2.9 Robustness/Susceptibility to Interference

RKD is highly resistant to temperature fluctuations, shocks, moisture, etc., because the hardware does not contain any mechanical components. RKD therefore does not require any maintenance of the devices, which is always security sensitive. If an RKD device ever breaks down, it can be easily and inexpensively replaced with a new one. The compatibility of the hardware also makes it easy to change manufacturers. This means that the devices can be easily replaced with other models or by other manufacturers/suppliers.

4.2.10 Suitability for Mobile End Devices

RKD systems are perfect for mobile applications, as dynamics in the system are a fundamental prerequisite for key generation. These dynamics are created by signal variations that must be generated by at least one moving communication partner. In satellite systems, this is done by the satellite itself through its orbit. The laptop example described above shows that RKD devices can generate key bits even when the device is switched off during movement because it is supplied with the necessary energy by its own battery.

4.2.11 Standardization

There is currently no formal standardization initiative for RKD technologies, and none is expected in this decade. The external interface of the only product available is a standardized USB interface. Only hardware parts from the mass market are used (the user can therefore easily exchange and replace components).

4.2.12 Certification

Certification according to [EUCC][13] is currently being prepared for the first available product.

4.3 Advantages/Disadvantages of the Technology

The main advantages are low cost and suitability for mobile applications. The technology is based on mass-market hardware.

The main disadvantages of RKD are the mandatory dynamics, the short range, and the low number of key bits per second. A maximum of 2–8 bits per second limits its applicability to mathematical encryption methods (e.g., AES-256). Long distances via satellite are conceivable, but there is no empirical data or results available yet.

4.4 Man-in-the-Middle Attacks

4.4.1 Passive Man-in-the-Middle ("Eve")

A passive eavesdropper (Eve) is theoretically able to reconstruct parts of the key material if specific spatial and environmental conditions are met.

- In urban scenarios and indoor scenarios with multiple reflective surfaces (buildings, vehicles, walls), Eve must position herself in close proximity (less than 1 m) to one of the legitimate communication partners. The complex multipath propagation patterns result in highly localized channel characteristics, whereby even small spatial distances lead to significant decorrelation. However, this condition is difficult to maintain in practice without being detected, especially if the key exchange partners move for several minutes, which is a prerequisite for key generation.
- In scenarios without significant reflections (open field, water), the requirements for Eve are less restrictive. Here, it is sufficient if the distance between Eve and one of the communication partners approximately corresponds to the distance between Alice and Bob (geometric equidistance). However, for the same reasons, an attacker can hardly maintain this state for a sufficiently long period of time.

In satellite-based RKD implementations, the satellite represents a man-in-the-middle due to the nature of the system, as it amplifies and retransmits received signals with its transparent transponder.

[13] https://certification.enisa.europa.eu/certification-library/eucc-certification-scheme_en.

4.4.2 Active Man-in-the-Middle

An active man-in-the-middle can only be prevented by suitable authentication of both communication partners.

4.5 Protection Goals

4.5.1 Authentication

The same conditions apply to authentication as to QKD. RKD itself does not offer authentication of communication partners. This means that shared secrets must be used, and procedures such as the Wegman-Carter procedure [Weg81].

4.5.2 Integrity

The integrity of the key results from the algorithms used in RKD and the exchange of information between the two communication partners.

4.6 Special Challenges

The challenges lie in synchronizing the measurements between the communication partners, optimizing the parameters for different environmental conditions, and ensuring sufficient channel dynamics for continuous key generation. In addition, the complex signal and data processing steps (LOESS transformation, grid quantization, privacy amplification) require precise implementation and calibration for different application scenarios.

4.7 Brief Description of the Technology

RKD is a physical method for generating and distributing cryptographic keys that exploits the physical properties of radio channels. By measuring signal strength variations (RSSI) between two communication partners, identical random sequences are created, which are transformed into cryptographically secure 256-bit keys using algorithms (e.g., LOESS smoothing, grid quantization, cascade error correction, and Toeplitz-based privacy amplification). The system offers high security at low cost when implemented with mass-market radio modules.

4.8 Literature Analysis

RKD (radio signal key distribution) is referred to in various ways in the scientific literature, e.g., as "wireless physical layer key agreement."

If two communication partners in wireless transmission have access to a common random source, e.g., by measuring a changing channel state, they can agree on a secret key. In doing so, they convert their measured values into identical key bits. This method, also known as key agreement at the physical layer, has gained popularity, particularly in research on wireless communication security [Yener15,[14] Zeng15[15]].

The shared random source exploits two fundamental properties of radio channels: channel reciprocity and inherent unpredictability. These properties can be captured by wireless communication terminals. If an attacker does not have access to the shared measurements, they cannot extract any information about the secret keys. Security therefore lies not in assumptions, but in physical laws.

Current research on key agreement at the physical layer can be divided into five main categories:

1. Measurement techniques (not covered below).
2. Key generation algorithms.
3. Resistance to attacks.
4. Advanced key agreement methods.
5. Experimental validation efforts.

The following overview covers scientific work from the period 2007–2024.

4.8.1 The Four Basic Phases of Key Generation

The conversion of measured radio channel characteristics into secret key bits takes place in four basic phases:

- Channel exploration and synchronization.
- Key bit extraction.
- Error correction.
- Privacy enhancement.

4.8.2 Phase 1: Channel Exploration and Synchronization

In the first phase, the communication partners exchange short messages via the wireless channel and then measure the radio channel characteristics from the received signals. Various signal characteristics were examined for channel detection:

[14] https://doi.org/10.1109/JPROC.2015.2459592.

[15] https://doi.org/10.1109/MCOM.2015.7120014.

- Received signal strength (RSS) [Mathur08,[16] Premnath14,[17] Aono05[18]].
- Amplitude [Wilson07[19]].
- Phase angle [Mathur11,[20] Wang11[21]].
- Envelope [Azimi07[22]].
- Angle of arrival [Badawy15[23]].
- Time of arrival [Marino14[24]].
- Channel impulse response [Liu12[25]].
- Channel frequency response [Hon13[26]].

In addition, adaptive measurement strategies have been developed that automatically track changing channel conditions [Yas08[27]].

Since some wireless packets may be lost during channel measurements, Alice and Bob must first ensure that the individual measurements are present on both sides and that they are performed within the small measurement time window. Synchronization methods are helpful in ensuring this. The first option is to use counter values, whereby Alice adds a running integer to the channel measurement packet. If Bob can capture the packet, he stores his channel measurements along with the received integer and responds to Alice with the same integer value. Since Alice can capture Bob's packet, she now knows that she and Bob have both successfully performed a measurement, and the running integer is incremented by Alice. At the end of the measurements, Bob only needs to remove duplicate measurements, i.e., measurements associated with duplicate counter values.

Alternatively, a timestamp comparison can be used to achieve the same result. Here, Alice and Bob perform time synchronization before the channel measurements, e.g., via the Internet using an NTP server. First, a timestamp is added to each measurement value during the measurements. Bob then compares his timestamps with Alice's and discards values with large deviations. Bob informs Alice of the discarded values, whereupon Alice also removes the discarded values from her measurement set.

---

[16] https://doi.org/10.1145/1409944.1409960.

[17] https://doi.org/10.1145/2541289.

[18] https://doi.org/10.1109/TAP.2005.858853.

[19] https://doi.org/10.1109/TIFS.2007.902666.

[20] https://doi.org/10.1145/1999995.2000016.

[21] https://doi.org/10.1109/INFCOM.2011.5934929.

[22] https://doi.org/10.1145/1315245.1315295.

[23] https://doi.org/10.1109/VTCSpring.2015.7146072.

[24] https://doi.org/10.1109/ICUWB.2014.6958955.

[25] https://doi.org/10.1109/TIFS.2012.2206385.

[26] https://doi.org/10.1109/INFCOM.2013.6567117.

[27] https://doi.org/10.1109/ISITA.2008.4895646.

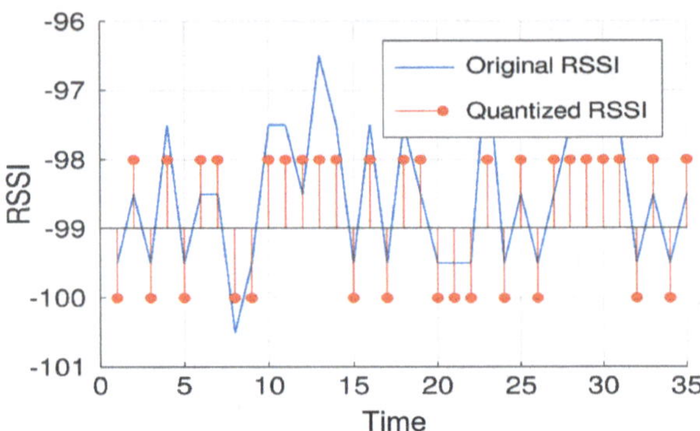

Fig. 4.7 1-bit quantizer

4.8.3 Phase 2: Key Bit Extraction

The actual process of converting RF measurements into binary values is called quantization. Here, Alice and Bob apply a quantization rule to the measured values, which converts them into secret key bits on both sides. One of the simplest rules compares a single measurement to a specified tolerance value. If a measurement is above or below the tolerance value, a key bit of one or a zero is generated. To illustrate the effect of this rule in practice, Fig. 4.7 shows a series of measured RSSI values and the corresponding quantized RSSI values after applying the above quantization rule.

On the other hand, slightly more sophisticated quantization algorithms can generate multiple bits per measurement and are robust against noise and distortion. The algorithms used include:

- Simple 1-bit quantizers with one threshold [Aono05[28]] or two thresholds [Mathur08[29]].
- Multi-bit quantizers [Patwari10,[30] Ambekar12[31]].
- Adaptive quantizers [Hamida09[32]].
- Vector quantization [Hong17[33]].
- Singular value decomposition-based quantizers [Furqan16[34]].

In addition, digital signal processing algorithms [Patwari10,[35] Yasukawa08[36]] can be used to reduce deviations between measured values caused by noise or hardware inaccuracies.

[28] https://doi.org/10.1109/TAP.2005.858853.
[29] https://doi.org/10.1145/1409944.1409960.
[30] https://doi.org/10.1109/TMC.2009.88.
[31] https://doi.org/10.1109/ISSSE.2012.6374318.
[32] https://doi.org/10.1109/NTMS.2009.5384826.
[33] https://doi.org/10.1109/TIFS.2017.2656459.
[34] https://doi.org/10.1109/ISWCS.2016.7600974.
[35] https://doi.org/10.1109/TMC.2009.88.
[36] https://doi.org/10.1109/ISITA.2008.4895646.

4.8.4 Postprocessing

Correction algorithms and privacy enhancements are then applied to ensure further error correction and resistance to eavesdropping attempts. After key bit extraction, Alice and Bob already have secret key bits that could be used for encryption and decryption. However, due to slight deviations in the measurements, some key bits on Alice's side do not match Bob's key bits. Error correction is therefore necessary. However, this reveals a small amount of information to Eve. This is counteracted by privacy amplification. For details on these procedures, see Sect. 8.3 Privacy Amplification.

Before the extracted key can be used in cryptographic algorithms, its quality, in particular the randomness of the bits, must be evaluated.

The statistical tests recommended by the US National Institute of Standards and Technology (NIST) [Rukhin10[37]] include the following:

- Mono-bit Frequency Test: Checks the ratio of zeros and ones in the key.
- Runs Test: Evaluates the independence of consecutive bit sequences.
- Spectral Test: Analyzes the discrete Fourier transform of the key stream.
- Additional tests have been developed specifically for wireless key generation:
- Maurer's Statistical Test: Particularly suitable for short key sequences [Maurer92[38]].
- Online Entropy Estimation: Designed for lightweight hardware implementations and directly monitors the randomness of channel parameters [Zenger16[39]].

4.8.5 Protection Against Attacks

More complex key generation schemes have been developed to improve resistance to various attacks. Works such as [Jana09,[40] Eberz12[41]] investigate the effects of passive and active man-in-the-middle attacks. In these scenarios, a skilled attacker takes control of the key generation process by manipulating channel conditions or injecting fake probing packets.

Similar attacks, including signal masking during channel reconnaissance and corresponding countermeasures, are discussed in [Zafer12[42]]. Further studies have shown that the so-called pilot randomization technique can successfully convert active signal injection attacks into less harmful reactive jamming attacks [Mitev19[43]].

[37] https://doi.org/10.6028/NIST.SP.800-22r1a.

[38] https://doi.org/10.1007/BF00193563.

[39] https://doi.org/10.1109/GLOCOMW.2016.7849064.

[40] https://doi.org/10.1145/1614320.1614356.

[41] https://doi.org/10.1007/978-3-642-33167-1_14.

[42] https://doi.org/10.1109/TNET.2012.2183146.

[43] https://doi.org/10.1109/GLOBECOM38437.2019.9013816.

This technique has also been recently investigated for advanced communication systems:

- Wireless relay communication [Letafati23[44]].
- Protection against attacks on smart reflective surfaces [Hu23[45]].

4.8.6 Advanced Key Agreement Methods

A second group of advanced methods aims to reduce the communication overhead during channel exploration. This is achieved through various advanced measurement techniques:

- Synchronized measurements in collaboration with wireless sensor networks [Premnath14[46]].
- Multiple-input multiple-output (MIMO) antennas for parallel channel detection [Wallace10[47]] and beamforming [Huang13[48]].

Both approaches have also shown improvements in key generation rates in static communication scenarios.

The MIMO concept was extended in [Jiao18[49]] to mm Wave massive MIMO configurations, as used in 5G networks. Here, angle-of-arrival interference leads to a significant increase in the secret key rate.

4.8.7 Modern Communication Technologies

Recent advances in wireless communication systems have been investigated to improve key generation:

Reconfigurable parasitic antenna arrays [Mehmood12[50]] and intelligent reflecting surfaces (IRS) can increase the randomness of channel measurements. One example is the electronically controllable parasitic array radiator antenna, which uses random beam steering for faster key generation [Aono05[51]].

Intelligent reflecting surfaces consist of large passive arrays of reflecting antenna elements and were originally used to increase channel capacity. As shown in [Ji21[52]],

[44] https://doi.org/10.1109/OJVT.2023.3315216.

[45] https://doi.org/10.1109/LWC.2023.3330809.

[46] https://doi.org/10.1145/2541289.

[47] https://doi.org/10.1109/TIFS.2010.2052253.

[48] https://doi.org/10.1109/INFCOM.2013.6567033.

[49] https://doi.org/10.1109/GLOCOM.2018.8647588.

[50] https://doi.org/10.1109/EuCAP.2012.6206173.

[51] https://doi.org/10.1109/TAP.2005.858853.

[52] https://doi.org/10.1109/TVT.2020.3045728.

appropriate control of the array elements can maximize the secret key capacity for users with single antennas, even in the presence of non-cooperative eavesdroppers.

This concept was extended to mmWave MIMO systems in [LiH23[53]], where IRS combined with compressive sampling outperformed conventional channel state-based methods at low signal-to-noise ratios.

4.8.8 Full-Duplex Transceivers

Wireless key generation has also been investigated for full-duplex transceivers—devices that enable simultaneous transmission and reception on the same channel [Vogt19[54]]. Under certain conditions, full-duplex mode reduces the ability of eavesdroppers to extract key material from legitimate parties, thereby strengthening attack resistance.

However, as shown in [Luo23[55]], the achievable key capacity and performance gains over half-duplex methods depend heavily on analog self-interference suppression.

4.8.9 Practical Applications

Various approaches have been developed to bring key agreement techniques closer to real-world applications:

- Low-power IoT Devices: Tailored solutions have been proposed in [Zenger14,[56] Zenger15[57]].
- Vehicle Systems: [Huth16[58]] developed key generation to secure vehicle communication.
- LoRaWAN Systems: For power-efficient wide-area networks, [Ruo20[59]] presented a reconfigurable antenna-based key transmission chain and provided extensive experimental results for indoor and outdoor scenarios.

[53] https://doi.org/10.1109/VTC2023-Fall60731.2023.10333834.

[54] https://doi.org/10.1109/TCOMM.2018.2868714.

[55] https://doi.org/10.1109/JSAC.2023.3287610.

[56] https://doi.org/10.1109/SIoT.2014.7.

[57] https://doi.org/10.1145/2841113.2841117.

[58] https://doi.org/10.1016/j.comnet.2016.06.014

[59] https://doi.org/10.1109/JIOT.2019.2946919.

References

[WP-RSSI] Wikipedia contributors, Received signal strength indicator, Wikipedia, the Free Encyclopedia. https://en.wikipedia.org/wiki/Received_signal_strength_indicator

[Mau93] U.M. Maurer, Secret key agreement by public discussion from common information. IEEE Trans. Inf. Theory **39**(3), 733–742 (1993). https://doi.org/10.1109/18.256484

[Ruo18] H. Ruotsalainen, S. Grebeniuk, Towards wireless secret key agreement with LoRa physical layer, in *Proceedings of the 13th International Conference on Availability, Reliability and Security (ARES '18)*, (2018) https://doi.org/10.1145/3230833.3232803

[WP-CSI] Wikipedia contributors, Channel state information. Wikipedia, the Free Encyclopedia. https://en.wikipedia.org/wiki/Channel_state_information

[WP-SDR] Wikipedia contributors, Software-defined radio. Wikipedia, the Free Encyclopedia. https://en.wikipedia.org/wiki/Software-defined_radio

[WP-LoRa] Wikipedia contributors, LoRa. Wikipedia, the Free Encyclopedia. https://en.wikipedia.org/wiki/LoRa

[WP-ISM] Wikipedia contributors, ISM radio band. Wikipedia, the Free Encyclopedia. https://en.wikipedia.org/wiki/ISM_radio_band

[WP-ERP] Wikipedia contributors, Effective radiated power. Wikipedia, the Free Encyclopedia. https://en.wikipedia.org/wiki/Effective_radiated_power

[EUCC] European Union Agency for Cybersecurity (ENISA). EUCC Certification Scheme (EU Cybersecurity Certification Scheme on Common Criteria) (certification library web page). No date. https://certification.enisa.europa.eu/certification-library/eucc-certification-scheme_en

[Weg81] M.N. Wegman, L. Carter, New hash functions and their use in authentication and set equality. J. Comput. Syst. Sci. **22**, 265–279 (1981). https://doi.org/10.1016/0022-0000(81)90033-7

[Yener15] A. Yener, S. Ulukus, Wireless physical-layer security: Lessons learned from information theory. Proc. IEEE **103**(10), 1814–1825 (2015). https://doi.org/10.1109/JPROC.2015.2459592

[Zeng15] K. Zeng, Physical layer key generation in wireless networks: Challenges and opportunities. IEEE Commun. Mag. **53**(6), 33–39 (2015). https://doi.org/10.1109/MCOM.2015.7120014

[Mathur08] S. Mathur et al., Radio-telepathy: Extracting a secret key from an unauthenticated wireless channel, in *Proceedings of the 14th ACM International Conference on Mobile Computing and Networking (MobiCom '08)*, (ACM, New York, NY, USA, 2008), pp. 128–139. https://doi.org/10.1145/1409944.1409960

[Premnath14] S.N. Premnath et al., Efficient high-rate secret key extraction in wireless sensor networks using collaboration. ACM Transactions on Sensor Networks **11**(1) (2014). https://doi.org/10.1145/2541289

[Aono05] T. Aono et al., Wireless secret key generation exploiting reactance-domain scalar response of multipath fading channels. IEEE Trans. Antennas Propag. **53**(11), 3776–3784 (2005). https://doi.org/10.1109/TAP.2005.858853

[Wilson07] R. Wilson, D. Tse, R.A. Scholtz, Channel identification: Secret sharing using reciprocity in ultrawideband channels. IEEE Trans. Inf. Forensics Security **2**(3), 364–375 (2007). https://doi.org/10.1109/TIFS.2007.902666

[Mathur11] S. Mathur, R. Miller, A. Varshavsky, W. Trappe, N. Mandayam, ProxiMate: Proximity-based secure pairing using ambient wireless signals, in *Proc. 9th Int. Conf. Mobile Syst., Appl., Services (MobiSys)*, (Washington, DC, USA, 2011), pp. 211–224. https://doi.org/10.1145/1999995.2000016

[Wang11] Q. Wang, H. Su, K. Ren, K. Kim, Fast and scalable secret key generation exploiting channel phase randomness in wireless networks, in *Proceedings IEEE INFOCOM*, (Shanghai, China, 2011). https://doi.org/10.1109/INFCOM.2011.5934929

[Azimi07] B. Azimi-Sadjadi, A. Kiayias, A. Mercado, and B. Yener. Robust key generation from signal envelopes in wireless networks, in Proceedings of the CCS '07. ACM, New York, NY, USA, 401–410, 2007. https://doi.org/10.1145/1315245.1315295

[Badawy15] A. Badawy, T. Khattab, T. El-Fouly, A. Mohamed, D. Trinchero and C. -F. Chiasserini, Secret Key Generation Based on AoA Estimation for Low SNR Conditions. in 2015 IEEE 81st vehicular technology conference (VTC spring), Glasgow, UK, 2015. https://doi.org/https://doi.org/10.1109/VTCSpring.2015.7146072

[Marino14] F. Marino, E. Paolini, M. Chiani, Secret key extraction from a UWB channel: Analysis in a real environment, in *2014 IEEE International Conference on Ultra-WideBand (ICUWB)*, (Paris, France, 2014). https://doi.org/10.1109/ICUWB.2014.6958955

[Liu12] Y. Liu, S.C. Draper, A.M. Sayeed, Exploiting Channel diversity in secret key generation from multipath fading randomness. IEEE Trans. Inf. Forensics Secur. **7**(5), 1484–1497 (2012). https://doi.org/10.1109/TIFS.2012.2206385

[Hon13] H. Liu, W. Yang, J. Yang, Y. Chen, Fast and practical secret key extraction by exploiting channel response, in proceedings of IEEE INFOCOM. IEEE, Turin, Italy **3048–3056** (2013) https://doi.org/10.1109/INFCOM.2013.6567117

[Yas08] S. Yasukawa, H. Iwai, H. Sasaoka, Adaptive key generation in secret key agreement scheme based on the channel characteristics in OFDM, in *Proceedings of the International Symposium on Information Theory and Its Applications, Auckland*, vol. 2008, (2008), pp. 1–6. https://doi.org/10.1109/ISITA.2008.4895646

[Patwari10] N. Patwari, J. Croft, S. Jana, S.K. Kasera, High-rate uncorrelated bit extraction for shared secret key generation from channel measurements. IEEE Trans. Mob. Comput. **9**(1), 17–30 (2010). https://doi.org/10.1109/TMC.2009.88

[Ambekar12] A. Ambekar, M. Hassan, H.D. Schotten, Improving channel reciprocity for effective key management systems, in *Proceedings of the International Symposium on Signals, Systems, and Electronics (ISSSE)*, (Potsdam, 2012), pp. 1–4. https://doi.org/10.1109/ISSSE.2012.6374318

[Hamida09] S. Hamida, J. Pierrot, C. Castelluccia, An adaptive quantization algorithm for secret key generation using Radio Channel measurements, in *Proceedings of the 3rd International Conference on New Technologies, Mobility and Security*, (Cairo, 2009), pp. 1–5. https://doi.org/10.1109/NTMS.2009.5384826

[Hong17] P. Hong et al., Vector quantization and clustered key mapping for channel-Based secret key generation. IEEE Trans. Inf. Forensics Secur. **12**(5), 1170–1181 (2017). https://doi.org/10.1109/TIFS.2017.2656459

[Furqan16] H.M. Furqan, J.M. Hamamreh, H. Arslan, Secret key generation using channel quantization with SVD for reciprocal MIMO channels, in *2016 International Symposium on Wireless Communication Systems (ISWCS)*, (Poznan, Poland, 2016), pp. 597–602. https://doi.org/10.1109/ISWCS.2016.7600974

[Rukhin10] A. L. Rukhin & et al., A Statistical Test Suite for Random and Pseudorandom Number Generators for Cryptographic Applications, in Tech. Rep. of National Institution of Standards and Technology, Gaithersburg, MD, USA, 800–822, 2010. https://doi.org/https://doi.org/10.6028/NIST.SP.800-22r1a

[Maurer92] U.M. Maurer, A universal statistical test for random bit generators. J. Cryptol. **5**, 89–105 (1992). https://doi.org/10.1007/BF00193563

[Zenger16] C. Zenger, H. Vogt, J. Zimmer, A. Sezgin, and C. Paar, The Passive Eavesdropper Afects My Channel: Secret-Key Rates under Real-World Conditions. In 2016 IEEE Globecom Workshops, 1–6, 2016. https://doi.org/10.1109/GLOCOMW.2016.7849064

[Jana09] S. Jana et al., On the effectiveness of secret key extraction from wireless signal strength in real environments, in *Proceedings of the 15th Annual International Conference on Mobile Computing and Networking (MobiCom '09)*, (ACM, New York, NY, USA, 2009), pp. 321–332. https://doi.org/10.1145/1614320.1614356

[Eberz12] S. Eberz et al., A practical man-in-the-middle attack on signal-Based key generation protocols, in *Proceedings of the 17th European Symposium on Research in Computer Security (ESORICS '12)*, (Springer, 2012) https://doi.org/10.1007/978-3-642-33167-1_14

[Zafer12] M. Zafer & et al. Limitations of generating a secret key using wireless fading under active adversary. IEEE/ACM Transactions of Networking, 20(5), pp. 1440–1451, 2012. https://doi.org/10.1109/TNET.2012.2183146

[Mitev19] M. Mitev, A. Chorti, E.V. Belmega, M. Reed, Man-in-the-middle and denial of service attacks in wireless secret key generation, in *2019 IEEE Global Communications Conference (GLOBECOM)*, (Waikoloa, HI, USA, 2019), pp. 1–6. https://doi.org/10.1109/GLOBECOM38437.2019.9013816

[Letafati23] M. Letafati, H. Behroozi, B.H. Khalaj, E.A. Jorswieck, Learning-Based secret key generation in relay channels under adversarial attacks. IEEE Open J. Veh. Technol. **4**, 749–764 (2023). https://doi.org/10.1109/OJVT.2023.3315216

[Hu23] L. Hu, G. Li, A. Hu, D.W.K. Ng, Exploiting malicious RIS for secret key Acquisition in Physical-Layer key Generation. IEEE Wirel. Commun. Lett. (2023). https://doi.org/10.1109/LWC.2023.3330809

[Wallace10] J.W. Wallace, R.K. Sharma, Automatic secret keys from reciprocal MIMO wireless channels: Measurement and analysis. IEEE Trans. Inf. Forensics Secur. **5**(3), 381–392 (2010). https://doi.org/10.1109/TIFS.2010.2052253

[Huang13] P. Huang, X. Wang, Fast secret key generation in static wireless networks: A virtual channel approach, in proceedings of IEEE INFOCOM. Turin, pp **2292–2300** (2013) https://doi.org/10.1109/INFCOM.2013.6567033

[Jiao18] L. Jiao, N. Wang, K. Zeng, Secret beam: Robust secret key agreement for mmWave massive MIMO 5G communication, in *2018 IEEE Global Communications Conference (GLOBECOM)*, (Abu Dhabi, United Arab Emirates, 2018), pp. 1–6. https://doi.org/10.1109/GLOCOM.2018.8647588

[Mehmood12] R. Mehmood, J.W. Wallace, Experimental assessment of secret key generation using parasitic reconfigurable aperture antennas, in *2012 6th European Conference on Antennas and Propagation (EUCAP)*, (Prague, 2012), pp. 1151–1155. https://doi.org/10.1109/EuCAP.2012.6206173

[Ji21] Z. Ji et al., Secret key generation for intelligent reflecting surface assisted wireless communication networks. IEEE Trans. Veh. Technol. **70**(1), 1030–1034 (2021). https://doi.org/10.1109/TVT.2020.3045728

[LiH23] H. Li, L. Chen, T. Lu, A. Hu, Angular-domain secret key generation for RIS-aided mmWave MIMO systems, in *2023 IEEE 98th Vehicular Technology Conference (VTC2023-Fall)*, (Hong Kong, Hong Kong, 2023), pp. 1–6. https://doi.org/10.1109/VTC2023-Fall60731.2023.10333834

[Vogt19] H. Vogt, Z.H. Awan, A. Sezgin, Secret-key generation: Full-duplex versus half-duplex probing. IEEE Trans. Commun. **67**(1), 639–652 (2019). https://doi.org/10.1109/TCOMM.2018.2868714

[Luo23] H. Luo, N. Garg, T. Ratnarajah, A channel frequency response-Based secret key generation scheme in in-band full-duplex MIMO-OFDM systems. IEEE J Sel Areas Commun **41**(9), 2951–2965 (2023). https://doi.org/10.1109/JSAC.2023.3287610

[Zenger14] C.T. Zenger, M.J. Chur, J.F. Posielek, C. Paar, G. Wunder, A novel key generating architecture for wireless low resource devices, in *In 2014 International Workshop on Secure Internet of Things*, (2014), pp. 26–34. https://doi.org/10.1109/SIoT.2014.7

[Zenger15] C.T. Zenger, J. Zimmer, M. Pietersz, J.F. Posielek, C. Paar, Exploiting the physical environment for securing the internet of things, in *Proceedings of the 2015 New Security Paradigms Workshop*, (2015), pp. 44–58. https://doi.org/10.1145/2841113.2841117

[Hut16] C. Huth, R. Guillaume, T. Strohm, P. Duplys, I. A. Samuel, T. Güneysu, Information reconciliation schemes in physical-layer security: A survey, in computer networks, 109, Part 1, 84–104, 2016. https://doi.org/https://doi.org/10.1016/j.comnet.2016.06.014

[Ruo20] H. Ruotsalainen, J. Zhang, S. Grebeniuk, Experimental investigation on wireless key generation for low-power wide-area networks. IEEE Internet Things J. **7**(3), 1745–1755 (2020). https://doi.org/10.1109/JIOT.2019.2946919

Further reading

Below is an excerpt from other important literature with a brief description of the content:

- Description of error correction methods, W.T. Buttler, et al., Fast, efficient error reconciliation for quantum cryptography. Phys. Rev. A **67**(5), 052303 (2003) https://doi.org/10.1103/PhysRevA.67.052303
- Description of the cascade protocol for error correction in QKD. Explains the potential performance, strengths, weaknesses, and comparison of different modified versions of this method is also very interesting for RKD: Martinez-Mateo, Jesus, et al. Demystifying the information reconciliation protocol cascade, in arXiv preprint https://arxiv.org/abs/1407.3257, 2014. https://doi.org/10.48550/arXiv.1407.3257
- Description of a key generation system based on signal strength measurement, R. Lin, et al., Efficient physical layer key generation technique in wireless communications. EURASIP Journal on Wireless Communications and Networking **2020**(1), 13 (2020) https://doi.org/10.1186/s13638-019-1634-7
- Description of the entire key generation process and an analysis of various error correction methods. This method is also very interesting for RKD, A. Yamamura, H. Ishizuka, Error detection and authentication in quantum key distribution, in *Australasian Conference on Information Security and Privacy*, (Springer Berlin Heidelberg, Berlin, Heidelberg, 2001) https://doi.org/10.1007/3-540-47719-5_22
- Key generation for smart home devices. Adaptive method based on signal strength measurement. Complex quantization method, H. Zhao, et al., A physical-layer key generation approach based on received signal strength in smart homes. IEEE Internet Things J. **9**(7), 4917–4927 (2021). https://doi.org/10.1109/JIOT.2021.3119053
- Analysis of technology in the 5G sector. Description of the advantages of 5G, because eavesdropping is made more difficult by beamforming. Furthermore, the otherwise unused channel is very well suited to minimizing errors in the key, L. Jiao, et al., Physical layer key generation in 5G wireless networks. IEEE Wirel. Commun. **26**(5), 48–54 (2019). https://doi.org/10.1109/MWC.001.1900061
- Description of the challenges in the automotive sector, Explanation of how code overhead could be reduced. Simulation with remote-controlled vehicles, L. Jiao, et al., Physical layer key generation in 5G wireless networks. IEEE Wirel. Commun. **26**(5), 48–54 (2019) https://doi.org/10.1109/MWC.001.1900061
- Explanation of how RKD can also be used in static environments. Combination of local randomness and radio channel characteristics, N. Aldaghri, H. Mahdavifar, Physical layer secret key generation in static environments. IEEE Trans. Inf. Forensics Secur. **15**, 2692–2705 (2020) https://doi.org/10.1109/TIFS.2020.2974621
- Detailed comparison of several error correction methods and the expected loss of key bits that can be intercepted by third parties, M. Miralem, et al., Error reconciliation in quantum key distribution protocols, in *Reversible Computation: Extending Horizons of Computing*, ed. by I. Ulidowski et al., vol. 12070, (Springer, Cham, 2020), pp. 222–236. https://doi.org/10.1007/978-3-030-47361-7_11

BY

Chapter 5
MKD (Memory Key Distribution)

MKD (Memory Key Distribution) takes a completely different approach to QKD and RKD, where cryptographic keys are generated and distributed from transmitted photons or radio signals. With MKD, non-deterministic random number generators generate the cryptographic keys, and the keys are transmitted using highly secure hardware tokens (usually ISO7816 smart cards) or special portable storage media (usually SSDs) with highly secure access protection for the data. Only highly secure storage media can be used for a one-time pad [WP–OTP][1] (sect 6.2) for subsequent data encryption and thus for cryptography that is entirely free of mathematics (except for XOR).

5.1 Precursors to MKD

The history of MKD (Memory Key Distribution) began around 2500 years ago. At that time, encryption was carried out using the Scytale (staff) of Sparta [WP–Scy].[2] In the early days, the keys were usually transported by envoys, diplomatic couriers, messengers, priests, or soldiers, and their brains were usually the "memory." Later, paper, teletype paper tape, microfilm, film strips, etc. were mostly used. With the advent of electronic storage media, magnetic tapes, cassettes, CDs, etc. were also used. Steganographic methods [WP–Ste],[3] glued nut shells (Fig. 5.1), private folds (letter locking), sealed envelopes, personal diplomatic bags, sealed capsules, secure containers, and even armored suitcases (sometimes with self-destruction devices) etc. were often used for hiding. Special hardware-based encryption boxes were usually used for encryption.

---

[1] https://en.wikipedia.org/wiki/One-time_pad.

[2] https://en.wikipedia.org/wiki/Scytale.

[3] https://en.wikipedia.org/wiki/steganography.

E. Piller and H. Schölnast, *Data Encryption at the Intersection of Mathematics and Physics*, SpringerBriefs in Information Security and Cryptography,
https://doi.org/10.1007/978-3-032-24764-3_5

Fig. 5.1 A precursor to MKD

Storage media with their own high-security access protection did not come onto the market until the 1980s, with the introduction of high-security smart cards with processors [Rankl10][4] in accordance with ISO/IEC 7816 [WP–Iso],[5] as used in passports and payment transactions. However, due to their low storage capacity, they are only suitable for subsequent mathematical encryption methods. At that time, data encryption was usually carried out using the DES method or Triple DES [WP–3D].[6] Today, AES-256 [WP-AES][7] is mostly used for this purpose. In the high-security area, encryption is usually carried out in an HSM (Hardware Security Module [WP–HSM][8]; see https://cryptography.study/phys/HSM). MKD with smart cards for key exchange and a mathematical method for data encryption is very interesting today and will continue to be so in the future if mathematical methods are accepted. Because this is usually the case today, MKD with smart cards and mathematical encryption is also the most widely used variant in practice.

Cost-effective portable storage media with highly secure access protection and internal data encryption for the use of a one-time pad [[Rij22],[9] Bell11,[10] [Bor12][11]] are achievements of this century. In this book, which deals with physical methods and, for security reasons, includes all cryptographic security objectives, i.e., data encryption for confidentiality, MKD prefers MKD-capable portable storage media with sufficient storage capacity for one-time pads.

It was not until 1976 that the first mathematical method for generating and distributing cryptographic keys over insecure channels was published by Diffie and Hellman [[WP–DH],[12] [Diff22][13]], which is now also available in quantum

---

[4] https://www.wiley.com/en-us/Smart+Card+Handbook%2C+4th+Edition-p-9780470743676.

[5] https://en.wikipedia.org/wiki/ISO/IEC_7816.

[6] https://en.wikipedia.org/wiki/Triple_DES.

[7] https://en.wikipedia.org/wiki/Advanced_Encryption_Standard.

[8] https://en.wikipedia.org/wiki/Hardware_security_module.

[9] https://ciphermachinesandcryptology.com/papers/one_time_pad.pdf.

[10] doi:10.1080/01611194.2011.583711.

[11] https://ieeexplore.ieee.org/abstract/document/6387923.

[12] https://en.wikipedia.org/wiki/Diffie-Hellman_key_exchange.

[13] doi:10.1145/3549993.3550007.

computer-secure variants. Due to the logistical effort required for the physical distribution of keys, MKD, i.e., the purely physical distribution of cryptographic keys, continued to lose importance. In particular, MKD became completely uninteresting in the mass market. Mathematical methods in the form of asymmetric cryptography have revolutionized cryptography, but the generation and distribution of keys using physical methods remain relevant where very high data security is required.

5.2 MKD

As mentioned above, MKD can use highly secure smart cards, such as those used today in payment cards, passports, etc., to generate and distribute cryptographic keys. However, the low storage capacity is only sufficient for data encryption using a mathematical method such as AES-256, which is sufficient for most applications today. This also applies to key exchange with an HSM or asymmetric key exchange in conjunction with a pre-shared key (PSK) in a stationary HSM.

In the following, MKD in conjunction with a one-time pad is preferred for encryption because this is the only way to ensure absolute data security throughout, from key generation and key exchange to the cryptographic security goals of confidentiality and integrity of the data.

This MKD with a one-time pad consists of at least two required devices and several process steps. The devices are MKD-capable portable storage media and non-deterministic random number generators. For security reasons, highly secure smart cards are usually used in addition, which contain a PIN (Personal Identification Number [WP–PIN][14]) for accessing the smart card and the keys used to encrypt the key bits on the storage media. The components required for MKD with a one-time pad, such as MKD-enabled storage media, random number generators, and smart cards, are available as mass-produced goods on the global market. This has a very positive effect on price, global availability, deliverability, maintenance, service, manufacturer change, supplier change, compatibility, and security assessments.

5.2.1 MKD-Capable Portable Storage Media

MKD-compatible portable storage media (Fig. 5.2) consist of at least six important components and requirements in terms of security technology:

1. Storage medium, currently implemented as a memory stick, SSD (solid state disk), or NVMe SSD (non-volatile memory express SSD). NVMe SSDs are characterized by particularly high read/write speeds, currently up to approx.

[14] https://en.wikipedia.org/wiki/Personal_identification_number.

Fig. 5.2 MKD-compatible portable storage medium

7 GB/sec. Memory sticks are currently available on the market with capacities of up to 256 GB, SSDs and NVMe SSDs with capacities of up to 16 TBytes.

2. PIN input device for PIN entry directly on the storage medium. A PIN change is only possible after entering the correct PIN. PIN checks can be performed on the external smart card and/or in the storage medium. Solutions where only a PIN check is performed in the storage medium and no smart cards are required are not recommended. There are also providers offering fingerprint recognition.
3. Smart card reader in accordance with ISO 7816. This reader is used to transfer the PIN entered on the storage medium to the smart card and to transfer the key from the smart card to the integrated AES-256 HW encryption unit via the smart card reader.
4. Integrated AES-256 HW encryption unit. All key bits sent from outside for storage in the storage medium are encrypted by the HW encryption unit and are decrypted again when read. In the better products, the encryption/decryption key comes from the external smart card, but it can also be stored in the storage medium. However, the smart card solution is more secure because it operates

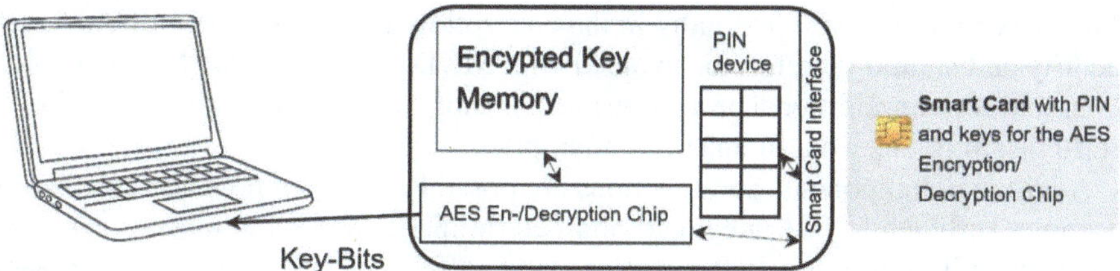

Fig. 5.3 Activation of a secure storage medium with PIN and smart card

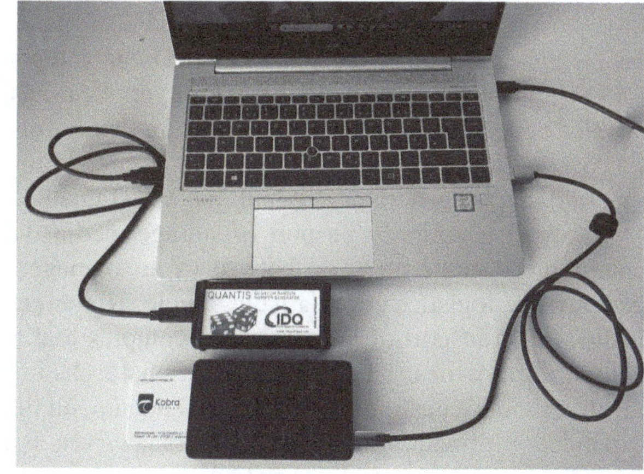

Fig. 5.4 Laptop with TRNG (true random number generator) and an MKD-compatible portable storage medium with a smart card

separately from the storage medium and therefore the encryption/decryption key is always missing in the event of a physical attack on the storage medium.

5. Certifications.
6. SATA or USB interface to the outside for data transfer.

Most products available on the market are also water-, dust-, and shock-resistant. This means they can also be used in harsher environments and, with security restrictions, can be transported using public service providers.

In addition to the storage media, high-security smart cards with processors in accordance with ISO/IEC 7816 [Rankl10][15] are required. The keys for encrypting/decrypting the data on the storage media are generated on these smart cards, and the keys are PIN-protected with an error counter (e.g., 3 attempts); see Fig. 5.3. Figure 5.4 shows a laptop with a random number generator and MKD-enabled storage media.

If the number of failed attempts is exceeded, the keys are no longer accessible. When the correct PIN is entered, the keys are transferred to the storage medium and used there to encrypt/decrypt the stored key bits by the internal AES HW encryption unit. Usually, two smart cards are used for one storage medium. There are also high-security SSDs and NVMe SSDs without these smart cards. In these, the key for AES

[15] https://en.wikipedia.org/wiki/ISO/IEC_7816

HW encryption is stored internally in the encryption unit. This variant offers lower security and should therefore be avoided with MKD. There are also MKD-enabled SSDs that contain additional protection mechanisms, such as zeroization [WP–Zer][16] (self-erasure in the event of an attack attempt).

Additional components and functions are possible. The components include, for example, sufficiently fast integrated non-deterministic random number generators, which are still far too slow in the current market offerings. HSMs are only necessary for telecommunications applications in conjunction with PCs (e.g., laptops), servers, etc., and MKD with a one-time pad if the PC is not protected.

In practical application, each user must have an MKD-capable portable storage medium on site where the data is encrypted/decrypted, e.g., on a desktop PC, laptop, etc., with/without an HSM. Another MKD-enabled portable storage medium is used for key transport. For telecommunications applications, each user requires an MKD-enabled portable storage medium and a non-deterministic random number generator. For data storage applications, only role administrators require a non-deterministic random number generator and multiple MKD-enabled storage media.

If key distribution (transport of storage media) takes place in person between communication partners or between role managers and role-access-authorized persons, the logistics are relatively simple. However, with multiple system participants, this transport of keys becomes complex and is usually carried out with the help of third parties. This requires additional tasks in the logistics process. A documented chain of custody (chronological documentation of evidence [WP–COC][17]), expanded with additional necessary tasks, serves as a model for this. A chain of custody comes from the legal field and describes the secure and traceable process from the identification of evidence, e.g., by the police, to its presentation in court. Details on the logistics of secure key transport are provided in Chapt 7.3, which covers topics and aspects such as typical procedures, documented chain of custody for MKD processes, process steps, sender and recipient authentication, confirmation of receipt, recall mechanisms, documentation requirements, and technological support for the logistics process.

5.2.2 TCG Opal Standard

In addition to the above requirements for MKD-enabled storage media, there is also an international standard that describes how MKD can be applied with a one-time pad. It is called TCG Opal [[WP–Opa],[18] [TCGOpa][19]]. TCG stands for Trusted

[16] https://en.wikipedia.org/wiki/Zeroisation

[17] https://en.wikipedia.org/wiki/Chain_of_custody.

[18] https://en.wikipedia.org/wiki/Opal_Storage_Specification.

[19] https://trustedcomputinggroup.org/resource/storage-work-group-storage-security-subsystem-class-opal/.

Computing Group [WP–TCG],[20] which develops open, vendor-neutral, industry-standard specifications for trusted computer components and software interfaces on multiple platforms, and is operated by leading companies in the computer industry. Opal was developed to increase the security of storage media and is designed to make hardware encryption integrated into storage media simple and secure. The storage media are called Opal SEDs (self-encrypting drives). SEDs are self-encrypting drives based on hardware encryption (usually AES-128 or AES-256). MKD-enabled storage media that comply with TCG Opal SSC specifications have the following features relevant to MKD with a one-time pad:

- The encryption of data—in the case of MKD, the key bits—is always performed by hardware on the storage medium itself. According to Opal, the key for this hardware encryption is also stored on the storage medium. Some of the storage media suitable for MKD allow this key to be stored externally on a smart card, and the key is not stored on the storage medium (only used during encryption/decryption). This extension of Opal is strongly recommended for MKD with a one-time pad.
- SEDs based on Opal 2.0 implement extended key management via both an authentication key (AK) and a second-level data encryption key (DEK). Key management takes place within the disk controller chip.
- Since encryption is always active, the controller automatically decrypts the contents of the permanent memory during the read process. If greater security is desired, an additional ATA password can be set. However, if this password is lost, it is no longer possible to read the stored data—in the case of MKD, the key bits— which is not a problem for MKD with a one-time pad in telecommunications applications, but it is a problem for data storage applications.
- Opal enables sector-specific authorizations with separate access rights. Each area can be created, edited, and deleted independently. In telecommunications applications, this allows different communication partners to be separated, and in data storage applications, different roles (each role has its own keys). This highly secure separation offers major security advantages for MKD, especially the separation between telecommunications and data storage.

5.2.3 Security Certification According to CC (Common Criteria) and EUCC

For security certifications according to CC[21] and EUCC,[22] there are also CC profiles, e.g., BSI-CC-PP-0081-2012, Portable Storage Media Protection Profile (PSMPP), Version 1.0 [BSI12].[23]

---

[20] https://en.wikipedia.org/wiki/Trusted_Computing_Group.

[21] https://www.commoncriteriaportal.org/index.cfm.

[22] https://certification.enisa.europa.eu/certification-library/eucc-certification-scheme_en1.

[23] https://www.commoncriteriaportal.org/files/ppfiles/pp0081b_pdf.pdf.

The TOE (Target of Evaluation) described in this protection profile is a portable, self-contained storage medium such as a USB stick or a portable SSD with a physical connection for a computer. It offers encrypted storage of user data (in the case of MKD, these are the key bits) and strong authentication to grant access to the encrypted data. This protection profile for mobile data carriers is divided into a "basic" part and an (optional) "extended package part." An extended package allows flexible adaptation to specific requirements, such as stronger authentication functionality, without having to completely revise the protection profile. The evaluation is carried out for two variants of the PP: for the basic part and for the extended package part. The data in the protected storage area of the portable storage medium must not be accessible to unauthorized persons if the medium is lost, misplaced, or stolen. To this end, the protection profile defines a basic set of security requirements to cryptographically ensure the confidentiality of the data in the protected storage area against logical or physical attacks. The default power-up state of the device only provides access to the authentication mechanism. An essential aspect of IT security is that the security functions are implemented entirely within the storage medium. Overall, the EVG implements the following important security features:

- Protection of the confidentiality of user data— in the case of MKD, the key bits for telecommunications and data storage applications— through encryption.
- Protection of TSF data (authentication data, internal encryption keys, etc.).

5.2.4 Non-deterministic Random Number Generators

Non-deterministic random number generators [[Vai23],[24] [John18][25]] use physical processes such as thermal noise, radioactive decay, or quantum-optical processes [[Meij19][26]] to generate random numbers. They provide truly random numbers (bit sequences) that represent non-reproducible number sequences (bit sequences). However, they are slower than deterministic generators because they rely on real physical processes. It is very important that at least two separate random number generators are always used, if possible from different manufacturers. This ensures that even a faulty or poor random number generator—possibly caused by an attacker or the manufacturer—cannot pose a security problem, because after an XOR operation on the generated key bits (random numbers), the better of the two generators always determines the minimum quality of the key bits. This is standard practice in MKD, but it also applies to QKD. Details on non-deterministic random number generators, including a current market overview, are available on the book's website at.[27]

---

[24] doi:10.1007/s11128-023-04175-y.

[25] doi:10.1515/9781501506062.

[26] doi:10.1109/SP.2019.00088.

[27] https://cryptography.study/phys/TRNG.

5.3 Process Steps for MKD

When it comes to the process steps of MKD with a one-time pad, a distinction must be made between telecommunications and data storage applications.

5.3.1 Telecommunications with MKD Using a One-Time Pad

In the field of telecommunications, two of these MKD-capable portable storage media are used on both sides (communication partners A and B). One of these is used for encrypting and decrypting the data on site (at A and B)—this storage medium is therefore called the encryption/decryption storage medium—and the second storage medium is used for key transport—this storage medium is called the transport storage medium. The transport storage medium has a size of 512 GB, for example, and the encryption/decryption storage medium has a size of 16 TBytes. This allows the key bits for telecommunications with 32 different communication partners to be stored on site.

In addition, highly secure smart cards in accordance with ISO-7816 with processors are used. Usually two per communication partner A and B are used.

Both communication partners A and B also require a non-deterministic random number generator to generate the necessary key bits (Fig. 5.5).

Process Steps

In the first process step, a smart card on both sides (communication partners A and B) generates a key for AES HW encryption in the portable storage medium and receives a start PIN. This key is then copied to a second smart card, which also receives a start PIN. To avoid copying the key to the second smart card, this process can also be carried out using a Diffie-Hellman key exchange procedure, which generates the key for AES HW encryption in both smart cards simultaneously and separately.

In the second process step, a random bit sequence (called S_A and S_B) is generated on both sides (communication partners A and B) using a non-deterministic random number generator, which is stored on each side (A and B) on a transport storage medium and on its own encryption/decryption storage medium (Fig. 5.5). During this storage process, the bit sequence is automatically encrypted in the storage medium itself using the smart card key before the storage process (process step 1).

Fig. 5.5 MKD during key generation

In the third process step, each of the two transport storage media and one of the two smart cards are transported to the other side (from A to B and from B to A) in person, by a trusted courier, or by a public parcel service. When using a public parcel service, the storage medium and smart card must be transported separately, which is always advisable. The smart card can also be transported only once at the very beginning, before the first transport of the transport storage medium. Over time, e.g., annually, the smart card can be renewed, which again results in transport.

In the fourth process step, the key bits received by the transport storage medium are then stored on both sides—after internal decryption by the AES HW encryption unit with the smart card key—in the own encryption/decryption storage medium under the name of the sender. This means that the encryption/decryption storage medium on both sides A and B then contains the key bits S_A and S_B in two different files—the file name is always the name of the generator of the key bits.

These key bits are then used on both sides in the fifth process step for encrypting/decrypting the data (see Fig. 5.6). Communication partner A uses the key bits from file "A" for encryption, i.e.,S_A, and communication partner B uses the key bits from file "B," i.e.,S_B. It follows that the sender's key file is always used to encrypt and decrypt the transmitted data. This means that both communication partners can always use new key bits for encryption and no key bits are used multiple times, even though there is no synchronization between the two communication partners. The sender from whom the data to be transmitted originates is always responsible for the quality of the key used.

In a second variant of this key exchange, both communication partners do not use their own key bits for encryption, but rather the key bits are created by an XOR link between both communication partners, i.e., A and B jointly generate the key bits for both communication directions. In the second process step of this variant, two random bit sequences for the key bits are generated on both sides (A and B) with the aid of a non-deterministic random number generator, i.e., on side A, S_{A1} and S_{A2} are generated, and on side B, S_{B1} and S_{B2} are generated, which are stored on each side (A and B) on a transport storage medium and on their own encryption/decryption storage medium. After transport, in the fourth process step, the key bits received by the transport storage medium are stored on both sides in the encryption/decryption storage medium under the name of the sender on side A in the form S_{A1} XOR S_{B1} and on side B in the form S_{A2} XOR S_{B2}. This means that the encryption/decryption storage medium then contains the XOR-linked key bits of both communication partners A and B in two different files—the file name is A for S_{A1} XOR S_{B1} and B for S_{A2} XOR S_{B2}. In this second variant, both communication partners can determine the quality of the key bits for both communication directions.

Fig. 5.6 MKD at the terminal device for telecommunications and data storage

In this environment, MKD is ideally suited for generating, storing, and exchanging keys using exclusively physical methods and for subsequent high-security data encryption with a one-time pad. Data integrity can be guaranteed with a MAC (GCM, CCM, CBC, etc.; see sect 2.6.2), which, like the one-time pad, also operates with the XOR function. The GCM-MAC and CCM-MAC also contain authentication data. Furthermore, the authentication of both sides A and B is perfectly solved by the transport of the smart card, and possibly also the storage media. Even when transporting the transport storage media via public parcel services, access protection to the transport storage medium with PIN and smart card provides a highly secure solution. From a security perspective, it must be taken into account that the encryption of the key bits for the one-time pad is performed with AES-256, i.e., with a mathematical procedure. If this encryption, including the certified access protection to the transport storage media, is classified as insufficiently secure, the transport of the transport storage media must be carried out personally or by confidential third parties. This closes the last non-purely physical gap, and MKD with a one-time pad can be classified as mathematically secure (except for the XOR function), even though it contains a mathematical procedure with AES-256 within the storage media, which only provides additional protection.

MKD can be integrated very well into telecommunications protocols.

5.3.2 Data Storage with MKD with a One-Time Pad

There are many possible solutions for highly secure data storage. Basically, these always involve an access control system based on physical cryptography, where read protection is ensured by encryption with a one-time pad. Below is an example of a solution that is easy to implement in practice and uses exclusively physical cryptographic methods. It is based on an authorization concept with roles, i.e., role-based access control [WP–RBA].[28]

In this solution, each user employs an MKD-enabled portable storage medium. This is used for encrypting and decrypting data on site at the user's location with a one-time pad and is therefore referred to as an encryption/decryption storage medium, as in the case of telecommunications above. A second storage medium, which is only used by role administrators, is used for key transport and is therefore called a transport storage medium. The transport storage medium has a size of 512 GB, for example, and the encryption/decryption storage medium has a size of 16 TBytes. If the key bits for data storage from 16 different roles are then stored on site, half of the storage remains available for the extension of role keys (see below).

A solution variant is presented below as an example.

Figures 5.5 and 5.6, "MKD during key generation" and "MKD at the terminal device during telecommunications and data storage," are also applicable here.

[28] https://en.wikipedia.org/wiki/Role-based_access_control.

Process Steps

In this role-based solution, the central function of key generation is performed by a role administrator, but it can also be a central office, etc.

In the first process step, the role administrator instructs a smart card to generate a key for AES HW encryption, and it receives a start PIN from the role administrator. This key is then copied to a second smart card, which also receives a start PIN. To avoid copying the key to the second smart card, this process can also be carried out using a Diffie-Hellman key exchange procedure, which generates the key for AES HW encryption on both smart cards simultaneously and separately.

In the second process step, a non-deterministic random number generator generates a random bit sequence of sufficient length (e.g., 512 GB).

In the third process step, the role administrator copies the random bit sequence from process step 2 to several transport storage media, depending on the number of subjects (read/write-authorized persons) of the role.

In the fourth step of the process, each subject of the role (authorized person, etc.) receives one of these transport storage media and one of the two smart cards from step 1, either in person or via a trusted courier. When using a public parcel service, the storage medium and smart card must be transported separately, which is always advisable. The smart card can also be transported only once at the very beginning, before the first transport of the transport storage medium. Over time, e.g., annually, the smart card can be renewed, which again results in a transport.

In the fifth process step, each subject then reads the key bits from the transport storage medium after decryption by the AES HW encryption unit using the smart card key. Each subject then copies the key bits as a file (called a role file) with the name of the role, a sequence number, and a generation number to its encryption/decryption storage medium. This means that the encryption/decryption storage medium then contains a roll file with the roll name and a sequence and generation number for all rolls to which the subject has access rights (read/write rights), which contains the key bits for this roll. Because new key bits are required for each storage of new data for the necessary encryption of this data (the one-time pad prohibits multiple use of key bits), all key bits of a role may eventually be used up (however, with the specified encryption modes, this only applies to one mode; see Sect. 6.4.3). The role administrator must then deliver a new file with key bits using the transport storage medium. This new file has the same name (the name of the role) and the same generation number, but the sequence number is increased by one. This allows the key bits of a role to be extended. Because all key bits ever used for data encryption are required again during a read operation as long as the encrypted data is still in use, and because years may elapse between the write operation (including data encryption) and subsequent read operations (including decryption), these key bits must be stored locally in the encryption/decryption storage medium for a correspondingly long period of time.

When a user (subject) leaves a role, new key material must be used for all future encryptions, i.e., process steps 2 to 5 must be repeated. In this case, a role administrator must send a new key file to all remaining users (subjects) of a role. This invalidates the unused key bits, and the user who has left the role can no longer use them. However, before the sixth process step can be performed, a pause is required until all users in the role have received the new key bits. This pause can last a few hours, but also several days if the transport is over a long distance. During this pause, the old key bits are still valid. The user who has left the role can still read the data for which they still have the key bits. However, this is not a disadvantage, as they also had free access to this data before leaving the role. In the fifth process step, each user (subject) remaining in the role reads the new key bits from the transport storage medium. Each user (subject) then copies the key bits as a role file with the name of the role, a sequence number, and a generation number to their encryption/decryption storage medium, whereby the generation number is increased by one.

In the sixth process step, these key bits of the roll file are used for encrypting/decrypting the data. Sect 6.4 and https://cryptography.study/phys/modes presents four different encryption methods/modes for encrypting/decrypting the data, three of which are methods/modes newly developed specifically for QKD and RKD. The methods/modes, called OTPH, OTPS and XTSO, do not require any additional key bits for each subsequent encryption of data blocks, i.e., the key length for the one-time pad is constant (Key1 plus Key2 plus Key3) plus a special counter (Chap 6.4). These encryption methods/modes do not require a mechanism for extending the role file, i.e., the sequence number loses its meaning, but the generation number must be retained because when a user (subject) leaves a role, the role key (Key1, Key2, and Key3) must be changed. This means that when a subject leaves a role, the same amount of new key material, including the counter, is required, and the key bits, including the file, are stored in the role file with the name of the role and a generation number increased by one.

If the application requires the key to be generated from several different key bits, several role administrators can generate key bits separately and use an XOR operation to determine the final key, which is then stored on transport storage media for all subjects.

Since the sequence number of a key file becomes larger and larger over the years, but much of the stored data is no longer used because it has already been deleted or replaced by new data, for example, for efficiency reasons, the sequence number can be restarted from the beginning by re-encrypting the data that is still relevant, and all old key bits of the file can be deleted. This applies to all three specified encryption methods/modes.

A problem with the data storage application can occur in networks when several users modify and thereby encrypt data in the same file or database at roughly the same time. This can lead to synchronization errors, which are not possible in the telecommunications application because each user uses their own key bits. However, if handled correctly, these synchronization errors do not have to lead to any errors. In encryption mode 3 (one-time pad), they can lead to individual key bits being used multiple times in exceptional cases. This problem can only be solved perfectly if, as in telecommunications, each user uses their own key bits and a role administrator no longer generates and distributes them to all subjects. However, this leads to a significantly larger number of role files, because each role file contains not only the sequence and generation number but also the user name and must therefore be available more often.

5.4 Summary

With MKD for one-time pads, the physical generation and distribution of cryptographic keys can be implemented with a high level of security. This is supported by the extremely high data volume, currently up to 16 TBytes for a single transport, which takes a few hours to days, key rates currently up to 7 GB/sec, high robustness in terms of temperature, shocks, etc., extensive certifications, access protection to the key bits with PIN and smart card, extensive standardization (USB, SATA), unrestricted suitability for mobile end devices, and, above all, the low price (currently $1100 for 1 TB with smart cards, $3000 for 16 TB). In addition, there is the required non-deterministic random number generator, currently costing around $1100 for fast key generation based on quantum-optical processes; slower non-deterministic random number generators are currently available from $65.

There is currently a wide range of MKD-enabled portable storage media on the market that are used today as portable storage media for high-security data backup, but which are also suitable for MKD. More information about such storage media can be found on the book's website at.[29]

These features of MKD with a one-time pad and easy usability with today's end devices via the USB or SATA interface—with or without connection to an HSM—allow highly secure end-to-end encryption in telecommunications and on-site data storage (on a PC, etc.) with a one-time pad, even with common end devices such as PCs, laptops, etc. Data encryption can then be performed in an HSM or directly on the PC.

MKD with a one-time pad also allows use in mobile devices for telecommunications and on-site data storage, thanks to the portable storage medium for all required key bits. This means that on a laptop—with or without a connection to an HSM—cryptography based entirely on physical processes (key generation and distribution, data encryption/decryption, MAC calculation, data authentication) can be implemented for seamless, highly secure data security, even during a train journey, flight, etc. The security requirements always lie with the end device and the MKD-enabled storage medium. This also applies to mobile IT systems in locomotives, cars, ships, weapon systems, etc.

With a 1 TB (1 TByte) MKD-compatible storage medium, telecommunications can be encrypted with a one-time pad for a long period of time with provable 100% security. The background software is very simple, as is the synchronization between the two communication partners (each partner uses only its own key bits for encryption). Decryption by an attacker on the communication link is completely impossible today and in the future, even for intelligence services. The "data storage" solution is

---

[29] https://cryptography.study/phys/memory.

more complex (see above). The "data storage" solution is more complex. However, the LISA solution (see Sect. 7.1.1), which was used for the MKD- tests, shows that data storage in a PC environment (even without the use of an HSM) can also be highly secure and function perfectly.

5.5 Counterarguments to MKD

Considering Memory Key Distribution (MKD) as a method for generating and distributing cryptographic keys requires explicit consideration of objections that arise less from the cryptographic idea and the physical possibilities themselves than from questions of scaling, organizational embedding, logistical processes, and legal framework conditions. These aspects relate to the implementation level and have a decisive influence on how MKD can be handled in practice in larger structures.

- **Scalability.** As with all methods involving paired-shared secrets, the organizational effort increases quadratically with the number of communication partners involved. For n participants, this results in a requirement for $n \cdot (n-1)/2$ independent key relationships in the worst case. This n^2 dependency is also found in the same form in QKD and RKD systems, which in the case of QKD is counteracted by KMS networks with trusted nodes, but this increases the attack surface. With MKD, this problem only affects the upstream key provisioning. With MKD, ongoing operation is not limited by continuous key rates (as with QKD and RKD), but by the one-time provisioning of sufficiently large key material. Scaling thus becomes an organizational issue (see Sect. 7.3) rather than a physical-technical limitation.
- **Logistical and Procedural Risks.** Such risks must be taken into account, particularly in connection with the physical transport of storage media. Possible vulnerabilities include interruptions in the documented chain of custody, loss, theft, or improper handling of data carriers. These risks are real and inherent, but differ fundamentally from attack vectors in transmission-based methods such as QKD and RKD. However, risks in MKD are concentrated in clearly definable process steps. The security-critical period is limited in time and space. This makes risks easily visible, verifiable, and addressable at the organizational level.
- **Organizational Fault Tolerance.** The effectiveness of MKD depends on clearly defined responsibilities, clean documentation, and disciplined process execution (see also Sect. 7.3). Human error or organizational oversights can compromise security. However, this dependency is not unique to MKD, but characterizes all high-security procedures whose protective effect is not exclusively enforced by technical means. In contrast to complex, continuously operated technical systems, deviations from defined processes in MKD do not lead to creeping security losses over long periods of time. Errors take effect immediately and force a clear response, such as the reevaluation or replacement of key material.

- **Regulatory and Liability Issues** relating to MKD primarily concern the handling of physical data carriers, personal access devices, and transport services. In many jurisdictions, there are established regulations for this from related areas such as confidentiality, data carrier classification, or high-security logistics. MKD thus operates within known regulatory patterns instead of opening up new, technically elusive problem areas. Liability issues can be clarified on the basis of specific process responsibilities. Security-related events are linked to physical actions, times, and responsibilities and are therefore fundamentally traceable. This differs from scenarios in which security breaches can only be identified retrospectively and without a clear analysis of the causes.

These counterarguments show that the challenges of MKD do not lie at the level of cryptographic security, but rather in scaling, organization, and logistical implementation. These challenges are clearly identifiable, analytically accessible, and not obscured by idealized assumptions about technical components or transmission channels. MKD thus deliberately shifts security-related issues into an area that is characterized by processes, responsibilities, and control and differs fundamentally from transmission-based physical processes.

5.6 Security Considerations

Portable MKD-enabled storage media for small amounts of data, where mathematical cryptographic methods are subsequently used, are primarily high-security smart cards with processors in accordance with ISO/IEC 7816, as used in passports, SIM cards, and payment transactions [Rankl10]. They are all available with high-security certifications (CC EAL4+) in various designs, such as cards, USB sticks, wristbands, chips, etc.

Portable storage media available for MKD with a one-time pad[30] contain at least one access protection, integrated AES HW encryption, a PIN input device, smart cards, etc., are security certified and are currently available up to 16 TB. Additional security features are available in some cases. When transporting storage media personally or through a trusted third party, the transport route and, above all, the very important authentication of the partners are additionally secured.

The number of security-critical components and the security of each of these components are also interesting from a security perspective, because no manufacturer develops and produces all of these components themselves (for details, see Sect. 7.2).

In contrast to QKD, MKD with a one-time pad contains only a few security-critical components. At the highest level, this involves the non-deterministic random number generator and at the lower levels access protection for the storage medium with the necessary components. This also applies to side-channel attacks, which represent a wide field of activity for attackers in QKD and RKD and are difficult to assess

[30] https://cryptography.study/phys/memory.

completely due to their high complexity in some cases. With MKD using a one-time pad, side-channel attacks are easy to understand and assess due to their simplicity. Side-channel attacks via measurement of radiation and power consumption are only possible during operation and only immediately next to the device. If the storage medium remains switched on or in standby mode after operation and the internal AES key is still in the RAM, an attacker could read the RAM by physically cooling it down. However, this is hardly feasible in practice because the RAM is protected in the AES chip and the AES chip is built into the storage medium.

When transported personally or by a trusted third party, the device is never in an operational state and therefore there is no radiation or power consumption and no possibility of reading the RAM, and the storage medium is always under control.

Transportation by a public service provider allows for an attack scenario that requires a great deal of effort, leads to the destruction of the storage medium, but then fails at the level of AES encryption in the storage medium because the encryption key is stored on another storage medium (the smart card) (hence the requirement for a smart card for key transport for AES HW encryption). However, if the AES encryption itself becomes a successful attack scenario because it is a mathematical encryption method, MKD must be transported personally or by a trusted third party, because this transport also reliably prevents this attack scenario.

However, the central security component of an MKD solution is the non-deterministic random number generator. Particular attention must be paid to the quality of the random numbers, because the random numbers determine the quality of the key and thus the data encryption. Because key quality is very difficult to verify, high-security certifications are particularly important here. The environment, i.e., the supplier, etc., should also be checked (see Sect.7.2) and several different random number generators should be used.

5.7 Practical Criteria

5.7.1 ***Market Readiness***

Suitable portable storage media for MKD[31] with one-time pads and non-deterministic random number generators are already widely available on the market.[32] A suitable complete software solution for data storage with and without HSM is also available on the market (see Sect.7.1.1). Integration into web browsers is not known for MKD with one-time pads, although it is easy to implement.

---

[31] https://cryptography.study/phys/memory.

[32] https://cryptography.study/phys/TRNG.

5.7.2 Key Rates

Key rates depend on the read speed. For MKD-enabled NVMe SSDs, they are currently around 7 GB (GBytes) per second. This key rate is well above the key rates of QKD and RKD and can be guaranteed for MKD throughout.

This does not take into account the generation of the key bits. To "fill" a 1 TB storage medium with non-deterministic random numbers, very fast non-deterministic random number generators that use quantum-optical processes (240 Mbit/sec, price approx. $3600) are required, which take around 9 hours. Non-deterministic random number generators with a USB interface, which also use quantum-optical processes and are in the price range of around $1100, only deliver slightly more than 4 Mbit/sec, which requires around 23 days for a 1 TB storage medium. Slow random number generators usually require an upgrade to a hybrid generator to reduce the time required, i.e., additional numbers are calculated from the non-deterministic numbers using a suitable algorithm so that the rate can be increased, for example, 20fold. However, this reduces data security, which may be relevant.

5.7.3 Distance of Key Transmission

The distance only affects the duration of transport of the portable storage medium and ranges from a few hours to several days. This means that with MKD using a one-time pad, up to 16 TB of random key material can currently be exchanged nationally and worldwide in a few hours to days in a highly secure manner between "n" participating partners/end devices. With MKD, the destination address can change regularly because the storage medium is physically transported, which requires extensive preparation and costs with QKD.

5.7.4 Cost Framework

The cost of MKD-enabled portable storage media currently ranges from approximately $1,100 for 1 TB with smart cards to $3,000 for 16 TB (see the book's website at[33]). For HSMs, the cost is approximately $1600 for the PC solution (see the book's website at[34]). In addition, there is the required non-deterministic random number generator, which costs from around $1,100 and, in some applications or application environments, can be provided by trusted central units and can therefore be more expensive and thus faster. Fast non-deterministic random number generators

[33] https://cryptography.study/phys/memory.

[34] https://cryptography.study/phys/HSM.

that operate on the basis of quantum-optical processes cost from $1100, and around $3,600 for very high bit rates (see the book's website at[35]).

During operation, the costs of transporting the storage media must also be taken into account. For public service providers, this amounts to only a few dollars per transport, and for transport with confidential third parties or personally over short distances, the costs are low, but for long distances, higher costs (time and travel expenses) may be incurred. With distribution of storage media, e.g., to company locations, all storage media at a location can be transported at the same time, thus saving on higher costs.

5.7.5 Compatibility (with Today's Technology, Interchangeability).

Because the available portable MKD-enabled storage media have a USB interface in the case of memory sticks and usually a SATA interface in the case of SSDs (SSDs with USB interfaces are also available), they can be plugged directly into any PC, laptop, HSM, etc., and the stored cryptographic keys can be read directly. The non-deterministic random number generators currently contain a USB interface with a bit rate of up to 4 Mbit/sec and a standardized PCIe interface above that.

MKD-enabled storage media and non-deterministic random number generators are mass-produced goods on the global market and can therefore be easily replaced by other models or manufacturers/suppliers.

5.7.6 Robustness/Susceptibility to Interference

Portable storage media are very robust against temperature fluctuations, shocks, moisture, etc., because SSDs and memory sticks do not contain any mechanical components. MKD with a one-time pad therefore does not require any maintenance of the devices, which is always security-sensitive and involves extensive attack scenarios. If a portable storage medium breaks down, it can be easily and inexpensively replaced with a new one. Compatibility makes it easy to switch manufacturers, thus preventing delivery problems in the event of a supplier bottleneck.

[35] https://cryptography.study/phys/TRNG.

5.7.7 Suitability for Mobile Devices

Because portable storage media are very robust and relatively small and draw their power from PCs, laptops, HSMs, etc., they can also be used without any speed restrictions in mobile devices. This means that they can also be used without restriction in cars, rail vehicles, aircraft, ships, drones, etc. MKD with a one-time pad is therefore also suitable for telecommunications to and from aircraft (passengers or crew members), where highly sensitive/secret data is exchanged.

5.7.8 Randomness of the Keys.

The non-deterministic random number generator determines the randomness of the key on both sides when used for telecommunications. When generating the key, the sender of the data or both communication partners can equally determine the quality of the encryption, which leads to equality between both communication partners, which is often not the case with QKD.

In the data storage application, one or more role administrators take responsibility for the randomness of the key bits in the example solution described. They must use certified non-deterministic random number generators.

5.7.9 Standardization.

Because the available portable storage media have a USB or SATA interface and the data can be read directly by any operating system, no further standardization is necessary. USB adapters are also available for the SATA interface so that it can also be used with laptops, etc. The TCG-OPAL standard exists for functionality (Chap 5.2.2).

The USB interface is used for random number generators, while the PCIe interface is used for very fast generators; both are also standardized interfaces. However, the PCIe interface usually requires desktop PCs.

5.7.10 Certification

The available portable storage media, random number generators, and HSMs are all comprehensive and certified for high-security applications. Depending on the region, this involves Common Criteria (CC), EUCC, FIPS, etc., i.e., suitable certifications are a matter of course at MKD. From a purely security perspective, particular attention must be paid to the quality of the random number generators, as they determine the quality of the key and represent the central security component of an MKD solution.

5.7.11 Advantages/Disadvantages of the Technology

The main disadvantage of MKD is that physical transport of the storage media with suitable logistics is required. With few partners, this is not an issue, as this transport is only necessary at longer intervals (months, years) and is easy to implement. With devices such as aircraft, etc., the storage medium can be replaced during maintenance, for example. In a network with n partners or n end devices, $(n^2-n)/2$ storage media and a maximum of $(n^2-n)/2$ transports are required for a key exchange. When distributing the storage media, e.g., to company locations, all storage media at a location can be transported at the same time, significantly reducing the number of transports required.

Suitable logistics should always be used for this purpose (see Sect.7.3), but it is essential in many cases when there are a large number of end devices.

MKD requires no maintenance—damaged or old storage media are simply replaced with new ones. MKD is therefore a very durable solution that can also be gradually and cost-effectively converted to new storage technologies and standards (e.g., USB and SATA) without any impact on operations.

The sharp increase in the amount of data in telecommunications and data storage in IT over the past decades, which will continue, is not a problem for MKD with One-Time Pad, because portable storage media, such as SSDs, have always kept pace with this growth and will continue to do so in the future. Therefore, the one-time pad capability of MKD will remain intact in the future.

5.7.12 Man-in-the-Middle Attacks

Passive Man-in-the-Middle

A passive man-in-the-middle attack can be ruled out if the attacker is not located directly next to the storage medium.

Active Man-in-the-Middle

An active man-in-the-middle attack requires the attacker to intercept the portable storage medium during transport and crack the access protection. This is impossible if the medium is transported personally or by a trusted third party (partner).

Transportation by a public service provider allows for an active man-in-the-middle attack. In this case, the storage medium must be destroyed in order to gain direct access to the data. Then the AES-256 encryption of the storage medium must be cracked. If this encryption is not trusted because it is a mathematical process, MKD with a one-time pad must be transported personally or by a trusted third party, because this transport also reliably prevents this attack scenario.

A man-in-the-middle attack directly on the end device is effectively shifted to the one-time pad, where the plaintext data must always be located, and is therefore not an MKD-specific problem.

5.7.13 Authentication

Personal transport or transport by a trusted third party and the PIN and smart card required for access provide two-factor or three-factor authentication. However, even with a public service provider, two-factor authentication with a PIN and smart card is used. Another advantage of MKD with a one-time pad is that authentication can be renewed with each transport, i.e., it is long-lasting.

5.7.14 Integrity / Errors

The integrity of the key, which is a major challenge with QKD and RKD, is a matter of course with MKD with a one-time pad due to the nature of the system.

References

[WP-OTP] Wikipedia contributors "One-time pad," Wikipedia, The Free Encyclopedia, https://en.wikipedia.org/wiki/One-time_pad

[WP-Scy] Wikipedia contributors, "Scytale," Wikipedia, The Free Encyclopedia, https://en.wikipedia.org/wiki/Scytale

[WP-Ste] Wikipedia contributors, "Steganography," Wikipedia, The Free Encyclopedia, https://en.wikipedia.org/wiki/steganography

[Rankl10] W. Rankl, W. Effing, Smart Card Handbook, 4th edn. (Wiley 2010), ISBN: 978–0–470-74367-6, https://www.wiley.com/en-us/Smart+Card+Handbook%2C+4th+Edition-p-9780470743676

[WP-Iso] Wikipedia contributors, "ISO/IEC 7816," Wikipedia, The Free Encyclopedia, https://en.wikipedia.org/wiki/ISO/IEC_7816

[WP-3D] Wikipedia contributors, "Triple DES," Wikipedia, The Free Encyclopedia, https://en.wikipedia.org/wiki/Triple_DES

[WP-HSM] Wikipedia contributors, "Hardware security module," Wikipedia, The Free Encyclopedia, https://en.wikipedia.org/wiki/Hardware_security_module

[Rij22] D. Rijmenants, *The Complete Guide to Secure Communications with the One Time Pad Cipher*, 8.1 edn. (Self-published manuscript, 2022). https://ciphermachinesandcryptology.com/papers/one_time_pad.pdf

[Bell11] S. Bellovin, M. Frank Miller, Inventor of the one-time pad. Cryptologia **35**(3), 203–222 (2011). https://doi.org/10.1080/01611194.2011.583711

[Bor12] S. Borowski, M. Lesniewicz, Modern usage of old one-time pad, in *Military Communications and Information System Conference* (IEEE, 2012), pp. 1–5, https://ieeexplore.ieee.org/abstract/document/6387923

[WP-DH] Wikipedia contributors, "Diffie–Hellman key exchange," Wikipedia, The Free Encyclopedia, https://en.wikipedia.org/wiki/Diffie–Hellman_key_exchange

[Diff22] W. Diffie, M.E. Hellman, New directions in cryptography, in *Democratizing Cryptography: The Work of Whitfield Diffie and Martin Hellman*, (2022), pp. 365–390. https://doi.org/10.1145/3549993.3550007

[WP-PIN] Wikipedia contributors, "Personal identification number," Wikipedia, The Free Encyclopedia, https://en.wikipedia.org/wiki/Personal_identification_number

[WP-Zer] Wikipedia contributors, "Zeroisation," Wikipedia, The Free Encyclopedia, https://en.wikipedia.org/wiki/Zeroisation

[WP-COC] Wikipedia contributors, "Chain of custody," Wikipedia, The Free Encyclopedia, https://en.wikipedia.org/wiki/Chain_of_custody

[WP-Opa] Wikipedia contributors, "Opal Storage Specification," Wikipedia, The Free Encyclopedia, https://en.wikipedia.org/wiki/Opal_Storage_Specification

[TCGOpa] Trusted Computing Group (TCG). "Storage Work Group, Storage Security Subsystem Class: Opal" (specification web page). no date; https://trustedcomputinggroup.org/resource/storage-work-group-storage-security-subsystem-class-opal/

[WP-TCG] Wikipedia contributors, "Trusted Computing Group," Wikipedia, The Free Encyclopedia, https://en.wikipedia.org/wiki/Trusted_Computing_Group

[BSI12] BSI, "Protection Profile for Portable Storage Medie (PSMPP)", Common Criteria Protection Profile, BSI-CC-PP-0081-2012; https://www.commoncriteriaportal.org/files/ppfiles/pp0081b_pdf.pdf

[Vai23] V. Mannalath, S. Mishra, A. Pathak, A comprehensive review of quantum random number generators: Concepts, classification and the origin of randomness. Quantum Inf. Process. Springer Science and Business Media LLC. **22**, Nr. 439 (2023) https://doi.org/10.1007/s11128-023-04175-y

[John18] Johnston, David, *Random Number Generators—Principles and Practices: A Guide for Engineers and Programmers* (Walter de Gruyter GmbH & Co KG, 2018). https://doi.org/10.1515/9781501506062

[Meij19] C. Meijer, B. van Gastel, Self-Encrypting Deception: Weaknesses in the Encryption of Solid State Drives, in 2019 *IEEE Symposium on Security and Privacy (SP)* (IEEE, San Francisco, CA, USA, 2019), pp. 72–87. ISBN 978-1-5386-6660-9. ISSN 2375–1207, https://doi.org/10.1109/SP.2019.00088

[WP-RBA] Wikipedia contributors, "Role-based access control," Wikipedia, The Free Encyclopedia, https://en.wikipedia.org/wiki/Role-based_access_control

Chapter 6
Encryption Methods for QKD and RKD and XOR Operation

This chapter and https://cryptography.study/phys/modes introduce four new encryption methods and the one-time pad, all of which are based on the XOR operation. The new methods/modes limit the required key length and are therefore particularly interesting for QKD and RKD. Because hash functions are already used in QKD and RKD, no additional mathematical methods are required for data encryption. One of these four methods also generates a MAC for the security objectives of integrity and authenticity. Because these four methods are very simple in structure—they contain only the XOR function for data encryption (like the 100% secure one-time pad) and a hash algorithm/MAC—cryptanalysis is also easily possible.

The XOR function is not based on the laws of physics, but on Boolean algebra [WP–Boo].[1] Under certain circumstances, it can guarantee provable 100% security and is easy to implement in hardware. The XOR function plays an important role in cryptography. This is especially true

- in data encryption (security objective: confidentiality) when using the one-time pad, which consists solely of an XOR function, whereby each data bit is XORed with a key bit during encryption, resulting in a bit of encrypted data, and,
- in MAC calculation (security objectives: integrity and authenticity), where the XOR function is used in leading MACs such as CBC-MAC, CCM-MAC, and GCM-MAC.

6.1 Connection between the XOR Function and Physics

The XOR function is a logical operation of Boolean algebra. Boolean algebra is a mathematical model that can be used, among other things, to describe the behavior of digital circuits. Such circuits do not contain any software themselves, but are

[1] https://en.wikipedia.org/wiki/Boolean_algebra

E. Piller and H. Schölnast, *Data Encryption at the Intersection of Mathematics and Physics*, SpringerBriefs in Information Security and Cryptography,
https://doi.org/10.1007/978-3-032-24764-3_6

purely hardware components and, as such, physical systems. They form the hardware basis of many technical applications. Boolean algebra is used directly in classical mechanics and electrical engineering. It is a fundamental part of the development of digital electronics, where it is applied as switching algebra. Boolean algebra is the basis for digital circuits and computer technology.

Logical operations of Boolean algebra such as AND (written as $a \wedge b$), OR (written as $a \vee b$), NOT (written as $\neg a$) can be implemented in practice by combining transistors. The XOR function (eXclusive OR, written as $a \oplus b$) is a logical operation that compares two binary inputs and only outputs 1 if exactly one of the two inputs is 1. If both inputs are the same (both 0 or both 1), the result is 0. The following formula shows how the XOR operation is defined and how it can be formed from the elementary Boolean functions AND, OR, and NOT.

$$s = x \oplus y = x\, XOR\, y = (\neg x \wedge y) \vee (x \wedge \neg y)$$

Table 6.1 Truth table for the XOR operation.

Figure 6.1 shows how the XOR operation can be constructed from circuits for elementary Boolean operations. Figure 6.2 is a black box representation for the same function.

Table 6.1 provides an overview of all possible value combinations

x	y	$x \oplus y$
0	0	0
0	1	1
1	0	1
1	1	0

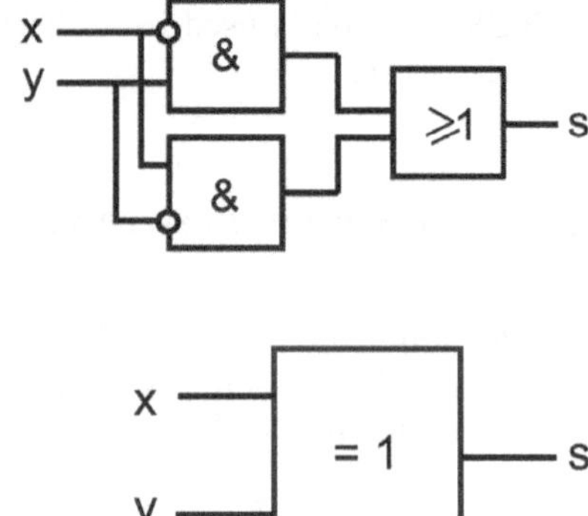

Fig. 6.1. XOR as the result of elementary operations

Fig. 6.2. Simplified circuit symbol for XOR

Table 6.2 shows an example of an XOR operation. Each bit from the unencrypted data is linked to the corresponding bit of the key. If both bits are the same, the value of the corresponding bit in the encrypted data is 0; if they are different, the value is 1

Unencrypted data	010011101010
Key	110011010111
Encrypted data	100000111101

6.2 One-Time Pad

The one-time pad was first mentioned in 1882 by Frank Miller and in 1885 by Joseph Mauborgne. However, it was only encrypted character by character. In 1917, Gilbert Vernam registered the one-time pad in its current form as a patent, which was commercialized by AT&T from the 1920s onward [Rij22][2]. As early as 1923, the German Foreign Ministry introduced the one-time pad in conjunction with physical distribution of the keys (see Chap. 5; MKD) for all diplomatic correspondence.

Vernam was also the first to mechanize the one-time pad. To do this, he used teletype paper tape containing randomly distributed character strings as key strips. The characters of the plaintext in the usual telegraph code were combined with those of the key strips using relays and the XOR function. Special devices were also built to generate these key strips on teletype paper tape. Another important factor here was the easier integration with telegraph traffic. After World War II, the Swiss company Crypto AG offered this solution worldwide as its own version of its C machines and became a market leader in this field. Although many different versions of these so-called "cipher machines" based on the one-time pad were developed and used worldwide, the literature is not very informative in this regard. The reason for this is that these cipher machines were mainly used in high-security areas, especially by secret services, and therefore the research and development results were usually not published.

With the first generations of computers and the representation of characters and numbers in bits, bitwise encryption with the XOR function finally became established [Bor12][3].

In bitwise encryption, each bit of the plaintext is XORed with a bit of the key. (See Table 6.1).

Table 6.2 Example of an XOR operation.

The 100% security of one-time pad encryption can be proven under these three conditions:

1. The key must be completely random, i.e., it must come from a non-deterministic random number generator.
2. The key must be at least as long as the unencrypted data. (If it is longer than the unencrypted data, only part of the key is used.)

[2] https://ciphermachinesandcryptology.com/papers/one_time_pad.pdf

[3] https://ieeexplore.ieee.org/abstract/document/6387923

3. New key bits must be used for each new encryption, i.e., the key must never be reused, not even parts of it.

The one-time pad can be used with all five physical methods / technologies described in this book if a sufficiently large amount of key material is available. If a maximum of a few megabytes of data per day is to be encrypted with a one-time pad, the key material that can be obtained at the same time with QKD devices available today can be used for this purpose, among other sources. However, at the beginning of 2026, the key rates that can actually be achieved by QKD devices will not be sufficient to encrypt significantly larger amounts of data generated daily with a one-time pad. In this case, key generation and distribution must be carried out using faster methods. Of course, established and standardized mathematical methods are available for this purpose, the more recent of which are even considered quantum computer-secure. However, this security classification is not based on rigorous mathematical proof, but "only" on the assessment of a commission of experts. If you also want to rule out the risk of error on the part of the commission of experts, you have to switch to physical methods, and then, due to the key rate, there is currently no way around MKD.

In practice, this means that QKD and RKD can only be used for telecommunications applications involving smaller amounts of data, and not for data storage. MKD is practically independent of the amount of data and the encryption mode, because MKD-capable storage media up to 16 TB are already available today.

In conjunction with a one-time pad, MKD-capable storage media for transporting cryptographic keys only became interesting with the application "secure and simple data backup" because this application ensured correspondingly low prices for storage media for a mass market with [BSI][4] [Gimbut13][5]. This marked the beginning of low-cost and easy-to-use MKD in conjunction with one-time pads and MKD-enabled storage media, followed by cryptography based exclusively on physical processes that covers the security mechanisms of confidentiality, integrity, and authenticity. Absolute cryptographic security, which is secure against computationally powerful adversaries and mathematical attack methods that are still unknown (unpublished) today, is thus also possible in the low-cost sector and can be implemented easily and in a user-friendly way in practice. But in conjunction with MKD, logistics (see Sect. 7.3) must ensure that sufficient key material is always available.

[4] https://www.bsi.bund.de/EN/Topics/Consumers/Information and recommendations/Cyber security recommendations/Backing up, encrypting, and deleting data/Data encryption/Software and hardware-based encryption/software and hardware-based encryption.html?nn = 921,724#doc921720bodyText2

[5] doi:10.1007/s11623-013-0212-0

6.3 Data Encryption for Data Storage

Data encryption using physical methods for data storage involves different conditions than those for telecommunications. The use of a one-time pad requires a very high number of key bits, because new key bits are required for encryption every time the data is changed (see Sect. 6.4). For example, MS Word constantly performs temporary saves, and user-initiated saves can also occur regularly. MS Word automatically saves 6 times per hour, although the user can reduce this interval to 10 minutes. Working with MS Word for five hours means at least 30 save operations, which, with average file sizes of, say, 200 kB, requires 6 MB of key material. This key material is required for a pure one-time pad. If this very high amount of key material is to be avoided, special encryption modes with a one-time pad are possible, though these do not constitute a pure one-time pad. They are presented in Sect. 6.4 and in the appendix https://cryptography.study/phys/modes and allow for a restriction on the key length. One of these new modes, called OTPM, also incorporates the security objectives of integrity and authenticity and additionally randomizes the entire encryption process. They are also considered highly secure, although no mathematical proof is known for this assessment. One of these new encryption methods is based on the XTS encryption mode, which is briefly introduced below. Since they are structurally simple—they contain only the XOR operation (like the 100% secure one-time pad) and a hash/ MAC algorithm for data encryption—cryptanalysis is also easily possible.

6.3.1 XTS Mode

XTS (XEX-based Tweaked CodeBook mode with Ciphertext Stealing) [WP–XTS][6] [Ball12][7] is an encryption mode of operation developed for encrypting data in permanent storage devices such as hard disks, SSDs, USB sticks, virtual storage, etc. It was created by Phillip Rogaway [Rog04][8] with a few minor modifications. XTS mode uses two independent keys. XTS was approved by NIST for data storage protection and standardized in 2007 as quasi-standard IEEE 1619 [WP–IEE] [9] [IEEE18][10].

In XTS mode, the data to be encrypted, referred to below as m, is divided into blocks of 128 bits in length; the last block may be shorter. The variable j indicates the block number, starting with j = 0, i.e., the individual data blocks are m_j. The encrypted data blocks are called C_j.

The variable i indicates the location of the data block in the permanent memory (e.g., logical sector number) or the location of the data block within a file or a

---

[6] https://en.wikipedia.org/wiki/Disk_encryption_theory#XTS

[7] doi:10.1080/01611194.2012.635115

[8] doi:10.1007/978-3-540-30,539-2_2

[9] https://en.wikipedia.org/wiki/IEEE_Security_in_Storage_Working_Group

[10] https://standards.ieee.org/ieee/1619/11552/

database/table of a database, etc. However, linked to the location of the data block, it must also contain the name of the permanent memory or the file or database/table.

- α is a generator polynomial in $GF(2^{128})$, defined by the polynomial j.
- $\otimes$ represents the multiplication of two polynomials (α and AES-result) in the Galois field $GF(2^{128})$, where the multiplication is performed modulo $x^{128} + x^7 + x^2 + x + 1$
- Key_1 is the encryption key (256-bit) of the data m_j (plaintext block j).
- Key_2 is the second key (256-bit) for encrypting the variable i.

The left image shows the data encryption of the individual blocks. The right image shows the data encryption of the last two data blocks.

Figure 6.3 shows that the data is encrypted three times. First with the XOR function with the encrypted variable i (which is also linked to the value of variable j by Galois multiplication), then with the AES algorithm, and finally once again with the encrypted variable i. The encryption therefore corresponds to the following link:

$$C_j = AES_{Key_1}\left(m_j\ XOR\ \left(AES_{Key_2}(i) \otimes j\right)\right) XOR\ \left(AES_{Key_2}(i) \otimes j\right)$$

In XTS mode, identical plaintext blocks P_j result in different ciphertext blocks C_j because the block position is included in the encryption. This makes partial encryption, i.e., the encryption of individual data blocks independently of other data blocks, quick and easy to perform. Figure 6.3 illustrates the processes for the last two data blocks. This shows that no padding (filling the last data block to a length of 128 bits) is required for the last data block (ciphertext stealing). XTS mode also allows for easy parallelization in hardware, which is ideal for large amounts of data and

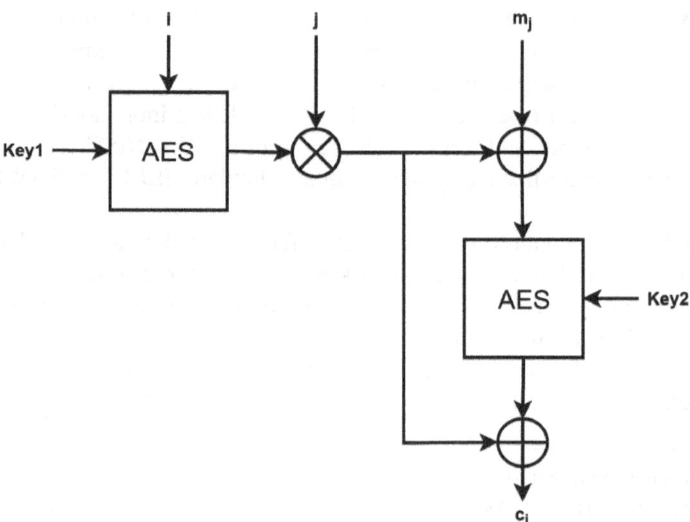

Fig. 6.3 XTS with one block

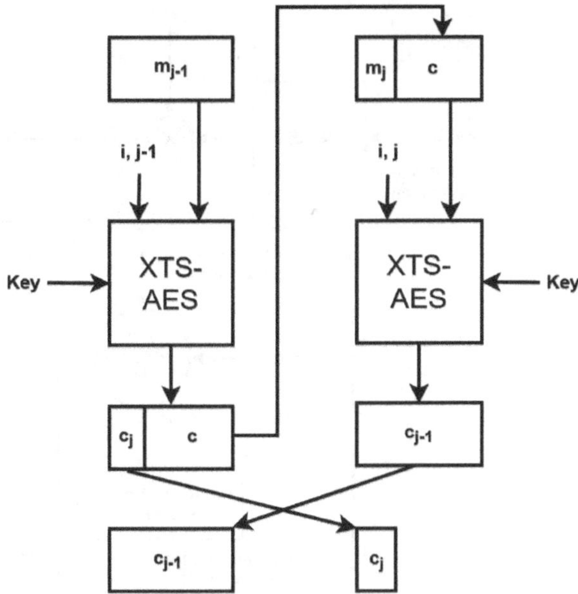

Fig. 6.4 XTS with the last two blocks

hardware acceleration (e.g., AES-NI). The double application of the AES encryption function requires double the key length and half the speed. XTS mode is used today, for example, in TrueCrypt, FreeBSD, OpenBSD softraid disk encryption software, Mac OSX Lion's FileVault, SPYRUS Hydra PC Digital Attaché, and Kingston DataTraveler.

6.4 Encryption Methods/Modes for QKD and RKD

6.4.1 OTPH Encryption Method

In the OTPH the upper section of Fig. 6.5 containing the two AES ciphers and the first XOR operation is omitted. For OTPH, only the area in Fig. 6.5 marked with a dotted line applies. The OTPH extends the One-Time Pad with a cyclic buffer (ring buffer) and a HMAC, based on RFC5869 Key Derivation Function (HKDF). The choice of HMAC is flexible in OTPH. We use the standardized HMAC-SHA3-512 (ISO/IEC 9707 und 10188). In OTPH, the non-deterministic—i.e., completely random—key is treated as a cyclic buffer. This means that the Key 3 (see Fig. 6.5) is considered a "cyclic buffer with modulo addressing" [WP–Cir],[11] [NSCL][12].

[11] https://en.wikipedia.org/wiki/Circular_buffer

[12] https://docs.frib.msu.edu/daq/newsite/nscldaq-10.2/c5.html

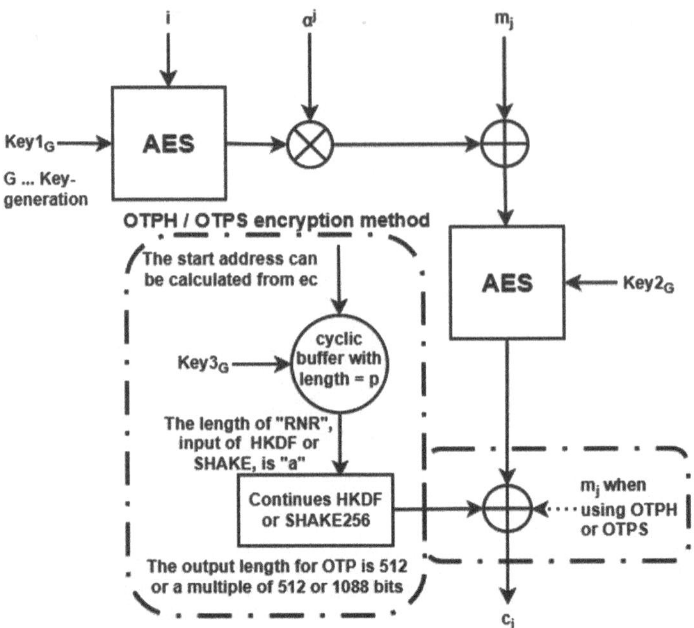

Fig. 6.5 OTPH, OTPS and XTSO

The key bits of Key 3 are read cyclically (in a loop), and the address pointer when reading Key3 is calculated modulo “p”. The length of the cyclic buffer must be a prime number, hereinafter referred to as “p”. In the first step, the key bits of Key 3 are read bit by bit with a spacing of “d=1” (d denotes bit spacing)—that is, the bits are read right next to each other—and in blocks (block length is "a") from the cyclic buffer, starting from an address derived from “ec” (encryption counter) using a simple algorithm (see website). These blocks are subsequently referred to as “RNR” and are extended using the HKDF-Expand function. This results in T_1, T_2, T_3, T_4, etc., each of which is 512 bits long due to SHA3-512. right next to each other.

The following function is used for this: $T_1 = HMAC_{RNR}$(„First Part“ || 0x01), $T_2 = HMAC_{RNR}$(T_1 || „Second Part“ || 0x02), $T_3 = HMAC_{RNR}$(T_2 || „Third Part“ || 0x03), and so on. This results in the Key for the One-Time Pad, which provides the actual key bits for the XOR operation used in data encryption.

Key for One-Time Pad = $T_1 \parallel T_2 \parallel T_3 \parallel T_4 \parallel T_5 \parallel T_6 \parallel$ ....

For the last data block, which may of course be shorter, correspondingly fewer bits from the Key for the One-Time Pad are used, and thus no padding is required. After the first “p” rounds, the value of “d” is changed, i.e., the interval between the bits read from the cyclic buffer. The new value of “d” is specified by the first three bytes in the cyclic buffer. However, “p” must be greater than 16,777,216; otherwise, two bytes must be used. After another “p” rounds with the new “d”, a new “d” is determined, which is specified in the second three bytes in the cyclic buffer, and so on. For example, if “d=10,” only every tenth bit is read sequentially from the cyclic buffer. This means that the three bytes in the cyclic buffer specify the value of "d," and all "d" values used must be different. If this is not the case, the corresponding three-byte block is ignored and the next one is used. A further separation occurs when the values of "d" are not part of the key bits in the cyclic buffer, i.e., they are stored separately. The combination of HKDF and "d-variation" allows the key length—i.e., the number of key bits—to be significantly increased, e.g., from 100 KByte to TBytes.

The block length for the data encryption is 512 bits. No padding is required for the last block, meaning it may be shorter. If there is only one block that is shorter, there is no security issue. OTPH allows partial encryption, i.e., the encryption/decryption of individual data blocks, and identical unencrypted data blocks $m_i = m_j$ result in different encrypted data blocks $c_i \neq c_j$. These four characteristics are important advantages of the encryption method OTPH.

When performing cryptanalysis on OTPH, one can refer to the HKDF (RFC5869). This applies fully to the first round with "d=1". Because the value of "d" is also completely random in subsequent rounds, the selection of bits in the cyclic buffer is non-deterministic and there are no deterministic dependencies.

6.4.2 OTPS Encryption Method

For OTPS, only the area in Fig. 6.5 marked with a dotted line applies. OTPS (OTP with SHAKE256) is the same as OTPH, except that SHAKE256 is used instead of HKDF. SHAKE256 has been standardized as an SHA-3 variant. SHAKE256 has an extendable output function (XOF), where the length of the hash value is not fixed, but any number of hash data can be extracted. The input length is "a = 1088," and the output length is a multiple of 1088, e.g., 4352 bits, which corresponds to seventeen 256-bit data blocks in data encryption. That is, the key is extended as early as the first round of OTPS. If, after the end of the first round, there is still insufficient key material available, further rounds are performed as described above.

The block length for the data encryption is 512 bits. No padding is required for the last block, meaning it may be shorter. If there is only one block that is shorter, there is no security issue. OTPS allows partial encryption, i.e., the encryption/decryption of individual data blocks, and identical unencrypted data blocks $m_i = m_j$ result in different encrypted data blocks $c_i \neq c_j$. These four characteristics are important advantages of the encryption method OTPS. When performing cryptanalysis on OTPS, one can refer to the SHAKE256. This applies fully to the first round with "d=1". Because the value of "d" is also completely random in subsequent rounds, the selection of bits in the cyclic buffer is non-deterministic and there are no deterministic dependencies.

For every "d" where "$0 < d \leq p-1$" the following applies to OTPH and OTPS: During sequential reading of a constant amount "a" of bits from the cyclic buffer, "p" different input blocks "RNR" can be read. According to the rules of combinatorics, this results in "$p^2 - p$" different input blocks "RNR" which can be read from the cyclic buffer. Key expansion is primarily based on the HKDF or SHAKE256. The rounds are intended only in the event that too few key bits are available for the One-Time Pad after the first round. Due to the theoretical maximum of "p^2 - p" rounds, in practice the OTPH and OTPS always provides a sufficient number of key bits if "p" is greater than one hundred thousand. This is a significant (quadratic) key expansion that, for example, increases the key length from the original 100 KByte to the TByte range when HKDF or SHAKE256 is included.

For OTPH and OTPS: An encryption counter "ec" is also required, which is stored for subsequent encryption operations. Using this counter "ec", a simple algorithm can determine the current bit position within the cyclic buffer and the parameters "r" (round counter) and "d" (read distance / spacing between two bits in the cyclic buffer) at any time (see https://cryptography.dot/phys/modes). The value "a" represents the length of the input to the HKDF or SHAKE256, while the value "ol" (output length) represents the length of the output of the HKDF or SHAKE256 (see Fig. 6.5). This output is used sequentially to encrypt the bits of the data blocks using the XOR operation. The value "ol" is a multiple of 512 (or 1088). Whenever all bits from this output have been used up—i.e., after "ol / 512" encrypted data blocks—the value "ec" (encryption counter) must be incremented by one, and "a" bits must be read from the cyclic buffer and processed with HKDF or SHAKE256.

When a new key (Key 3) of length "p" is loaded into the cyclic buffer, "ec" is reset to one ("ec = 1"). The parameters "a", "ol", and "p" must remain constant at least until a new key is loaded into the cyclic buffer. Due to the multiple use of Key 3, an HSM or another security module is required. Since modern HSMs have storage capacities in the GByte range, a specific (first) memory area within the HSM can be used to store the new key bits—such as those currently being generated via QKD or RKD—while the current key in the cyclic buffer is used for data encryption in a separate memory area. As soon as the first memory area in the HSM is filled with new key bits, a switch can be made, thereby reducing the number of rounds required.

6.4.3 XTSO Encryption Mode

XTSO (XTS with One-Time Pad, see Fig. 6.5) corresponds exactly to the XTS mode of operation (see Fig. 6.3 and 6.4), with the following difference: The second XOR function receives its input from an OTPH or OTPS, i.e., Key 3 with a cyclic buffer and HKDF or SHAKE256.

$$C_j = AES_{Key_1}\left(m_j\ XOR\ \left(AES_{Key_2}(i) \otimes j\right)\right) XOR\ OTPH/OTPSresult$$

The representation in Fig. 6.4 for the last two blocks therefore applies unchanged to this encryption mode as well, that means no padding is required, as with the XTS. Compared to XTS, the new XTSO encryption mode is much more secure due to the integration of the OTPH or OTPS encryption method.

Key generations in data storage application: The keys Key 1, Key 2, and Key 3 can be changed together, e.g., if a subject leaves a role-based authorization system and therefore loses read authorization (decryption authorization). These keys therefore also include the specification of the respective key generation G ($Key1_G$, $Key2_G$, $Key3_G$). For reasons of clarity, however, this has been deliberately omitted from the above description. Further details on OTPH, OTPS and XTSO can be requested from the first author or can be found at https://cryptography.study/phys/modes, which describes another encryption mode that includes a MAC for the security objectives of integrity and authenticity and is based on OTP, OTPH and OTPS.

References

[WP-Boo] Wikipedia contributors, "Boolean algebra," Wikipedia, The Free Encyclopedia. https://en.wikipedia.org/wiki/Boolean_algebra

[Rij22] D. Rijmenants, The complete guide to secure communications with the one time pad cipher, in *Self-Published Manuscript*, 8.1 edn., (2022). https://ciphermachinesandcryptology.com/papers/one_time_pad.pdf

[Bor12] S. Borowski, M. Lesniewicz, Modern usage of old one-time pad, in Military Communications and Information System Conference (IEEE, 2012), pp. 1–5. https://ieeexplore.ieee.org/abstract/document/6387923

[BSI] Bundesamt für Sicherheit in der Informationstechnik, "Verschlüsselung mit Software & Hardware; Hardware-based encryption," Online. https://www.bsi.bund.de/EN/Themen/Verbraucherinnen-und-Verbraucher/Informationen-und-Empfehlungen/Cyber-Sicherheitsempfehlungen/Daten-sichern-verschluesseln-und-loeschen/Datenverschluesselung/Soft-und-hardwaregestuetzte-Verschluesselung/soft-und-hardwaregestuetzte-verschluesselung.html?nn=921724#doc921720bodyText2

[Gimbut13] L. Gimbut, Datensicherheit: Was leisten externe verschlüsselte Festplatten? Datenschutz und Datensicherheit—DuD **37**(8), 526–529 (2013). https://doi.org/10.1007/s11623-013-0212-0

[WP-XTS] Wikipedia contributors, "Disk encryption theory; XTS," Wikipedia, The Free Encyclopedia. https://en.wikipedia.org/wiki/Disk_encryption_theory#XTS

[Ball12] Ball M.V, C. Guyot, J.P. Hughes, L. Martin, L. C. Noll, The XTS-AES disk encryption algorithm and the security of ciphertext stealing. Cryptologia (2012). https://doi.org/10.1080/01611194.2012.635115

[Rog04] P. Rogaway, Efficient instantiations of tweakable blockciphers and refinements to modes OCB and PMAC, in *International Conference on the Theory and Application of Cryptology and Information Security.* (Berlin, Heidelberg: Springer Berlin Heidelberg, 2004). https://doi.org/10.1007/978-3-540-30539-2_2

[WP-IEE] Wikipedia contributors, "IEEE Security in Storage Working Group; XTS," Wikipedia, The Free Encyclopedia. https://en.wikipedia.org/wiki/IEEE_Security_in_Storage_Working_Group

[IEEE18] IEEE. IEEE Std 1619-2018: "IEEE Standard for Cryptographic Protection of Data on Block-Oriented Storage Devices. IEEE ndards Association (IEEE SA)" standard web page. (2018). https://standards.ieee.org/ieee/1619/11552/

[WP-Cir] Wikipedia contributors, "Circular buffer," Wikipedia, The Free Encyclopedia. https://en.wikipedia.org/wiki/Circular_buffer

[NSCL] Facility for Rare Isotope Beams (FRIB), Michigan State University. "NSCL DAQ Software Documentation (NSCLDAQ 10.2): Chapter 1 Introduction," no date. https://docs.frib.msu.edu/daq/newsite/nscldaq-10.2/c5.html

Chapter 7
Data Storage, Procurement, Distribution Logistics

This chapter deals with three practical aspects:

1. Data encryption for data storage on PCs.
2. Procurement of QKD, RKD, and MKD products with consideration for IT security.
3. Distribution logistics for MKD: Secure logistics for the distribution of storage media for MKD.

7.1 Role-Based Data Encryption

Data is usually stored in databases or files. Role-based or attribute-based access control systems are typically used for access control. These determine rights such as read, write, and delete. In conjunction with cryptography, cryptographic access control systems are required which, in role-based or attribute-based systems, only recognize encryption/decryption rights, from which read rights in particular can then be directly derived (reading is only possible through successful decryption). Only users (subjects) who have read rights for a specific role receive the corresponding key to decrypt the data that the role contains as objects—they cannot therefore decrypt and read any other data. For reasons of speed, only symmetric methods such as AES or the one-time pad with different encryption modes (see Chap. 6.4) are suitable for encryption/decryption and MAC calculation. In contrast to telecommunications, the keys must be retained for as long as the encrypted data is stored and relevant for reading. This can be many years.

The required keys are determined based on roles/attributes. In a role-based system, each role is assigned a key, which usually originates from administrators (role managers) of the role. When authorized users (subjects) leave a role, a new key must be determined by an administrator of the role. Once all data relevant to this role has been re-encrypted, only the new role key is required. In the other case, which is

E. Piller and H. Schölnast, *Data Encryption at the Intersection of Mathematics and Physics*, SpringerBriefs in Information Security and Cryptography,
https://doi.org/10.1007/978-3-032-24764-3_7

common in decentralized systems, all older role keys must also be retained. In this case, the number of required keys increases constantly. Over the years, this can result in a large number of keys, all of which must be stored securely over a long period of time. For details, see also Chap. 5.3.2.

7.1.1 MKD Solution LISA

There is currently only one product available on the market called "LISA".[1] It is the only product that can fully meet the processes described in Chap. 5.3 and the requirements for MKD (see Chap. 5) and the encryption modes (see Chap. 6.4). LISA is available for PC operating systems and was developed, among other things, to enable the full use of MKD for data storage on desktop PCs, laptops, tablets, etc.

In addition to a solution with smart cards, TPM chips, and AES encryption, LISA also offers completely math-free cryptography (except for the XOR function) with a one-time pad for highly sensitive data through the complete implementation of MKD technology. This applies on a role-based basis to all files and individual elements of the rows and columns of a database. LISA is also available as a LISA workstation with the entire LISA software (see above), in which conventional PCs from the market, e.g., laptops, can be operated with several parallel virtual workstations with different security levels at the operating system level, from open (as is usual for PCs) to closed (highly secure).

7.2 Procurement of QKD, RKD, and MKD Products with Consideration for IT Security

Physical methods always require hardware for implementation in practice. This means that hardware and software are always required for QKD, RKD, and MKD in practical use. With regard to the mathematical methods used in physical methods, strict care must be taken to ensure that all methods used are secure against mathematically very strong opponents and mathematical attack methods that are still unknown (unpublished) today. For a purchaser and user of the devices and software, hereinafter referred to as the product, this is only possible if the mathematical methods used in each product are fully disclosed. Security certifications alone are not sufficient to provide an adequate picture.

Security certifications are important in the high-security sector, but they only cover part of the picture, as successful attacks in the past have shown. They show only a snapshot of a specific environment at the time of certification and not in the user's later overall system or at a later point in time. Past experience has shown that not only have attack scenarios expanded and were not included in the original

[1] https://www.insitu.software

certification process, but that vendors also made changes to the product without new certification. In the past, these changes have also included targeted sabotage and espionage functions. These targeted and significant product deteriorations after certification have also been carried out by reputable providers and in the context of high-security products.

For products (hardware and software from QKD, RKD, and MKD), there is also the problem of supply chains. Hardware and software supply chains are becoming increasingly global and complex, posing major challenges and dependencies for manufacturers, suppliers, and end customers. Multiple components designed, developed, and manufactured in different countries are combined to produce a single piece of hardware or software, which is then purchased by a procurer through a single vendor/supplier. Every player in the global product supply chain has a responsibility to ensure the necessary security and resilience of the product against attacks. However, due to the complexity of the product and the supply chain, effective assurance and verification of defined security are often only possible to a limited extent. This creates the risk that procurers are often unaware of the security level and security vulnerabilities of the products and have no or only limited traceability and control over the products. They may purchase products with integrated sabotage or espionage functions, deliberate vulnerabilities, etc.

The simpler a product is, the more manageable the supply chains and the traceability of security assessments usually are. For example, MKD with One-Time Pad consists of only three main components: the storage media, the random number generators, and the smart cards. In addition, all three of these main components are available as mass-produced goods on the global market. (In terms of hardware, RKD also consists only of mass-produced goods from the global market.) This circumstance has a very positive effect on price, availability/deliverability, maintenance/service, manufacturer/supplier change, and, to a limited extent, security assessments. The smart cards pose the lowest risk because they come from global payment transactions, mobile communications, and passports, which have a very high attack potential, and are certified and regularly tested accordingly. The random number generators are the main component at MKD with the greatest risk of attack and are therefore the central security component. Anyone who succeeds in influencing the generation of random numbers does not need to attack the storage media, the third main component. The random number generators contain an internal mechanism with a few suppliers of subcomponents, which in turn have further suppliers. The entropy of the generated bits (randomness) is the essential performance criterion and can be checked externally, at least to a limited extent, without knowing the current inner workings of a product. From a security perspective, it must also be noted that entropy does not only apply for a limited period of time in order to pass tests. Therefore, checks should also be repeated at a later date. Then there is the danger of artificial radiation that has been deliberately integrated into the product. In MKD, multiple different random number generators are always used, and the random numbers (key bits) are XORed so that an attack or a faulty generator does not affect the key quality (see Sect. 5.2.4). The third and most complex main component in MKD is the storage medium. In terms of security, the main concern here is the AES-256 HW encryption unit. The rest are

MKD-enabled memory sticks or SSDs from the global market. If the key for the internal HW encryption unit is not stored in the storage medium, the only question is whether the encryption unit works according to specifications and does not contain any artificial radiation, etc. Because this is a unit built into the product by a supplier, the supplier must be trusted. Regular monitoring of this supplier by the manufacturer of the MKD-compatible storage medium is important, but often cannot be carried out by the purchaser, or only to a limited extent.

This brief description, which is not yet complete for MKD, shows how quickly complexity can increase and limitations can become insurmountable. RKD is already more complex, and QKD in particular contains a significantly larger number of individual components that come from different suppliers, who in turn require further suppliers, and which can open up security gaps for themselves and the entire product. QKD primarily involves highly complex components such as photon sources, photon detectors, etc., the mathematical methods used for key post-processing and protocols, transmission paths, highly complex trusted nodes, satellites, etc. QKD also enables a variety of side-channel attacks that must be taken into account. QKD is far more complex than MKD and RKD and thus involves issues such as supply chains, the security of individual components and suppliers, etc.

In addition, in the high-security sector, the security offered should also be verifiable by the purchaser at any time, which already poses some challenges with MKD, as mentioned above, with few subcomponents, suppliers, and no mathematical procedures whatsoever.

In the field of high-security cryptography, purchasers are often ministries, military, intelligence services, companies with data that is critical to their survival, etc. who also want to carry out security checks relevant to them at any time—i.e., not only upon initial delivery— and want to have an up-to-date overview of the threat situation at all times.

Therefore, the following minimum requirements have been developed for QKD, RKD, and MKD, which every provider/supplier of a product must offer:

- The product requires the necessary security certifications (CC—Common Criteria, EUCC—European Cybersecurity Certification, FIPS, etc.) from independent, recognized certification institutes.
- Availability of current and time-critical information on vulnerabilities and security risks affecting the product, in particular that providers/suppliers inform purchasers as soon as possible if another customer with the same product identifies and reports any, or if the supplier or one of its suppliers or customers has identified any.
- Disclosure of all known side-channel attacks at the time of the procurement process and later if new ones become known.
- Disclosure of all mathematical procedures and protocols in the product.
- Liability on the part of the provider/supplier and its subcontractors for unreported security vulnerabilities and lack of controls in the supply chain.
- Contractual agreements (service level agreements) with the provider/supplier of a product regarding risk management measures, handling of cybersecurity incidents, and patch management.

In addition to the mandatory requirements listed above, the following recommended requirements are helpful:

- The purchaser should be given sufficient opportunity to conduct its own security checks and security evaluations, which cover the suppliers and their subcontractors and are not limited to the beginning of the life cycle, but can also be carried out regularly at a later stage. To this end, the purchaser should be informed of all components of the product that are critical to security during the procurement process and later, if changes occur. This also includes all components where sabotage or espionage functions and deliberate security vulnerabilities can be integrated.
- Notification of the various suppliers of security-critical components and minimum verifiability of these suppliers (also by purchasers and not only by vendors/ suppliers).
- A purchaser should not only know their supplier, but also, upon request, receive relevant information about the entire supply chain affected by security-critical components. In Europe, the EU Supply Chain Regulation [EU24[2]], which is currently the subject of heated debate and controversy, deals with similar aspects, even if the reasons behind it are different. There are many known cases where products have been tampered with during the supply chain by integrating espionage or sabotage functions into the devices during transport. The topic is usually addressed under terms such as supply chain attacks, hardware implants, supply chain manipulation, or hardware tampering [Hua17,[3] Huang17,[4], Perl21[5] Snow19,[6] BSINis2,[7] Scheme n23[8]].

In Europe, the NIS 2 Directive [EU22[9]] requires important and particularly important organizations to implement comprehensive risk management measures. This includes "the security of the supply chain, including security-related aspects of the relationships between the individual organizations and their immediate suppliers or service providers" (Article 21(2)(d) and Article 21(3) NIS 2 Directive).

In the case of QKD, RKD, and MKD products, the supplier or manufacturer of the product determines the security requirements of the product. This means that the purchaser can only make specifications to the supplier or manufacturer during the product selection process, where they compare their security requirements with the products on offer and in terms of the measures to be taken. In the case of these

---

[2] https://data.europa.eu/eli/dir/2024/1760/oj

[3] doi:10.5555/3153234

[4] https://www.kea.nu/files/textbooks/humblesec/thehardwarehacker.pdf

[5] https://thisishowtheytellmetheworldends.com

[6] https://en.wikipedia.org/wiki/Permanent_Record_(autobiography)

[7] https://www.bsi.bund.de/DE/Themen/Regulierte-Wirtschaft/NIS-2-regulierte-Unternehmen/NIS-2-Infopakete/NIS-2-Lieferkette/NIS-2-Lieferkette_node.html

[8] https://www.theguardian.com/commentisfree/2013/sep/05/government-betrayed-internet-nsa-spying

[9] https://data.europa.eu/eli/dir/2022/2555/oj

measures, the purchaser often only has comparison options that influence the procurement decision, and they can regulate some aspects of the purchase, leasing, or rental agreement, insofar as this is possible with the supplier. Trust in the supplier and the origin of the product also play a role. The purchaser must be able to rely on the fact that the products delivered have not been tampered with and do not have any hidden functions or deliberately built-in vulnerabilities. A trustworthy supply chain means: verified origin, tested components, and traceable processes. Incidents not only jeopardize sensitive information, but also a company's trust, ability to act, and reputation. The origin of a product and the suppliers (subcontractors) of security-critical components often have a direct influence on the trust placed in the product. One reason for this is the numerous reports and books. Research into such articles gives the impression that products from certain countries are particularly affected by these cases.

Further details on the consideration of security aspects in procurement are described in [Pill16[10]].

7.3 Distribution Logistics

With MKD, key exchange does not take place via telecommunications, e.g., using asymmetric cryptography (e.g., Diffie-Hellman key exchange), or light quanta (QKD), or radio waves (RKD), but rather by transporting the storage media. The storage media can be high-security smart cards, etc. or MKD-enabled portable storage media for encryption with a one-time pad. Therefore, the major challenges of MKD lie in the scaling, organization, and logistical implementation of physical key distribution. These challenges are clearly identifiable, analytically accessible, and not obscured by idealized assumptions about technical components or transmission channels. MKD thus deliberately shifts security-related issues to an area characterized by processes, responsibilities, and control.

Therefore, the logistics of distributing storage media play an important role in MKD. In the following, no distinction is made as to whether the storage medium is a smart card or an MKD-enabled storage medium.

This chapter is devoted to this logistics, taking into account not only the distribution of smart cards as key data carriers for mathematical procedures or MKD-enabled storage media with key bits, but also the separate distribution of smart cards used to distribute the key for the internal encryption unit of MKD-enabled storage media. Because MKD is not of interest to the mass market, but primarily to the high-security sector, the number of end devices will usually not be very high in practice, and the distribution of storage media and smart cards will therefore remain manageable. Nevertheless, it must be noted that in telecommunications, each possible pair of

[10] https://www.springerprofessional.de/beschaffung-unter-beruecksichtigung-der-it-sicherheit/12357132

communication partners requires its own key pair, which means a maximum of $(n^2 - n)/2$ key pairs for n end devices.

With MKD, it must also always be borne in mind that cryptographic keys are generated and distributed here, which are then used later to encrypt potentially secret or strictly confidential data. Improper generation of keys or distribution of storage media and smart cards can therefore have legal consequences and cause significant political or economic damage.

The following aspects are discussed below:

- Documented chain of custody (CoC) for MKD.
- Selection by third parties or communication partners.
- Special case of timely distribution (only required for key renewal in the event of subject deletions).
- IT support.

7.3.1 Documented Chain of Custody (CoC) for the Creation and Distribution of Storage Media and Smart Cards

This chapter is completely independent of MKD and of whether the keys are distributed using high-security smart cards or MKD-compatible storage media.

With a CoC, the generation of keys and distribution of key media and smart cards are seamlessly documented, enabling precise tracking. Today, a CoC is essential in areas such as medical devices, forensics, justice, quality management, and supply chain certification, but it is also important for MKD due to its use in high-security areas.

7.3.2 What Does a Documented CoC Include?

It includes the following:

- **Chronological Trail:** Every handover and check is seamlessly documented with a time stamp, location, and responsible person and/or device (laptop, desktop PC, etc.). These processes must be recorded with IT support (e.g., using a smartphone) so that an up-to-date overview can always be accessed. Electronic CoC systems (known as eCOC) are available for this purpose. These processes must be documented flawlessly and in full at all times. Otherwise, tracking is impossible.
- **Identification of the Storage Medium and Transfer Location:** Unique identification, e.g., by means of a QR code (ISO/IEC 18004) or matrix code (ISO/IEC 16022 and 24,720), on all storage media and smart cards, to avoid confusion. In addition, the transfer location must be entered. This can be a terminal

device (laptop, desktop PC, etc., with a QR or matrix code), but also just a location where the storage medium or smart card was handed over. There must be no confusion, because highly secure cryptographic keys are being handed over here. Even though in practice, with MKD-enabled storage media, the actual handover of the keys only takes place via the smart card, the handover of the storage media must also be carried out correctly, or at least be precisely traceable.

- **Responsibilities:** All roles in key generation, distribution and handover of storage media and smart cards, IT processing, etc. must be defined in advance, e.g., via the policy, and it must be possible to determine who did what with which storage media and smart cards and when. All resulting documentation must be traceable and verifiable. This also enables complete auditability of the CoC and, subsequently, the entire generation and distribution of keys at any time.
- **Security Measures:** Access restrictions to the storage media must be defined in advance (e.g., as part of the policy) and, above all, they are technically controlled in a highly secure manner in the real environment via the smart cards that contain the keys for the integrated AES encryption. In addition, the entire IT-controlled input and processing of the CoC must be sufficiently secured so that it cannot be manipulated. Therefore, the most important step when using MKD-enabled storage media is the correct distribution of smart cards, which must be done only once and, if possible, in person by the communication partners in telecommunications and role administrators in data storage. Trusted third parties are also possible here, but should only be the second choice, except for longer distances, and public service providers should absolutely not be allowed.
- **Training of all Parties Involved:** All parties involved, including users of storage media and smart cards, must be adequately trained to ensure that the policy is fully implemented and the CoC is implemented professionally and securely. Training must also be updated.

There are eCoC tools on the market that can detect certain errors in a real eCoC and automatically send out warnings.

7.3.3 Selection by Third Parties or Communication Partners

When storing data with a role-based access control system, the keys are generated by role administrators.

In telecommunications, keys can be generated by the communication partners themselves, but also by selected third parties.

A policy and the exact CoC procedure must be established for the generation and distribution of storage media and smart cards. It must also be specified whether and when public service providers may be used for distribution.

7.3.4 Timely Distribution

This is necessary when a subject leaves a role in a role-based system. In this case, the role key must be replaced with a new one in a solution variant—when using a one-time pad, a larger number of key bits (e.g., 1 TB) must be replaced. This key change must be carried out for all subjects (authorized persons) of the role within a general synchronization pause of a few seconds at a precisely defined point in time. Therefore, when determining this point in time, MKD must take into account the maximum time required for physical key distribution to all active subjects. Currently, passive subjects, e.g., those who are on vacation, can be excluded from this.

7.3.5 IT Support

These processes must be recorded with IT support so that an up-to-date overview can always be accessed. Electronic CoC systems (known as eCoC) are available for this purpose.

For MKD with one-time pads, such an eCoC has just been developed that takes into account all the special features of MKD and supports distribution for storage media and smart cards (see https://cryptography.study/phys/eCoC). Smartphones are used as end devices for the eCoC, and any PC can serve as a server. This solution is to be used in conjunction with the solution described in the chapter "Practical implementation in telecommunications and data storage."

References

[EU24] European Parliament; Council of the European Union. "Directive (EU) 2024/1760 of 13 June 2024 on corporate sustainability due diligence and amending Directive (EU) 2019/1937 and Regulation (EU) 2023/2859." Off. J. Eur. Union, L 2024/1760, (2024). https://data.europa.eu/eli/dir/2024/1760/oj

[Hua17] A. Huang, *The Hardware Hacker: Adventures in Making and Breaking Hardware* (No Starch Press, San Francisco, CA, 2017). https://doi.org/10.5555/3153234

[Huang17] Huang, Andrew, *The Hardware Hacker: Adventures in Making and Breaking Hardware*. (No Starch Press, 2017), ISBN 978–1–59327-758-1. https://www.kea.nu/files/textbooks/humblesec/thehardwarehacker.pdf

[Perl21] N. Perlroth, This Is How They Tell Me The World Ends: The Cyberweapons Arms Race. (Bloomsbury Publishing, 2021), ISBN 9781526629852. https://thisishowtheytellmetheworldends.com

[Snow19] E. Snowden, *Permanent Record*," Metropolitan Books / Henry Holt, (2019), ISBN 978–1250237231. https://en.wikipedia.org/wiki/Permanent_Record_(autobiography)

[BSINis2] BSI. "#nis2know Sichere Lieferkette", (web page), no date; https://www.bsi.bund.de/DE/Themen/Regulierte-Wirtschaft/NIS-2-regulierte-Unternehmen/NIS-2-Infopakete/

NIS-2-Lieferkette/NIS-2-Lieferkette_node.html[Schn23] S. Bruce, The US government has betrayed the internet. We need to take it back," (2013). https://www.theguardian.com/commentisfree/2013/sep/05/government-betrayed-internet-nsa-spying

[EU22] European Parliament; Council of the European Union. "Directive (EU) 2022/2555 of 14 December 2022 on measures for a high common level of cybersecurity across the Union, amending Regulation (EU) No 910/2014 and Directive (EU) 2018/1972, and repealing Directive (EU) 2016/1148 (NIS 2 Directive)." Off. J. Eur. Union, L 333, (2022). https://data.europa.eu/eli/dir/2022/2555/oj

[Pill16] E. Piller, *Berücksichtigung der IT-Sicherheit bei der Beschaffung*. (Springer-Vieweg, 2016). https://www.springerprofessional.de/beschaffung-unter-beruecksichtigung-der-it-sicherheit/12357132

Chapter 8
Mathematical Key Postprocessing

In both QKD and RKD, raw keys are generated that are subject to errors. In order to remove errors from the keys, i.e., to ensure that both sides have identical keys, error correction is necessary after the actual key exchange. To perform this error correction, the two parties who carried out the key exchange need to exchange additional data. This data could fall into the hands of a listening attacker and provide them with information that could help them guess the true key more quickly and reliably. To prevent this, privacy amplification is also performed in QKD and RKD technologies after error correction.

8.1 Error Estimation

Before the actual error correction, the quality of the raw data generated is estimated. The aim of this step is to determine the extent to which the raw bit sequences available to the two communication partners differ and whether key generation can be continued securely under the given conditions.

For the security assessment, it is conservatively assumed that every error that is later eliminated by error correction is to be regarded as information that has potentially become known to an attacker. Even though it is clear that a significant proportion of these errors are caused in practice by noise, attenuation, and other physical effects.

To this end, selected parts of the raw data or statistical parameters derived from it are exchanged via the public communication channel. On this basis, an error or deviation rate is determined, which indicates how many bits of the two raw sequences are likely to not match. In QKD, the quantum bit error rate (QBER) is typically used for this purpose, while in RKD a corresponding bit deviation rate derived from the measured values is used. The underlying principle is identical in both cases.

E. Piller and H. Schölnast, *Data Encryption at the Intersection of Mathematics and Physics*, SpringerBriefs in Information Security and Cryptography,
https://doi.org/10.1007/978-3-032-24764-3_8

The quality indicator found determines both the effort required for error correction and the necessary reduction in key length within the framework of privacy amplification.

8.2 Error Correction

Alice and Bob send each other bit sequences that are much shorter than the raw keys, but contain statistical information about these keys that the respective other party can use for error correction. The information transmitted for the purpose of error correction can essentially be thought of as parity information or, more generally, redundancy information, i.e., in the broadest sense, something like check digits. In practice, interactive methods such as cascade [Tup23][1] or unilateral methods such as LDPC/Polar codes [Kik20][2] are used. However, a detailed description of these methods will not be provided here.

With the help of the exchanged parity or redundancy information, Alice and Bob can identify the positions where they have differing bits in their bit sequences, and they can also use this information to agree on identical bit values at these positions without directly transmitting the specific positions or bit values. At the end of the error correction process, they calculate short hash values from the bit sequences they have received, which they send to each other and compare in order to be absolutely sure that they now have exactly identical bit sequences. In fact, despite these measures, there remains a minimal residual risk of receiving different keys. However, the size of this residual risk is adjustable and is usually so extremely small that it can be considered practically secure.

Eve can read the exchanged parity information and hash values. This does not give her any information about specific individual bits in the key, but if Eve knew before the error correction that the key consisted of, for example, 300 bits, and the information exchanged for the error correction was 30 bits long, then the number of possible keys is reduced from 2^{300} to 2^{270}. This is still an astronomical number, but it is only about one billionth of the original number of possible keys. This reduction in the number of keys is systematically taken into account in the next step through privacy amplification.

8.3 Privacy Amplification

By publicly disclosing the error correction data, Eve obtains a certain amount of information that is also contained in the now corrected and identical raw keys. (In the example above, the information content of this amount of information is 30

[1] https://doi.org/10.1103/PhysRevApplied.20.064040.

[2] https://doi.org/10.1109/LCOMM.2020.3021142.

Shannon because it is 30 bits long and cannot be compressed.) Although this is essentially only general parity information, if you have enough of it, you can make well-founded assumptions about the finished key, which, at least in theory, make it a little easier for the attacker to reconstruct parts of the key.

To prevent this, the information-theoretical amount of information in the finished key must be reduced, at least by the amount of information contained in the error correction data. To stick with the example: The 300-bit-long non-compressible raw key has an information content of 300 Shannon, the error correction data contains 30 Shannon, so the key must be reduced to such an extent that it can only hold a maximum of 270 Shannon. This amounts to a reduction to a maximum of 270 bits, but you cannot simply delete 30 bits; instead, you must distribute the original information evenly across all remaining bits.

Another reason for this step is the errors themselves. Although it is known that most errors occur without any involvement from an attacker, it cannot be ruled out with certainty for any single different bit that it may have been caused by eavesdropping. Therefore, it is always decided to assume that every error is information that has fallen into Eve's hands. This is handled in a similar way to error correction data, which is also assumed to be known to the attacker: the amount of information in the keys is reduced by at least the maximum amount of information that an attacker could have obtained. This step is called "privacy amplification." The preceding estimation of the amount of information that an attacker could have obtained in the worst case (i.e., the number of bits by which the key must be shortened) is usually referred to as "leakage accounting" [Tom12].[3]

The Basic Procedure Is as Follows:

First, Alice and Bob exchange small parts of their keys to determine the quantum bit error rate (QBER, see above), and they count how much information they have exchanged with each other due to error correction. They subtract these two values and an additional security buffer from the raw key length to obtain the desired length of the final key.

Alice then uses a random number generator to create a random bit sequence that must not be related to the key currently being processed. This means that it must not be derived from this key in the form of a hash value or by other methods, but must be independent of it. However, it may be derived from a previously exchanged key, which may no longer be used for encryption afterwards. This random bit sequence is as long as the input key length plus the output key length. Alice transmits this bit sequence to Bob via the public classical side channel. From this, Alice and Bob generate the same matrix (a Toeplitz matrix over the residue field Z2 [WP–Toe,[4] WP–Res[5]]). They interpret the key they received after error correction as a vector, multiply it by the Toeplitz matrix, and thereby obtain a new vector in the desired shorter length, which they interpret again as a bit sequence. This matrix multiplication acts as a

[3] https://doi.org/10.1038/ncomms1631.

[4] https://en.wikipedia.org/wiki/Toeplitz_matrix.

[5] https://en.wikipedia.org/wiki/Residue_field.

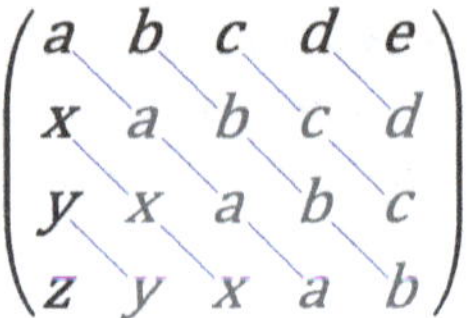

Fig. 8.1 General form of a Toeplitz matrix

universal hash function here. If the matrix was chosen randomly and independently of the key to be processed, each bit of the finished key depends equally on all bits of the input key, and the original amount of information was distributed completely evenly across all result bits. (Changing a single bit of the input key will, in the most likely case, flip exactly 50% of all bits in the finished key. The following also applies: if you want to change only a single bit of the result, you normally have to flip around 50% of all bits of the input key.)

Even if Eve was able to make certain assumptions about individual bits or bit combinations after error correction, she now has no information whatsoever about individual bits or bit combinations in the finished key.

Example of Multiplication with a Toeplitz Matrix

A Toeplitz matrix is completely defined by its values on the left and top edges. The value of every other cell is identical to the value of its neighbor diagonally above the cell, as shown in Fig. 8.1.

In privacy amplification, all entries in the Toeplitz matrix are bit values (0 or 1), with the values on the left and top edges being random values and the others being as described.

In the following example, the key after error correction is 5 bits long and is interpreted as a column vector. It is multiplied from the left by a 3x5 Toeplitz matrix with the properties described above in order to obtain a 3-bit-long secure key after privacy amplification. (The length is thus reduced by 2 bits.)

$$\begin{pmatrix} 1\,1 & 0\,1\,1 \\ 0\,1 & 1\,0\,1 \\ 1\,0 & 1\,1\,0 \end{pmatrix} \begin{pmatrix} 0 \\ 1 \\ 1 \\ 0 \\ 1 \end{pmatrix} \bmod 2 = \begin{pmatrix} 0 \\ 1 \\ 1 \end{pmatrix}.$$

In a "normal" matrix multiplication, the result would have been $\begin{pmatrix} 2 \\ 3 \\ 1 \end{pmatrix}$, but "mod 2" takes the remainder when dividing by 2, resulting in the result shown.

Since these are bit values that can only be 0 or 1, the individual elementary multiplications can also be interpreted as logical AND operations. And if, instead of the usual summation, an XOR operation is performed on the intermediate results, the desired bit values are obtained immediately. The entire process can therefore be reduced to very simple logical operations that can be performed at very high speed in specialized hardware and also deliver very high performance in standard processor chips.

References

[Tup23] Tupkary, Devashish, L. Norbert, Using cascade in quantum key distribution. Phys. Rev. Appl. **20**(6), 064040 (2023). https://doi.org/10.1103/PhysRevApplied.20.064040

[Kik20] Kiktenko, O. Evgeniy, et al., Blind information reconciliation with polar codes for quantum key distribution. IEEE Commun. Lett. **25**(1), 79–83 (2020). https://doi.org/10.1109/LCOMM.2020.3021142

[Tom12] Tomamichel, Marco, et al., Tight finite-key analysis for quantum cryptography. Nat. Commun. **3**(1), 634 (2012). https://doi.org/10.1038/ncomms1631

[WP-Toe] Wikipedia contributors, "Toeplitz matrix," Wikipedia, The Free Encyclopedia. https://en.wikipedia.org/wiki/Toeplitz_matrix

[WP-Res] Wikipedia contributors, "Residue field," Wikipedia, The Free Encyclopedia. https://en.wikipedia.org/wiki/Residue_field

Chapter 9
Concluding Remarks and Summary

9.1 Achievability of Security Objectives

9.1.1 Confidentiality

As already explained at the beginning (in sect.2.6.1), mathematically provable confidentiality can only be achieved with the one-time pad method. All other encryption methods only achieve a certain degree of practically achievable confidentiality for which there is no rigorous proof, meaning that the possibility of a breach of confidentiality cannot be completely ruled out. The physical methods for generating and distributing cryptographic keys described in this book do not change this.

So, if you are not satisfied with practically achievable confidentiality for which there is no solid proof, you have to use the one-time pad, which in practice means that you need at least as much key material as you want to send or store in encrypted data.

QKD

The key rates currently achievable with QKD are sufficient for key material that can be used for AES encryption with frequently changing keys. (AES-256 is often used for this purpose.) The rate at which these AES keys can be changed depends on the key rate. If an average of 1000 bits/sec is generated, this is sufficient for approximately 4 key changes per second, which already achieves an extremely high level of practical confidentiality. But as mentioned, provable confidentiality can only be achieved with one-time pad encryption.

In QKD with entangled photons, the key rate for a one-time pad is also usually too low, especially in connection with satellites, where only a few bits per second can currently be achieved. For transmissions using optical fibers, the key rates for QKD are currently limited to a maximum of a few kilobits per second over longer distances (see Chap.3). For 1 TB of data, a key rate of 10 kbit/sec requires around

E. Piller and H. Schölnast, *Data Encryption at the Intersection of Mathematics and Physics*, SpringerBriefs in Information Security and Cryptography,
https://doi.org/10.1007/978-3-032-24764-3_9

25 years of continuous key exchange. However, significant improvements in this area are expected for QKD over the next ten years. But as the past has shown, data volumes are also constantly increasing, which means that this race may only ever lead to limited success for QKD.

RKD

With RKD, a one-time pad cannot be used for data encryption because the key rate is very low. (Feasible values are a few bits per second, and this key rate can hardly be improved). However, AES encryption with frequently changing keys can still be implemented at very low cost if one is satisfied with changing the key every minute or less frequently.

MKD

Only MKD can currently exchange up to 16 TB of key material per transfer with a data carrier in a cost-effective and highly secure manner, thus guaranteeing the ideal use of the one-time pad. Today, very fast generators based on quantum mechanics require around 9 hours to generate non-deterministic random numbers for 1 TB of key material. MKD in conjunction with one-time pads therefore makes it possible to fully achieve the protection goal of mathematically provable confidentiality with today's state-of-the-art technology, at comparatively low cost, for large amounts of data, and without having to accept any losses due to the distance between the communication partners. And even if the amount of data to be encrypted should exceed the capacity of today's data carriers in the future, it can be assumed that the capacities of data carriers will grow at approximately the same rate.

9.1.2 Integrity and Authenticity

During Key Generation with QKD and RKD

In the case of QKD and RKD, integrity and authenticity during key generation must be ensured on the public channel by one of the methods already mentioned in sect.2.6.2., for example, by the Wegman-Carter method [1].[1] These methods derive their security from the mathematically strictly limited collision resistance of the hash function used, which in turn can be increased arbitrarily by enlarging the MAC tag [2].[2] However, MAC tags longer than a few hundred bits do not increase the actual overall security that can be achieved, because above a certain length of MAC tags, the probability of a hash collision is already so extremely low that other risks dominate (e.g., undetected implementation errors in the hardware or software of the communication devices). But the good news here is that although an attacker can use brute force methods to try to cause a hash collision in order to attach a MAC tag

[1] https://doi.org/10.1016/0022-0000(81)90033-7.

[2] https://en.wikipedia.org/wiki/Message_authentication_code.

generated by the legitimate sender to a manipulated message without being noticed, it can be mathematically proven that it is impossible to develop an algorithm for this that is significantly more efficient than blind trial and error. (This assumes that the hash function used meets certain criteria, which are met in all common implementations.)

For the key exchange methods examined, this means that a certain portion of the key material must be branched off to ensure integrity. This portion represents a small percentage of the key set used for encryption and is therefore proportional to it. This in turn means that, from an integrity standpoint, nothing can be said about QKD, RKD, and MKD that does not already apply due to confidentiality.

During Key Transport with MKD

In the case of MKD, key generation and key transport are separate steps. Since key generation takes place before transport with the help of non-deterministic random number generators and excludes other partners, no special measures are necessary to secure this step. The same applies to the merging of the self-generated material with the partner's key material in the XOR link after transport.

With MKD, the transport itself is carried out physically and separately in two stages, with the storage medium containing the encrypted key being transported separately from the smart card. The smart card contains the key used to encrypt the key on the storage medium. Integrity can be achieved through cryptographic methods, but is also physically ensured by access protection to the storage media and smart cards. Authenticity is ensured by the smart card with a PIN and by the authentication of the start and destination addresses during transport (see Sect. 7.3 eCoC).

9.2 Comparison According to Criteria Relevant to Practice

9.2.1 Technological Maturity and Availability

The physical methods considered for generating and distributing cryptographic keys vary considerably in terms of their technological maturity. These differences stem less from the fundamental functionality of the underlying physical principles than from the degree of their technical maturity, system integration, and long-term operational experience. For this reason, experimental concepts, pilot applications, and systems with limited usability are considered separately.

Some of the quantum-based methods/technologies, in particular selected QKD approaches, have clearly moved beyond the stage of pure laboratory research. Integrated systems exist for these methods that can be operated under controlled conditions in test networks or in clearly defined application scenarios. However, these forms of application are often limited by specific infrastructural requirements, limited ranges, or increased operational requirements. Other QKD variants, on the other hand, are still in the experimental testing or conceptual development stage, where essential properties have been demonstrated in principle, but it is not yet possible to make a reliable statement about their suitability for everyday use.

The state of research for RKD is also very advanced, but only one manufacturer is currently known to have a marketable product, which has not yet been certified for security.

For MKD, all the necessary components are available on the market in a wide range. They are security-certified (up to classified information) and available worldwide at low cost.

When assessing the degree of maturity, it is crucial to determine whether a process/technology is available as a closed, reproducible system or is primarily implemented as a combination of specialized individual components. Processes/technologies based on complex, sensitive, or only partially standardized components require considerable integration and operational effort in practice that goes beyond a mere demonstration of functionality. In contrast, physical approaches based on simple, well-understood, and independently verifiable components are easier to understand, implement, and manage organizationally, even if they are less formalized.

The state of standardization is another indicator of maturity, but it is not synonymous with broad applicability. While standardized interfaces and protocols can facilitate integration, they say little about long-term maintainability, operating costs, or dependencies on specific implementations. For a reliable assessment of technological maturity, it is therefore always necessary to consider the interplay between system availability, operational stability, integration effort, and organizational viability.

9.2.2 Key Rates, Range, and Scaling

Key rates and ranges are difficult to compare not only technologically but also conceptually in the methods/technologies under consideration: In the literature, "raw key," "sifted key," and "secret key rate (SKR)" are not always used consistently, and it is not always clear whether post-processing (error correction, privacy amplification) has already been fully taken into account. Where possible, the following information therefore explicitly uses values that are identified as secret key rates. Otherwise, they are classified as practical orders of magnitude or boundary conditions.

Technology class	Typical distance or attenuation	Practical key rate (order of magnitude)	Comments
DV-QKD	approx. 10–20 km (2–5 dB)	several kbit/s to several tens of kbit/s	advantageous conditions, short distances
	approx. 50–80 km (10–26 dB)	usually 100–1000 bit/s	typical for field tests and continuous operation

(continued)

(continued)

Technology class	Typical distance or attenuation	Practical key rate (order of magnitude)	Comments
	approx. 120–200 km (24–40 dB)	usually 10–100 bit/s	border range, only usable to a limited extent
CV-QKD	up to approx. 40 km (up to 8 dB)	usually 1–10 kbit/s	short distances, sensitive to noise
	approx. 50–100 km (10–20 dB)	usually 10–100 bit/s	practical working range
QKD with entanglement	approx. 10–50 km (2–10 dB)	usually 10–100 bits/s	highly dependent on source and detection
	over 70 km	less than 100 bits/s	experimental limit range
RKD	local radio connection, usually under 15 km	usually 1–10 bit/s	systemically limited, hardly scalable
MKD	physical transport of a data carrier	up to 16 TB per transfer; up to 240 Mbit/s (also 7 Gbit/s) during creation	not limited by transport, but by generation

For QKD over fiber optics, field tests and cross-manufacturer evaluations consistently show that the actual usable secret key rate (final key rate) drops sharply as channel attenuation increases. In the range of approximately 10–20 dB, practical values are often in the upper double-digit to lower four-digit bit/s range; at 25–30 dB, only a few hundred bit/s or less are often achieved. These orders of magnitude are found independently of the specific product and reflect the physically induced losses.

RKD is classified in this book as fundamentally very cost-effective and suitable for mobility (RKD requires movement), but at the same time as severely limited in terms of key rate and distance.

MKD follows a different metric: the "key rate" is effectively derived from the combination of

1. The amount of non-deterministic key bits that can be generated (e.g., 1 TB in approx. 9 hours with very fast random number generators) and.
2. Logistical transferability. The capacity per transfer is stated as up to 16 TB of key bytes, although there is no reason why several data carriers cannot be transported at the same time.

In the case of MKD, this shifts the performance limit from transmission losses, etc. to generation and logistics parameters. In order to classify MKD in terms of key rates, it must be taken into account that transporting a single, handy, and comparatively inexpensive 16-TB data carrier involves exchanging as much key material as QKD (at 1000 bit/s) does in more than 4000 years. Even if fast QKD solutions reaching speeds of 1 Mbit/s were to become available in a few years, they would have to be operated for four years to keep up with the physical transport of a single data carrier.

Therefore, the key rates for MKD are also sufficient for the use of a one-time pad and thus for provably 100% secure data encryption.

9.2.3 Operating Conditions and Robustness

The operating conditions of the methods/technologies under consideration differ significantly and have a direct impact on stability, availability, and organizational controllability. Optical QKD methods/technologies, regardless of whether they work with discrete variables, continuous variables, or entangled photons, are sensitive to environmental and system influences. In optical fibers, temperature changes, mechanical stress, or aging effects lead to polarization and phase drift, which must be continuously compensated for. In free-space and satellite-based connections, atmospheric effects (aerosols, fog, clouds, etc.), alignment errors, and background light also occur, which can lead to significant temporal fluctuations in the key rate or to interruptions. These influences are physically determined and can only be reduced to a limited extent by technical measures.

The ongoing operation of optical QKD systems therefore requires precise calibration, exact time and phase synchronization, and regular readjustment. These requirements tie up human and technical resources, especially over longer distances or in changing environmental conditions. Different QKD variants differ in detail, but share the need for continuously monitored and actively controlled operation. Deviations outside defined tolerances typically do not lead to gradual quality losses, but to a sharp drop in the key rate or complete termination of key exchange.

In comparison, RKD has very low requirements for precision calibration and synchronization, but is highly dependent on the characteristics of the radio channel. Interference from multipath propagation, shadowing, or foreign radio signals can further reduce the already low key rates or make them temporarily impossible. Robustness here results less from technical stability than from the ability to flexibly adapt procedures to changing conditions.

MKD is a special case in this respect. Although the generation of key bits is subject to the operating conditions of the random number generators used (which are optimized for security through the separate use of multiple generators), the actual transport is independent of sensitive transmission channels. Robustness is primarily determined by organizational and logistical factors, such as the secure handling, and transport of data carriers. In operation, this results in a very high fault tolerance, i.e., robustness against environmental and system influences, but is combined with a discrete rather than continuous provisioning model for the key material.

9.2.4 Security Assumptions and System Risks

The methods/technologies under consideration are based on different security models, each with its own assumptions and limitations. Quantum-based methods/technologies aim to trace the security of key generation and distribution back to the laws of quantum mechanics. In idealized form, they allow statements to be made about information-theoretical security against certain attacker models. However, these statements only apply under clearly defined conditions and are abstracted from practical implementation details. In contrast, RKD and MKD do not pursue quantum physical security models, but are based on classical physical properties of radio channels, hardware-based random number generators, storage media, smart cards, and processes, as well as organizational measures.

A key difference between the approaches lies in the number and type of additional assumptions. Optical QKD methods/technologies require that the devices used operate as specified, that detectors and sources are not tampered with, and that certain side channels are adequately controlled. In network-like structures, additional assumptions are often made, such as trust in intermediate stations or key management systems. In addition, all QKD variants require initial authentication, which in turn is based on pre-shared secrets or classical cryptographic methods. These additional assumptions relativize the formal security gain without necessarily negating it.

Post-processing (error correction, privacy amplification), which is based purely on mathematical methods, also plays an important role in QKD and RKD.

RKD also requires assumptions about the properties of the radio channel and about an attacker's ability to completely control or eavesdrop on it. Security here does not result from strict theoretical proofs, but from the practical difficulty of certain attacks.

MKD largely shifts the security assumptions to the organizational realm: the confidentiality of the key depends primarily on the secure generation, storage, and physical transport of the data carriers. In practice, attack surfaces do not arise from mathematical or physical weaknesses that determine non-deterministic random number generators and MKD-capable storage media, but from processes, personnel, and logistics.

Systemic risks arise in all processes/technologies from implementation, operation, and integration into existing infrastructures. Complex systems with many components and interfaces generally offer more points of attack than simple, clearly defined processes/technologies. With QKD in particular, side-channel attacks (see Chap. 3.8), misconfigurations, and post-processing (error correction and privacy amplification; see Chap.8) can result in practical security falling significantly short of theoretical expectations. Conversely, with MKD, the risks shift to organizational weaknesses, which, unlike with QKD, are easy to manage and control even without special expertise.

The comparison thus shows a clear difference between theoretical security and practical vulnerability. High formal security guarantees at the procedural/technological level are no substitute for robust implementation and controllable operating models. For a realistic assessment, it is therefore crucial to consider not only the underlying security model, but also the entirety of assumptions and risks that come into play in concrete use.

9.2.5 Cost and Infrastructure Dependencies

The cost and infrastructure profiles of the procedures/technologies under consideration differ significantly and have a major impact on their practical applicability. Optical QKD procedures (DV-QKD, CV-QKD, and entanglement-based approaches) require highly specialized hardware on both sides of a connection. The investment costs are typically in the high five- to six-figure dollar range per link, plus installation, integration, and ongoing operating costs. Highly sensitive detectors, precision optical components, and (in certain cases) cryogenic cooling are particularly cost-relevant. In addition to energy and maintenance, operating costs also include qualified personnel for monitoring and troubleshooting.

These processes/technologies also require suitable physical infrastructure. Fiber-optic QKD requires access to dedicated or at least controllable fiber-optic lines; coexistence with data traffic is possible, but technically challenging. Free-space and satellite applications require clear lines of sight (i.e., no clouds, fog, etc.), precise alignment, and suitable locations. The resulting dependencies on network infrastructure, site conditions, and permits have a direct impact on costs, flexibility, and rollout.

In contrast, RKD has very low investment costs because it can rely on comparatively simple radio hardware and existing communications infrastructure. Operating costs remain manageable, but are offset by the very low key rates and distances, which limit its use to specific scenarios— mostly with moving devices. Additional infrastructure requirements arise primarily from the need for controlled radio environments.

MKD follows a fundamentally different cost model. The technical costs for generating large quantities of key material are very low and scale with the performance of the random number generators and storage systems used. The dominant cost factor lies in the organizational and logistical area: secure data carriers, transport, storage, and access control. In return, there are no requirements for continuous transmission infrastructure and highly specialized technology during operation. The economic evaluation here depends heavily on existing logistics structures and organizational integration.

Overall, it is evident that increasing technical complexity is accompanied by significantly higher investment and operating costs as well as greater infrastructure dependencies, while simpler physical approaches shift costs and risks more strongly into the organizational sphere.

9.3 Consolidated View

The preceding sections show that the methods/technologies considered cannot be classified along a linear scale of "better" or "worse," but rather represent different security, operational, and organizational paradigms. DV-QKD, CV-QKD, and entanglement-based QKD share the fundamental goal of securing the generation and distribution of keys via a physical transmission channel, but differ in their technical design, achievable performance, and operational complexity. RKD and MKD, on the other hand, pursue approaches in which security primarily results from the physical properties of devices, radio channels, or processes, as well as from organizational measures.

Quantum-based methods/technologies are characterized by a high degree of formal security at the method/technology level, which allows far-reaching security-theoretical statements under idealized assumptions. However, this strength is accompanied by structural limitations. The achievable key rates are limited and highly dependent on distance, attenuation, and operating conditions. In addition, the design and operation require complex systems with sensitive components, continuous calibration, and close monitoring. Practical applicability is therefore often limited to clearly defined scenarios in which the infrastructure, environment, and operation are controllable.

RKD occupies an intermediate position. The approach uses the physical properties of radio channels to extract keys, but does not provide the formal security guarantees of quantum-based methods/technologies. The strength of RKD lies in its comparatively low technical complexity and the possibility of using existing communication infrastructure. On the other hand, it has very low key rates and distances, a dependence on the respective radio environment, and dynamic requirements (movement of at least one device), which limits its use to niche applications.

MKD differs most significantly from the other approaches in terms of structure. Here, the generation and distribution of keys are decoupled from the actual use in terms of time and space. Very large quantities of key material can be generated independently of transmission channels and then physically distributed. This results in very high, effectively available key quantities with comparatively very low technical complexity during operation. At the same time, the security-related effort shifts to the organizational area: secure generation, storage, transport, and management of data carriers become the central control variables, which can be easily monitored and controlled without special expertise.

The characteristic strengths and weaknesses of the approaches cannot, therefore, be considered in isolation, but only in combination. Quantum-based methods/technologies offer conceptually elegant solutions for continuous key exchange over distance, but are very cost-intensive and operationally demanding. RKD is a technically simple but performance-limited alternative, but scores points in terms of mobile devices and costs. MKD offers exceptionally high key capacities, which also enable one-time pad encryption, and robust operating conditions at very low cost, but requires established logistical processes and clear organizational responsibilities.

Finally, for a comprehensive classification, it is crucial that the procedures/technologies differ not only in performance parameters but also in their fundamental understanding of the system. While QKD approaches and RKD primarily understand security as a property of an ongoing physical transmission process, MKD treats security as the result of controlled physical and organizational processes. These structural differences shape all other aspects, from costs and scalability to attack surfaces, and form the framework for the subsequent consolidation of key findings.

9.4 Condensed Key Statements

A comparison of the methods/technologies under consideration shows that physical methods of key provision do not form a uniform solution field, but represent different security and organizational concepts. A key finding is that the performance, operational requirements, and security assumptions of the methods vary greatly and cannot be compared without context. Statements about the "superiority" or "inferiority" of individual approaches are therefore only meaningful in relation to specific conditions of use.

Quantum-based methods/technologies achieve only limited key rates under realistic operating conditions and are sensitive to distance, attenuation, and environmental conditions. These limitations are physical in nature and independent of individual implementations. At the same time, their setup and operation are technically demanding and involve considerable investment and operating costs. It can be considered certain that QKD solutions are currently only practicable in clearly defined scenarios with controllable infrastructure.

RKD represents an approach with low technical complexity, but its performance is limited by very low key rates and distances. It is certain that RKD is not suitable for applications with high key requirements or longer distances, but is well suited for moving devices (vehicles, drones, moving IoT devices, etc.). However, it remains unclear to what extent RKD can provide additional benefits in specialized niches when combined with other methods.

MKD differs fundamentally from all transmission-based approaches. It is certain that the physical distribution of large quantities of key material can effectively achieve very high key capacities that far exceed the orders of magnitude of optical methods/technologies. It is also certain that the central security assumptions and risks here shift to the organizational and logistical areas and that the costs are low. It remains to be seen to what extent existing organizations can reliably integrate these processes.

Overall, it is clear that theoretical security models alone do not provide a sufficient basis for procurement decisions. Rather, the decisive factors are practical assumptions, systemic risks, and organizational controllability in real-world operations. Open questions relate in particular to future technological developments, possible advances in standardization, and the question of how different methods/technologies can be combined in a meaningful way. The present results thus provide a reliable basis for informed decisions, but do not replace a context-specific assessment of the respective application scenario.

Summary performance comparison of the five methods/technologies DV-QKD (quantum key distribution with polarization of individual photons), CV-QKD (quantum key distribution with a continuous photon stream), QKD (quantum key distribution) with entanglement, RKD (radio signal key distribution), and MKD (memory key distribution)

Criterion	DV-QKD	CV-QKD	QKD with entanglement	RKD	MKD
Distance	★★★★☆	★★☆☆☆	★★★★☆	★☆☆☆☆	★★★★★
Key rate for short distances	★★★☆☆	★★★☆☆	★★☆☆☆	★☆☆☆☆	★★★★★
Key rate at long distances	★☆☆☆☆	☆☆☆☆☆	★☆☆☆☆	☆☆☆☆☆	★★★★★
Market readiness	★★★★☆	★★★★☆	★★★☆☆	★★★★☆	★★★★★
IT security issues	M, S, T	M, S, T	M, S	M	T
Cost					
Robustness	★★☆☆☆	★★☆☆☆	★☆☆☆☆	★★★★☆	★★★★★
Manufacturer dependency	Yes	Yes	Yes	No	No
Authentication	Shared secret	Shared secret	Shared secret	Shared secret	Smart-card
Suitability for mobile devices	☆☆☆☆☆	★☆☆☆☆	☆☆☆☆☆	★★★★★	★★★★★
Disadvantages	Infrastructure	Infrastructure	Infrastructure	Transport	Transport

★★★★★ = excellent; ★★★☆☆ = moderate; ★☆☆☆☆ = very poor; ☆☆☆☆☆ = not

Explanation of IT security issues:

- M = Mathematical methods
- S = Side-channel attacks
- T = Risk via true random number generator (TRNG)

Explanation of disadvantages:

- Infrastructure: Complex communication infrastructure (fiber optics, free-space optics, satellites, ground stations, trusted nodes)
- Transport: Physical transport of storage media required

References

[Weg81] M.N. Wegman, L. Carter, New hash functions and their use in authentication and set equality. J. Comput. Syst. Sci. **22**, 265–279 (1981). https://doi.org/10.1016/0022-0000(81)90033-7

[WP-MAC] Wikipedia contributors, "Message authentication code," Wikipedia, The Free Encyclopedia. https://en.wikipedia.org/wiki/Message_authentication_code

Zeitfracht Medien GmbH
Ferdinand-Jühlke-Straße 7
99095 Erfurt, Deutschland
produktsicherheit@kolibri360.de